Kind Business

Values create Value

Reimagining a corporate world where people and
planet are placed at the heart of leadership decisions

Dr David Cooke

I pay respect to the traditional owners and custodians of the land on which I am residing and where this book was written, the Arakwal people of the Bundjalung Nation in the Byron Bay district of the Northern Rivers of coastal New South Wales, Australia, who have occupied this land for at least 22,000 years, and pay my respects to Elders past, present and emerging.

'Can business be both kind and profitable? David Cooke's *Kind Business* answers with a resounding yes. This powerful book bridges the gap between commercial success and compassionate leadership, serving as a roadmap for anyone ready to challenge the status quo and lead with heart.

'David's exceptional leadership in promoting these values sets a much-needed example for current and future leaders who dare to achieve sustainable profit without forgoing core values of empathy, decency, and kindness towards people and the planet. David's approach stands as a cornerstone for the future of ethical business practices – making it essential reading for visionary leaders.'

Cassandra Kelly – Member of the European Union Global Tech Panel, Chair Treasury Corporation of Victoria and co-founder of Pottinger

'David would be in the top drawer of Australian business leaders who have led profitable businesses with strong compassion and purpose. I am pleased he is taking the opportunity to reflect on his career and share with us many of his lifelong learnings.'

Tony Stuart – CEO, UNICEF Australia

'One of the most compelling and complete books on business, culture and sustainable performance available. This book is a must for any business leader looking to realise the benefits of a fully integrated approach to ESG.'

Alison Cameron – International Leadership Coach, author *Leadership for the New Millennium*

'This book is a refreshing antidote to growing distrust in business. David Cooke shows by powerful example how companies can do well when leaders have the courage to do good.'

Narelle Hooper – Non-executive Director The Ethics Centre, former Editor AFR *BOSS* and former Editor-in-Chief *Company Director* magazine

'Business as usual has put us on the road to ruin. If we are to rein in climate change and yawning inequality, then we need an alternative approach that doesn't put profit ahead of people and the planet. Dr David Cooke mounts a compelling case for kind business practices. He presents a wealth of evidence to show that if corporate leaders followed his advice, then they would lead happier and more fulfilling lives – and so would the rest of us.'

Peter Mares, Moderator, Cranlana Centre for Ethical Leadership, author of *No Place Like Home: Repairing Australia's Housing Crisis*

'Dr David Cooke remains one of the most forward thinkers in how we can restructure capitalism in a manner that prioritises kindness to provide better outcomes for people and planet. I strongly recommend this book to anyone currently leading, or having aspirations to lead a business, and particularly to those who have the courage to take the lessons Dr Cooke offers into the real world to enable our society to be net positive and thrive.'

Kylie Porter, Chief Sustainability Officer, and Business Ethics Fellow

'Written by a true purpose-leader and impact-enabler, *Kind Business* will shake up the corporate world and shift paradigms on how things are done and how they should be done. It will inspire businesses to embed kindness when our world needs it the most.'

Professor Debbie Haski-Leventhal – Author of *Make it Meaningful*

'In a world still dominated by "greed is good", Cooke challenges the status quo, asserting that profit and purpose can coexist. With compelling examples from corporate Australia, he advocates for a shift from shareholder primacy to stakeholder inclusion, redefining leadership with moral courage and empathy for a more sustainable future.'

Susan Mizrahi – Sustainability Thought Leader and Strategist,
Non-executive Director UN Global Compact Network Australia

'Far too many people follow Friedman's mantra that the only social responsibility of a business is to increase its profits, rashly ignoring his commentary on long-run interests earlier in the article in question. Unsurprisingly, many businesses have been decimated by a myopic focus on near-term results.

'David's timely book is part a cautionary tale of the grave perils of relentless short-termism, and inspiration for leaders looking to ensure their businesses thrive in the decade ahead. Even better, they will enjoy a much happier working environment along the way and be able to look the next generation in the eye when explaining the secrets of their success.'

Nigel Lake – Founder and Executive Chair Pottinger,
author of *The Long Term Starts Tomorrow*

First published in 2024 by
ESG Advisory
https://esgadvisory.com.au

A catalogue entry for this book is available from the National Library of Australia.

ISBN: 978-1-923225-01-5

Printed in Australia by Pegasus
Book production and text design by Publish Central
Cover design by Pipeline Design
Back cover photo by Kylee Ingram

The paper this book is printed on is certified as environmentally friendly.

Disclaimer

The material in this publication is of the nature of general comment only, and does not represent professional advice. It is not intended to provide specific guidance for particular circumstances and it should not be relied on as the basis for any decision to take action or not take action on any matter which it covers. Readers should obtain professional advice where appropriate, before making any such decision. To the maximum extent permitted by law, the author and publisher disclaim all responsibility and liability to any person, arising directly or indirectly from any person taking or not taking action based on the information in this publication.

For my beautiful daughters,

Beth and Nina

and wonderful grandson, Lucky

Contents

Introduction   xi

Part 1 Traditional Business

Chapter 1 The Nature of the Corporation   3

   History of the Corporation   3

   What Drives the Corporation?   4

   Shareholder Primacy   7

   Business as War   10

   Big Business   13

   Business Behaving Badly   23

   Profit Before People   26

   Bad Businesses or Bad Leaders?   33

Chapter 2 The Changing Face of Business   39

   Consumer Advocacy   39

   Corporate Social Responsibility   41

   Business and Human Rights   45

   Environmental, Social & Governance (ESG)   52

Chapter 3 Challenges   59

   Continuing Concerns   59

   Managing Expectations   63

   Investor-Driven Change   71

   Climate Change   73

   Eliminating Exploitation   81

   Good Tech Bad Tech   87

   Artificial Intelligence   95

Part 2 A New Paradigm

Chapter 4 It Makes Sense to be Kind   107

    Doing Good and Doing Well   107

    Profit and Purpose   113

    Gender Equality   118

    Employee Wellbeing   125

    Social Impact   130

    Partnerships   135

    A Culture of Curiosity   140

Chapter 5 Kind Leadership   145

    The Power of Kindness   145

    Qualities of a Leader   147

    Inclusive Leadership   150

    Conscious Leadership   152

    Authentic Leadership   154

    Selfless Leadership   160

    Quiet Leadership   163

    Courageous Leadership   170

    Self-awareness   175

    Corporate Awareness   178

Chapter 6 Creating a Kinder Future   182

    Resources and Support   182

    Finding Our North Star   191

    Final Thoughts   195

Part 3 A Case Study

Chapter 7 A Company that Cares   211

    Communication   211

    Purpose   214

    Cambodia   216

    Modern Slavery   219

    Thai Fishing Story   221

    Our Supply Chain   223

    Recognition   226

    Culture   228

    Wage Parity   230

    Parental Leave   231

    Domestic Violence Leave   233

    Respect at Work   234

    Commercial Success   236

    Moving the Dial   237

About the Author   241

Introduction

Welcome to kind business.

We are all familiar with the positive feelings that are generated when we exhibit kindness,[1] and yet this quality is rarely associated with business, which for many of us is where we spend most of our waking day. 'Kind' as a description of business scarcely exists, in fact the words 'kind' and 'business' rarely appear in the same sentence.

The purpose of this book is to provide an overview of how business could be conducted, if we are to respect people and planet while acknowledging the responsibility of business to produce returns for those who have invested in the company.

The book contains multiple references to authors, journalists, public speakers, researchers and advocates from a range of countries. In this sense it acts as a resource that helps to build the case for 'business done differently', including reports from CEOs who have experienced the transformative power of good business practice, and its effect of underpinning long-term sustainable returns for shareholders.

The book is designed to put forward thought-provoking concepts while inviting the reader to dive more deeply into any field that particularly takes their interest via the works and wisdom of the experts quoted. It is hoped that the book will not only further the reader's own

---

1   Ferrucci, P. (2006) *The Power of Kindness: The Unexpected Benefits of Leading a Compassionate Life*. Penguin Random House, London.

knowledge but also contribute to the transformation of the business world.

We begin with a short history lesson of how company structures came into being, the essential motivation of business and the way business evolved to focus on the short term.

We will see that this environment, characterised by ever-increasing demand for quarterly profits and shareholder returns, often drove poor and unethical decision-making. Short-termism is the curse of the capitalist system.

Nigel Lake, co-founder of global corporate advisory firm Pottinger, provides us with an alternative paradigm in his book, *The Long Term Starts Tomorrow*, when he states, 'long-term thinking + action = lasting impact.'[2]

Today, the impact of companies extends well beyond the simple model of a seller and a buyer engaged in a financial transaction. The responsibilities of companies start with the treatment of the people who work there and extends to their greater societal and environmental impacts. This presents challenges for boards and senior executives in balancing short-term shareholder interests, with environmental and human rights responsibilities affecting the lives of future generations.

The community is looking for large corporations to demonstrate that they are doing business in a way that is honest and transparent, and that this is embedded from the board down. The public are sick of scandals involving deceptive business practices, poor executive behaviour and corporate corruption.

While quoting case studies of poor business practice *Kind Business* highlights the positives as regards constructive leadership behaviour, and corporate cultures that enrich the lives of those who work within them, and builds a case for 'business done differently' becoming 'the new normal' with superior outcomes for all stakeholders.

---

2   Lake, N. (2014) *The Long Term Starts Tomorrow*. Frog Publishing, Sydney.

Revolutions tend to polarise and create 'us and them' environments. Hence this book is not about inciting a revolution; rather it advocates for logical, pragmatic reform. A process which may take longer, but if executed well, is guaranteed of greater lasting success, as we are likely to take more people on the journey.

This book is not a compilation of financial numbers, however, at times numbers do have a role to play. Quantitative and qualitative data are both important in building a case for change as different audiences respond more positively to the methodology that they are most aligned with.

For example, measuring turnover rates in a company will tell you *how many* people are leaving, but we need the stories of those people in order for us to understand *why* they are leaving. When measuring what's important we also need to respect the subjective, and often personal, nature of people's stories, as not everything of value can be measured, and not everything that can be measured is of value.

To help make this book as accessible as possible to those with different learning styles, much of the content comprises stories. This is deliberate as analysis of people's learning styles tells us that:

> ... *roughly 40 percent will be predominantly visual learners, who learn best from videos, diagrams, or illustrations. Another 40 percent will be auditory, learning best through lectures and discussions. The remaining 20 percent are kinaesthetic learners, who learn best by doing, experiencing, or feeling. Storytelling has aspects that work for all three types.*[3]

---

3   Boris, V. (2017) 'What Makes Storytelling So Effective for Learning'. Harvard Business Learning, December 20th.

This book is a compilation of many people's ideas, and every effort has been made to attribute all quotes and ideas to the original authors. These are all people who are seeking a better world. There are also many more people doing extraordinary work than it has been possible to include.

Placing good values at the heart of all cultures is not a radical idea, but nevertheless a powerful one. The corporate sector has enormous resources, brilliant people and vast reserves of capital. If even a small percentage are channelled into caring more deeply for our people and our planet, and into tackling some of society's most intractable problems, the world will be a better place for all of us.

I hope I have captured philosophies, perspectives and stories that will inspire the reader to adopt a different approach as to how they manage people and how they conduct business; or embolden them to keep up their existing efforts.

It all starts with embracing the philosophy of being kind and finding the courage within ourselves to put this philosophy into action. To quote Nelson Mandela:

What counts in life is not the mere fact that we have lived.
It is what difference we have made to the lives of others
that will determine the significance of the life we had.[4]

Books Referenced

- Boris, Vanessa, *What Makes Storytelling So Effective for Learning*. Harvard Business Learning, December 20th, (2017)
- Ferrucci, Piero, *The Power of Kindness: The Unexpected Benefits of Leading a Compassionate Life* (2006)
- Lake, Nigel, *The Long Term Starts Tomorrow* (2014)

---

4   https://www.nelsonmandela.org

PART 1

Traditional Business

Kindness is more than behaviour. The art of kindness means harbouring a spirit of helpfulness, as well as being generous and considerate, and doing so without expecting anything in return. Kindness is a quality of being. The act of giving kindness often is simple, free, positive and healthy.

S. Siegle
Art of Kindness – Mayo Clinic Health Systems

CHAPTER 1

The Nature of the Corporation

History of the Corporation

Companies in various forms have existed for thousands of years and have evolved through a variety of systems. They stretch from the simple structures of Mesopotamia in 3000 BCE, and the early loose trading arrangements that came into being around 2000 BCE, to modern-day complex shareholder structures and the growing trend toward ownership by private equity firms practising their leveraged buy-out strategies.[1]

The ancient Romans had their 'societates' or partnerships involving share holdings. Trading through company structures was also widespread throughout the East. The Chinese were particularly advanced in business, involving elaborate partnerships, the use of currency and generation of tax levies to benefit the Great Khan.[2]

By the 12th century the 'compagnia' of Florence had evolved in Italy. This word was formed from the Latin words *cum* and *panis*, meaning to break bread. This coming together and eating together signified the trust that each partner had in each other as an underlying basis for joint ownership. Company structures proliferated through

---

1   Micklethwait, J. & Wooldridge, A. (2003) *The Company: A Short History of a Revolutionary Idea*. Phoenix, London.

2   Komroff, M. (1926) *The Travels of Marco Polo*. Liveright, New York.

the ages, appearing in almost every culture. The guilds of the Middle Ages were dominant in the commercial life of Europe.

Chartered companies, which were combined private and government entities, then came into being, in an attempt by commercial speculators to capitalise on the riches of newly discovered lands.

The voyages of merchants were often funded by royal charters, with the monarch becoming a principal investor and even taking an equity position themselves. Situations where the venture was so high in risk and required such large investments, gave birth to limited liability structures created to entice potential shareholders otherwise reluctant to risk their capital.

The most famous model of the chartered firm was the Dutch East India Company, created in 1602. Unlike its predecessor, the English East India Company, in which individuals invested for one voyage at a time, investors in this new structure were part of a 21-year limited-liability company. A desire to share risk and reward was the primary motivation for moving beyond the single owner structure.[3]

What Drives the Corporation?

Today the directors of profit-making corporations, owned by shareholders, have the same underlying motive – to produce a return for those shareholders who have risked their funds in purchasing an interest in that company, and therefore provided the necessary capital for its operation and growth. Hence the modern corporation is primarily driven by the pursuit of profit, or the creation of shareholder value.

Company structures have come in for criticism around the lack of agency, or sense of control, felt by workers.[4] This has long been the

---

3   Micklethwait, J. & Wooldridge, A. (2003) *The Company: A Short History of a Revolutionary Idea*. Phoenix, London.
4   Kouzmin, A. (1980) *Control and Organisation: Towards Reflexive Analysis*.

focus of the union movement. It has been argued within the context of organisational theory that it is the hierarchical nature of organisational structure, and its search for order and control, that works against more egalitarian outcomes for workers.[5]

More recently there have been other concerns with the emergence of technology. The internet empowers us in many ways, facilitates participation and creativity while enabling us to connect with each other at high speed; yet does it also undermine true connectedness facilitated by human-to-human contact? Despite its indisputable power to rapidly allow access to information, it is difficult to see recent trends in technology increasing true human connectedness.

The historical motivations of large companies are a complex field embracing religion, politics and individual calling. These fields in turn each held subsets of differing opinions. This formed the basis of Max Weber's classic work *The Protestant Ethic and the Spirit of Capitalism*.[6] Here we see views regarding the purpose of work, attitudes towards consumption, and the profit motive advanced by the European churches of the Calvinists, Lutherans, Protestants and Catholics.

He further expanded on this in his later work *Churches and Sects in North America*, which included discussions of Protestant sects such as the Baptists and Quakers.[7] These books enabled us to gain insight into the link between the church and early capitalism.

Deeply religious men often populated the upper echelons of the commercial world. The Protestant asceticism which manifested in frugal and disciplined habits was motivated by a kind of self-denial, to ensure one was not distracted from God. In many cases this was linked to prosperity through the pursuit of commerce in a manner that was designed to accumulate wealth as a means of fulfilling one's duty to God.

---

5   Borham, P. & Dow, G. (Eds) (1980) *Work and Inequality*. Volume 2. Ideology and Control in the Capitalist Labour Process, Macmillan, Melbourne.

6   Weber, M. (1905) *The Protestant Ethic and the Spirit of Capitalism*. Penguin, New York.

7   Weber, M. (1906) *Churches and Sects in North America*. Penguin, New York.

The Freemasons, credited with being the oldest fraternal organisation in the world, is a secular membership-based group that goes back to the Middle Ages and whose membership often consisted of powerful business leaders. This may well still be the case; however, a high degree of privacy surrounds the organisation.

Business has transformed over time, and yet growth and the attainment of market dominance against competitors has always been fundamental to what drives strategy. Increased efficiency has been an evolving process and key to achieving growth ambitions through which business owners sought higher levels of productivity and higher returns.

German economist Werner Sombart is credited with coining the terms 'capitalism' and 'economic rationalism'.[8] He talks of the productivity of labour being enhanced through production methods that eliminated the inherent limitations of the human being.

It seems ironic that while the roots of business today were planted in historical religious philosophies, we would see mechanistic approaches take over where people were turned into units of labour and many of the finer aspects of humanity abandoned.

However, exploitative behaviours were always a part of the landscape of commerce and have been questioned for centuries, with the Christian Bible referring to the proceeds of business extracted in such a way as being 'mammon of unrighteousness'.

The desire for greater profits has always been a driving force in business, irrespective of negative impacts on workers. Perhaps it is too much to expect that business owners down through the ages would act in a moral manner given their desire for personal gain, irrespective of their religious convictions. This became particularly evident over the years as businesses grew in size and their owners' standing and influence in society increased.

---

8   Carosso, V. (1952) Werner Sombart's Contribution to Business History. *Business History Review*, Volume 26, Issue 1, pp. 27–41.

Shareholder Primacy

The term shareholder primacy denotes the concept that the interests of the shareholders, as the owners of a company, must always be paramount, and that the payment of a dividend to them must be the primary consideration as regards the allocation of company resources. This was the view proffered by Nobel Prize winning economist Milton Friedman and became known as the Friedmanite doctrine.

Friedman is often quoted as saying, 'the one and only business of business is maximizing profit, while playing within the rules of the game.'[9] As to corporate social responsibility, he stated, 'There is one and only one social responsibility of business, to use its resources and engage in activities designed to increase its profits.'[10]

In this scenario doing good in society and generating maximum profit are seen as competing considerations, yet we will investigate the fact that this view is being rapidly overtaken by a more progressive one.

One view often put forward is that the directors of companies are appointed by shareholders to make money for shareholders, not to donate it to charitable organisations. Companies should not decide what to do with shareholders' money. The argument is that these funds should be distributed to shareholders as increased dividends, and that in particular for a publicly listed company to engage in philanthropic activities is nothing more than shareholder theft.

However, it is questionable whether company funds do, in fact, belong to shareholders prior to the distribution of dividends. Dr Simon Longstaff, Founder and Executive Director of The Ethics Centre in Sydney, expressed strong views on this situation, taking exception to any notion that company funds belong to shareholders at all. He links

---

9   Friedman, M. (1970) A Friedman Doctrine – the social responsibility of business is to increase its profits. *New York Times Magazine*, September.

10 Ibid.

this to the privileged structure of limited liability, claiming, 'Firstly, it's not clear to me that the money does in fact belong to the shareholders.' He further states that:

> *A lot of this goes back to the origins of the limited liability company and the creation of the corporation as a separate legal person. Now limited liability and legal personhood of corporations both operate to provide to investors, to shareholders, an unnatural and extra-ordinary privilege. In that you can invest a dollar in a company and your upside is unlimited, but it doesn't matter what goes wrong or what damage is done to the world at large, all you are liable for is the investment you made.*

> *Now the only way a democratic society could possibly infer such an extraordinary privilege is if in fact it believes that in doing so it will lead to an increase in the stock of common good.*

> *The money that a company has, is its money, and it may be under an obligation to distribute it back in the form of dividends or in the event of winding up, following creditors being satisfied, to ensure there is a distribution to shareholders. So, it is arguable that it is not the shareholders' money that is being spent in any case.*[11]

In essence, shareholders can only claim ownership of company funds once they are turned into a dividend and land in their bank account, not during the day-to-day operation of the company.

---

11 Longstaff, S. (2007) Research interview conducted by author on August 24th, The Ethics Centre, Sydney.

When making the decision to buy shares, they ceded their rights to those funds to those who manage the company.

There is an argument that can be made to counter shareholder concerns that money they have invested is being used to support societal causes. Prior to electing to buy shares, an informed investor should already know that the company he or she is contemplating buying shares in is currently engaging in activities that support the community.

Jack Welch, the CEO of General Electric between 1981 and 2001, was considered to have turned shareholder primacy into an art form. He introduced extensive layoffs of workers, moved manufacturing offshore and championed outsourcing to reduce company headcount. For those wealthy enough to own shares in GE this was good news. Yet for workers, many of whom had been loyal to the company for years, this was devastating and led more broadly to massive socio-economic inequality.

Welch himself benefitted from this approach – he was listed on the Forbes list of 400 richest Americans despite being an employee himself, who didn't own the company and hadn't invented anything.

In David Gelles' 2022 book, *The Man Who Broke Capitalism: How Jack Welch Gutted the Heartland and Crushed the Soul of Corporate America – and How to Undo His Legacy*, he describes that Welch's relentless focus on the GE share price came at the expense of most other considerations.[12]

Welch was revered, much like many of our captains of industry are today, and as such his playbook was copied by many who worked under him. Three successive CEOs at Boeing served their 'apprenticeships' under Welch and seemed determined to turn Boeing into another GE.

---

12 Gelles, D. (2022) *The Man Who Broke Capitalism: How Jack Welch Gutted the Heartland and Crushed the Soul of Corporate America – and How to Undo His Legacy.* Simon & Schuster, New York.

Gelles, who is a *New York Times* journalist, sees this as leading to the lowering of quality and safety standards, with potential links to the 737 Max crashes. He highlights this with the statement that Boeing moved from a 100-year company venerated for its outstanding 'aeronautical engineering' to one focused on 'financial engineering'.

During congressional inquiries into the Boeing crashes, company memos were submitted into evidence that demonstrated the culture of 'stock price first, safety and quality second' had filtered down well into middle management ranks forming a part of the company's culture.

Welch's shareholder primacy philosophy has seen entire cities in the US, often in the mid-west, devastated and communities torn apart. Even the government's tax base suffered at the expense of corporate profits, thereby impacting the government's ability to provide essential health care and educational services to those who needed them.

Interestingly in 2009, eight years after leaving GE, and following the Global Financial Crisis, Welch said, '… maximizing shareholder value is the dumbest idea in the world.'[13]

Opinion is divided as to whether Welch really had a moment of 'conversion on the road to Damascus' in making a statement completely antithetical to the behaviour he exhibited throughout his entire career or whether he was simply a master of reading the room, and knowing when public opinion had turned against him.

Business as War

Since the development of large national corporations, particularly in the US in the early 20th century, a more complex ownership structure brought with it a heightened desire for profits in order to enrich the

---

13 Westerway, K. (2022) Jack Welch: The Man Who Broke Capitalism. *Forbes*, May 31st.

shareholders who had invested, often with little consideration as to any negative effects on people or planet.[14]

We have often seen a sort of corporate machismo operating, and even lauded, with the captains of industry, usually men, being placed on pedestals and adored for their toughness, even ruthlessness, never for their compassion.

'Greed is good' virtually became an acceptable mantra for business in the 1980s following the 1987 film *Wall Street*, in which merchant banker, Gordon Gekko, talks in positive terms of greed, 'it clarifies, cuts through and captures the essence of the evolutionary spirit.'[15]

'Take-no-prisoners' was another attitude admired in our business leaders. This is the mindset of a flawed personality type, obsessed with growth, even if it causes harm which may ultimately bring about the destruction of the entity itself.

As the US is the seat of capitalism, and home to many of the most revered corporate demi-gods, some have posited that they are a kind of substitute for the royal families of the UK and Europe. Who better to put up on pedestals than the wealthiest corporate class?

Growth at the expense of anyone else is all that's important in such a world. It is best typified by Ray Kroc, the former CEO of McDonald's, when he said, 'Business is war, it's dog eats dog, rat eats rat. If my competitor were drowning, I'd walk over and put a hose in his mouth.'[16]

Great warriors were often the role models for these captains of industry. General Electric's Jack Welch based his core strategy on the principles of Prussian General Helmuth von Moltke.[17] The Japanese

---

14 Garten, J. E. (2001) *The Mind of the CEO*. Basic Books and Perseus Publishing. New York.

15 Ure, A. (2012) Sustainability & greed unlikely bedfellows. https://reneweconomy.com.au. September 26th.

16 Beale, L. (2017) 'The Founder' is the latest film to give moguls a tough time. *LA Times*, January 23rd.

17 Welch, J. (2001) *Jack: What I've Learnt Leading a Great Company and Great People*. Headline Book Publishing, London.

General Sun Tzu became another mentor within corporate circles. The attainment of outcomes by the dominant individual, or coalition within a company, has been described in military terms as 'the art of the general'.[18]

How did we equate leading troops into war with the role of managing a business, and are we in danger of transposing the rules of one into the world of the other? Fostering an attitude of kill or be killed will not create kinder companies or a better world.

Invariably in civil and corporate warfare there are innocent casualties. Milton Friedman discussed what he called 'externalities' and defined these as the effect of a transaction on a third party who has not consented or played any role in the conducting of that transaction.[19]

Externalities in the pursuit of profit are responsible for countless cases of exploitation, illness, death, poverty and pollution. In this sense corporate externalities sound remarkably like 'collateral damage' – a phrase used in connection with civilian deaths in the Vietnam War, and then used again to sanitise civilian casualties during the invasion of Iraq.

Yet society can forgive these acts, perhaps due to the human species having an advanced ability to compartmentalise. Our brains have different compartments – we can park darker aspects of human behaviour in a certain compartment back in the recesses of the mind, while we get on with our lives unperturbed, via the primary compartment that we access day to day.

If we are not negatively affected ourselves, or perhaps if we even gain in some way, then we appear able to live with the abuse of others by our governments and corporations. This is not new, and probably explains why many in the 19th century believed slavery, which was

---

18   Kets De Vries, M. F. R. (1991) *Organizations on the Couch.* Jossey-Bass, San Francisco, CA.
19   CFI Team (2020) Externality of Production. *Corporate Finance Institute,* Vancouver, August 21st.

fundamental to commerce and the economy at the time, was justifiable. However, justifications made no reference to the abject misery of the human beings that were enslaved.

Looking back on previous generations with disdain concerning their standards of behaviour and what were accepted as societal norms, it is interesting to contemplate how future generations will judge us. One imagines harshly as regards our own tolerance of modern day slavery in corporate supply chains. It is also easy to imagine that our lack of action on human-induced climate change will prove to be unfathomable to future generations who are sentenced to live with the consequences.

Big Business

Today, big business, the huge global corporations with immense market power, have many worried due to their sheer size and influence. Simon Longstaff, founder of The Ethics Centre in Sydney, writes of society's concerns:

> ... the metaphor of the organisation as a "machine" ...
> in which the "logic of the machine" gives rise to entities
> with the power to harm the interests of humanity. This
> fear has been translated to the modern corporation – often
> portrayed as a kind of 'Frankenstein's Monster' that no
> longer serves, but ultimately commands, humanity. Indeed,
> it is portrayed as a threat to (rather than as an enabler of)
> our collective interests.[20]

---

20   Longstaff, S. (2021) The Ethical Foundations of Responsible Management. MBA course material. https://unsw.edu.au/news/2021/10/leading-the-way-in-responsible-and-sustainable-management

Sectors within the corporate world such as Big Pharma and Big Tech have come in for increasing public scrutiny. These descriptions are now seen as derogatory terms to describe sections of the corporate world that have simply grown too big and too powerful. During the Global Financial Crisis banks were described as 'too big to fail', indicating the survival of the world's economy was now tied to these entities.

Concerns regarding the pharmaceutical industry include a perceived drive for profit at the expense of public safety. The widescale marketing and over-prescription of the narcotic oxycodone hydrochloride may well have been seen as a commercial triumph but caused a public health nightmare resulting in an opioid epidemic, and an estimated 600,000 deaths.

In perhaps the highest profile case, OxyContin, a trade name of Purdue Pharma owned by the Sackler family, triggered the first wave of deaths. The company entered Chapter 11 bankruptcy; however, the Sackler family were granted immunity from prosecution in exchange for a six-billion-dollar settlement. They were described as 'the most evil family in America' and 'the worst drug dealers in history'.[21]

Chemical companies continuing to sell products with harmful chemicals, affecting millions of people globally well after their own research has uncovered this possibility, is another example. This was shown to be the case with DuPont, resulting in lawsuits which claimed that the company had poisoned drinking water by discharging the chemical PFOA into waterways from its plant in Parkersburg, West Virginia, causing multiple cases of cancer. This chemical had been used in the manufacture of Teflon, a coating used in frying pans and for other purposes.

This one product produced over $1 billion a year in profit for DuPont, and despite their own tests revealing the harm to human

21 Smith, D. (2021) 'A story people need to know': behind a shocking TV series about the opioid crisis, *The Guardian*, October 11th.

and animal health, they put profits first and continued to market this chemical.

It was through the courage and determination to pursue justice for victims by lawyer Rob Bilott that these cases even came to court. He took on the powerful legal teams at DuPont and won. His story is retold in the 2019 film *Dark Waters*, and as of that date DuPont had been forced to pay out over $670 million in claims with many more pending.

US firm Monsanto, whose assets were largely purchased by Bayer in 2018, was widely criticised for the negative impact of their agricultural and bio tech products. These included DDT, PCBs and agent orange, a defoliant used in the Vietnam War. Its business model focused on patenting seeds, to gain control over sections of the agricultural industry and the introduction of genetically engineered crops.

Additionally, potential ethical issues have surfaced with so-called 'independent research' funded by pharmaceutical companies and their degree of influence with governments and regulators.[22]

Western economists largely support how scale can bring efficiencies and productivity gains to the capitalist system or market economy. Ross Gittins is a respected economist and has been the Economics Editor of the *Sydney Morning Herald* newspaper since 1978 and celebrated his 50th year in journalism in February of 2024. Like many Western economists, he largely supports the understandable desire to achieve economies of scale being balanced against the more sinister side of ever-expanding corporate empires. Gittins says, '... that doesn't mean companies can't get too big, nor that all the jobs and income big businesses bring us, mean governments should manage the economy to please the nation's chief executives.'[23]

---

22   Kluger, J. (2023) 3M's Historic $10 Billion 'Forever Chemical' Payout Is Just The Tip of the PFAS Iceberg. https://time.com/6289893/3m-forever-chemical-pfas-settlement. June 23rd.

23   Gittens, R. (2023) Big business should serve us not enslave us. *Sydney Morning Herald*, September 13th.

The perspectives advanced by Gittins's writings are refreshing. He often challenges the status quo and conventional economic theory, especially around what he sees as the negative consequences of neo-liberalism and the assumption that business knows best. He believes, 'governments should manage the economy for the benefit of the many, not the few.'[24] One wonders if the influence of his parents, both officers in the Salvation Army, may be found in his writings.

In the tech sphere Google is an obvious example of a corporation of immense size and influence that is now embedded in our lives, due to the productivity gains that it brings us.[25] The Justice Department in the US has spent three years investigating Google and building its case that the company has illegally abused the power it has through its popular search engine to crush its competitors.[26]

This is regarded as the most significant anti-trust case brought by the US government in the last 20 years. The last time we saw action of this magnitude was in 2001, when Microsoft was sued, with the US government claiming that the tying of its Internet Explorer browser to Windows was illegal and part of a blatant campaign to destroy Netscape, maker of arguably the first web browser.

Perhaps somewhat ironically in October 2023, in a battle of the titans, Microsoft chief executive Satya Nadella called Google's claim that users have choice in internet search 'bogus' because of contracts that make Google the default search engine on mobile devices.[27]

Nevertheless 'big' is still seen as a positive with most of the public. One of the largest mining companies in the world, Australian miner BHP, promoted itself for many years in the media as 'The Big

---

24 Ibid.

25 Naughton, J. (2023) Has Google's monopoly on the search engine market finally timed out? *The Guardian*, October 1st.

26 U.S. V. Microsoft: Court's Findings of Facts. https://justice.gov/atr/us-v-microsoft-courts-findings-fact

27 Palma, S. (2023) Microsoft chief says Google default agreements make search choice bogus. *Irish Times*, October 2nd.

Australian'. Here we not only see the company proclaiming its size as a virtue but also linking itself with the whole country, appealing to national pride in the process.

Qantas Airways has traded off its market dominance and an appeal to national patriotism for years, with the subtext that it would be un-Australian to use any other airline when flying overseas.

However, the proposition that they are virtually synonymous with Australia only works if the company looks after all Australians in the process of conducting its business. The Australian Competition and Consumer Commission (ACCC) is an independent Commonwealth statutory body established by the government to administer the Competition and Consumer Act (2001). According to their 2023 data, Qantas was now Australia's most complained about company.

The company's refusal to return any of the government's $2 billion JobKeeper handout received during the Covid pandemic, despite achieving record profits of $2.5 billion in the 2022/23 financial year, left a bad taste in the mouths of most members of the public.

Qantas also demonstrated that they were unwilling to refund $2 billion in cancelled flights and have even been found guilty of selling tickets despite knowing that up to 8000 flights had already been cancelled. These have become known as 'ghost flights'. The ACCC alleged that the airline had engaged in false, misleading and deceptive conduct.

This type of corporate behaviour raises questions as to whether a culture that could tolerate this type of behaviour and the business model which drives it is fit for purpose in the 21st century.

Australian Financial Review editor and journalist Tony Boyd had this to say: 'My view is Qantas put too much emphasis on short-term profit maximisation, to the detriment of the company's longer-term interests.'[28] He is critical of aspects of the board's performance and

---

28 Boyd, T. (2023) Long-term lessons. *Company Director Magazine*, Australian Institute of Company Directors, November.

targets a poorly designed remuneration scheme as a root cause of the company's problems. Qantas has now moved to a weighting of 40 per cent each for attainment of financial targets, and customer satisfaction targets, for short-term executive bonuses.

The concept of a 'social licence to operate', a kind of informal approval from the public, came into being to both restrain companies from doing harm and to foster positive contributions to the broader society. This concept first came into being in connection with the mining industry.

Companies had obtained all necessary government approvals to operate and conducted their activities within the law. Yet they had aspects of their commercial business model drawn into question as regards the extraction of national resources, impact on the environment and treatment of local Indigenous populations.

Earning approval from the public is vital for companies to operate without constant interference. However, companies appear at times to either forget they operate under a social licence that can be withdrawn at any time, or have become so arrogant they believe they are 'now bigger than the game', and can get away with anything, even without public support.

To a degree the social licence concept has been replaced by one of a company offering 'social purpose' – this was pioneered by BHP. No longer is one party (the public) granting its approval to another (a business), but the business is an integral part of the whole. In this sense, the health of both is dependent on each other thriving.

Sometimes corporate backlash will take the form of moves to diminish the influence of the company in question. During a government senate inquiry in 2023 into the Australian aviation industry, the inquiry heard allegations of anticompetitive behaviour within Australia's aviation market. The inquiry found the government should consider regulatory reforms to strengthen competition, including potential divestiture powers to remedy any misuse of market power.

Highly respected former Australian Competition and Consumer Commission (ACCC) chair Allan Fels told the inquiry that he was strongly in favour of divestiture powers. 'I believe it would have a very big effect on behaviour, including by Qantas.'[29] One news article written at the time of Qantas's reputation plummeting during the latter years of Alan Joyce's reign as CEO, reports that:

> *Governance experts and investors say the turbulence around Qantas underlines the importance of 'social licence' – the idea that when companies operate with an informal agreement with the wider public that their activities are acceptable.*[30]

Australian Eagle Asset Management's chief investment officer, Sean Sequeira, said social licence had been a focus for companies for some time. He warned that turning around customer and investor perceptions often required more than merely a promise to do better or cosmetic remediation measures. 'It can be very difficult to turn around consumer perception of a company after it goes through a very bad period.'[31]

'People first' is a proven path to profit, but 'profit at the expense of people' is rarely sustainable in the long term. Once people feel taken for granted or that their loyalty is being exploited, then a company's halo slips very quickly, resulting in a tarnished brand and a long journey back to the top.[32]

---

29 Thompson, A. (2023) Aviation inquiry recommends Qantas break up powers. *Sydney Morning Herald*, October 9th.

30 Muroi, M. & Yeats, C. (2023) Qantas crisis puts social licence back on the corporate agenda. *Sydney Morning Herald*, October 7th.

31 Chanticleer (2022) Qantas brand damage is getting worse. *Australian Financial Review*, August 19th.

32 Kretser, A. & Aston, J. (2023) How Qantas fell to earth. *Australian Financial Review*, September 8th.

Qantas is likely to discover this with headlines such as the following appearing, 'New CEO Vanessa Hudson takes over an airline that makes more money than ever but is the most hated brand in the country. How did it get to this?'[33]

In the case of Qantas its woes also stretched to the regulators, with the company losing an appeal in the High Court. It was previously judged to have breached The Fair Work Act when it sacked 1700 workers, in favour of outsourcing those roles. Compensation is likely to be in the hundreds of millions, adding to the company's woes.[34]

It is becoming more common for companies to grow rapidly in size and power only to implode. German tech company Wirecard is a company that experienced rapid growth and achieved vast scale to become a global payments processor considered to be Europe's answer to PayPal. It represented the nation's challenge to Silicon Valley. However, after launching in 2000, by 2021 it had spectacularly collapsed amid allegations of lies, fraud, forged contracts and links to Russian intelligence.[35]

A recent study by McKinsey detailed the average lifespan of companies listed in Standard & Poor's 500 in different eras and included a projection that this trend of diminishing lifespan will continue:

- 1958 – average company lifespan 61 years
- 2023 – average company lifespan less than 18 years
- 2027 – 75 per cent of the companies currently quoted on the S&P 500 will have disappeared.[36]

---

33 Ibid.

34 Thompson, A. & McGuire, A. (2023) Qantas workers in compensation bid after airline's High Court loss. *Sydney Morning Herald*, September 13th.

35 Taub, B. (2023) How the biggest fraud in German history unraveled. *The New Yorker*, February 7th.

36 Garelli, S. (2016) Why you will probably live longer than most big companies. IMD Research & Knowledge. https://forbesindia.com/article/imd-business-school/why-you-will-probably-live-longer-than-most-big-companies. December 1st.

It is true that they may exist in some form having been absorbed into other organisations through M & A activity. However, some will have become insolvent such as energy giant Enron in 2001, following the accounting scandal and discovery of widespread fraud within the organisation, involving the concealment of billions of dollars of liabilities. This was also the catalyst for the disappearance of their auditor Arthur Andersen.

Lehman Brothers, whose collapse in 2008 triggered the Global Financial Crisis, is another huge corporation which fell following the largest bankruptcy filing in US history.

Equally there are global giants that have existed for an exceptionally long period of time and are household names, such as General Electric, ExxonMobil and Procter & Gamble. They are some of the oldest companies on the New York Stock Exchange.

The difference these days is that although they may still be operating, they have nowhere near the power or influence that they previously possessed, nor do they sit at the top of the heap as regards market capitalisation. That honour now goes to what Bank of America analyst, Michael Hartnett, has termed 'The Magnificent Seven'. These are Microsoft, Amazon, Meta, Alphabet, Apple, Nvidia and Tesla; although Apple and Tesla's performance in the latter part of 2023 proved disappointing to many.[37]

Staggeringly, at a time when Tesla announced that it would lay off 10 per cent of its global workforce to address investor performance concerns, the board sought the approval of shareholders to award CEO Elon Musk a $US56 billion dollar pay deal, based on the achievement of stock price levels.

Anders Bylund, from investment site Motley Fool, developed the mnemonic MAMA ANT to help us remember these seven market leaders.[38] The first four are software-based companies and the last three have a hardware focus.

---

37   https://money.usnews.com/investing/articles/magnificent-7-stocks-explainer

38   https://fool.com/investing/2023/07/31/mama-ant-helps-you-recall-the-magnificent-7-stocks/

Other companies peak, then struggle for relevance or competitive advantage and seem to fade. Blackberry, Yahoo and perhaps X (formerly Twitter) are possible examples of this phenomenon. Saab Automobile was bought by General Motors in 2000 and had been shut down by 2011.

Although the reason for the failure of huge companies is complex, and varies in each situation, there may be some underlying commonalities. In his book *Small Is Beautiful*, English economist E. F. Schumacher suggests that by their very size global behemoths will begin to struggle at a certain point in their growth. This not a statement based on commerce but on science. The second law of thermodynamics states that closed systems lose energy and therefore require to be fed with increased energy. This is not sustainable for business in the 21st century.

'Big' as a business model is almost doomed to fail. If any structure is built up to the point where it can no longer support itself, it falls over. As an article in *Forbes* magazine points out, corporate growth relies on access to an ever-increasing share of resources, yet the consumption/production equation eventually moves out of equilibrium. 'What characterizes modern industry is its enormous consumption to produce so little … It is inefficient to a degree that goes beyond imagination!'[39]

In Japan, there are more than 20,000 companies that are more than 100 years old, with some more than 1000 years old, according to credit rating agency Tokyo Shoko Research. The list includes Nissiyama Onsen Keiunkan, a hotel founded in 705, which is thought to be the oldest company in the world.[40]

The Japanese word for this phenomenon of corporate longevity is 'shinise'. Professor Makoto Kanda of Seijo University in Tokyo has

---

39 Schumacker, E. F. (2011) *Small Is Beautiful: A Study of Economics as if People Mattered*. Penguin, Melbourne.

40 Gittleson, K. (2012) Can a Company Last Forever? *BBC News New York*. https://bbc.com/news/business-16611040. January 19th.

studied shinise in great depth. He has concluded that the longevity of these companies is based on their lack of size. It's no surprise that they do not strive to be the biggest and most profitable. Longevity is more likely to be found among smaller companies.

They tend to embody principles known as 'kakun', focused on respect for tradition, 'sticking to the knitting' or core business, being conservative, even risk averse with financial management playing out as avoidance of debt and maintaining cash reserves. Valuing long-standing customer relationships is another hallmark of the shinise businesses. These appear to be such valuable guiding principles, however, differ markedly from the Western business obsession with growth and the startup mantra of 'fail fast'.

Small businesses will often have the capacity to be more personal, more connected and to address niche requirements of a particular client base or act as a conduit for specialised suppliers.

One instance of this in Australia can be found in the Indigenous business community. Naturally many businesses owned by Indigenous people may operate in the same sector as any other business, however, at times they will bring particular products to market, where they have distinctive expertise. This could be products incorporating Indigenous art used in the fashion industry and artworks and sculpture sold through Indigenous galleries or online sites as well as consulting firms, run by Indigenous Australians with unique lived expertise, to advise in this area.

Business Behaving Badly

The Corporation: The Pathological Pursuit of Profit and Power is the title of a book and film, in which companies are portrayed as the most powerful class of institution on earth.[41] The author, Joel Bakan,

---

41   Bakan, J. (2004) *The Corporation: The Pathological Pursuit of Profit and Power.* Free Press, San Francisco, CA.

attributes a personality to that entity, which is defective, in fact, pathological. The corporation is the heart of capitalism and so this description by Bakan is a fundamental attack on what is seen as a social system gone terribly wrong.

Unlike the principle behind democratically elected governments, corporations are not accountable to the whole of society. They receive considerable benefits over those extended to the individual, such as taxation concessions, and lower levels of accountability due to their incorporation as limited liability entities.

There is no better historical example of a purely profit-driven approach to business than the calculation that appeared in an internal General Motors memorandum, placed into evidence during the now infamous court case in 1999. It concerned safety breaches in connection with accidents involving fuel-fed fires in their vehicles.

General Motors cars were catching fire following accidents, and they had requested a report from Edward Ivey, an engineer in its Advanced Design Department. Five hundred fires had already occurred each year in connection with their vehicles.

Ivey's report, *The General Motors' (GM) Value Analysis of Auto Fuel Fed Fire Related Fatalities Report*, produced in June of 1973, included the following calculation:

Fatalities in GM vehicles per year 500 × $200,000 (the estimated payout per fatality) spread across 41,000,000 GM automobiles currently on the road = current cost to GM $2.44 per automobile in current operation.[42]

While the cost of compensation was estimated at $2.44 per vehicle, amortised across all vehicles sold, the cost to General Motors to undertake modifications, which would save lives, was estimated to be $8.59 per vehicle, amortised across the total fleet.

---

42 Geyelen, M. (1999) How a Memo Written 26 Years Ago is Costing General Motors Dearly. *Wall Street Journal*. https://wsj.com/articles/ SB9385366607816889. September 29th.

The motivation not to incur additional production costs led General Motors to pursue the less costly option of <u>not</u> undertaking modifications and instead paying compensation each time a vehicle caught fire and resulted in the death of their customers.

It is important not to depersonalise this decision by attributing it to an entity called 'the company'. Individuals, at high levels of the organisation, made this decision that would result in the deaths of many people who had put their trust in General Motors, and others within the company went along with it.[43]

Governments eventually realised that they could not rely on companies to self-manage their own behaviour and so built frameworks to govern corporate standards and mechanisms to monitor adherence. This required legislators to search for the right balance between free market autonomy and government intervention. In the US, regulation such as the Sarbanes Oxley Act was enacted in 2002 as a direct result of perceived widespread business malpractice.[44]

The Australian Competition and Consumer Commission (ACCC) are effectively the champions of ensuring that business is conducted fairly. It is disappointing that we need an external regulatory body to tell us how we should act; in essence, to define integrity and decency for us. Surely this is what the board and leaders of each organisation should be doing. Their role is to set a high bar rather than waiting nervously to see where government sets it, and then setting their plans accordingly.

However, regrettably we continue to see evidence that regulators need to be constantly vigilant. In 2023 fraudulent testing practices were uncovered at Daihatsu, a subsidiary of Japanese car maker Toyota. This involved 64 models and forced the shutdown of production lines at all of its factories while the Japanese government investigated.

---

43 Dunphy, D., Griffiths, A. & Benn, S. (2003) *Organizational Change for Corporate Sustainability*. Routledge, London & New York.

44 The Sarbanes-Oxley Act (2002). https://www.law.cornell.edu/wex/sarbanes-oxley_act

The posting of fake safety test results had apparently been going on for 30 years, suggesting there were surely many senior executives who were aware of this fraud.[45] It seems little had changed among some members of this industry since GM's appalling behaviour had surfaced some 50 years prior.

Profit Before People

Offshore manufacturing is now a favoured option, over the previous model of manufacturing in-country, and has presented a new set of problems. While delivering a lower cost of manufacture, this has also allowed some companies to remain at arm's length from the day-to-day practices of their sub-contractors and in many cases turning a blind eye to exploitation.

Manufacturer Foxconn is the single largest employer in China, and a key supplier in Apple's supply chain, assembling iPhones and other Apple products. Worker deaths at Foxconn is often quoted as an example of this where profit is seen to be placed ahead of the wellbeing of people.

In 2010, assembly-line workers began killing themselves. Worker after worker threw themselves off the towering dorm buildings, sometimes in broad daylight, in a tragic display of desperation, and in protest at the working conditions inside the factories.

These people were driven to use their own lives as bargaining chips to try and force their employer to improve the living and working conditions of staff and to stop the constant harassment and humiliation by supervisors.

Rather than a focus on improving working conditions, the company's immediate response was to erect a net around the buildings to catch workers as they jumped. It is hard to imagine that senior Apple

---

45 https://www.abc.net.au/news/2023-12-27/japan-auto-maker-daihatsu-suspends-production-safety-testing/103268528

executives, including Steve Jobs, CEO of Apple at the time, was not aware of the situation at Foxconn that drove workers to take their own lives, albeit Jobs was diagnosed with cancer around this time.

It has even been stated that leading up to the release of one iPhone model, Jobs changed the screen design as full-scale production was about to commence. It is claimed that he was not prepared to lengthen lead times for delivery by Foxconn, resulting in even greater pressure on already exploited workers. Steve Jobs is remembered as a genius of design and innovation, yet his apparent failure to use his power and influence to improve conditions for the exploited workers within the Apple supply chain is deeply disappointing.[46]

In encouraging signs for both the environment and human rights, in 2023 Tim Cook, the then current CEO of Apple, stated that the company has a long-term goal of not taking anything from the earth to make its products.[47] He stated that all cobalt now used in Apple watches comes from recycled material. This has positive ramifications for the eradication of child labour, as the largest supplier of cobalt used in most tech products is the Democratic Republic of Congo (DRC), a known area for child exploitation.

More recently Nike, Adidas and other global apparel brands have been accused of owing millions of dollars to Cambodian factory workers, mostly women, because of underpayments.[48] In research undertaken by Action Aid and The Centre for Alliance of Labour, 85 per cent of workers interviewed said they were not paid a living wage, 50 per cent said they were unable to afford sufficient food and 25 per cent said they were being paid less in 2023 than they were in 2020.

46 Merchant, B. (2017) Life and death in Apple's forbidden city. *The Guardian*, June 18th.

47 Lipa, D. (2023) Dua Lipa: At Your Service, Interview with Tim Cook. *BBC Sounds*, November 19th.

48 Hardefeldt, S. & York, B. (2023) Stitched Under Strain. *Action Aid*. Sydney. https://actionaid.org.au/resources/new-report-stitched-under-strain. September 21st.

If consumers refuse to buy products made with the labour of exploited workers, global brands will respond and take action to improve conditions within their supply chains and the exploitation will cease.

Amazon, another global powerhouse employing over one million people, has been criticised for alleged exploitation of workers. It has been accused of driving workers to achieve unrealistic productivity levels, the underpayment of workers and the systematic termination of longer-term employees who would likely qualify for pay increases for years of service.[49]

Examples include sorters on the outbound shipping dock having to inspect and scan a mandated rate of 1,800 packages per hour, packers having to pack 700 items per hour and pickers at 400 items per hour.

'I would rather go back to a state correctional facility and work for 18 cents an hour than do that job,' said Jimpat Lacewell, a sorter. 'I'm sure Mr Bezos couldn't do a full shift at that place as an undercover boss.'[50]

Ilyer Geller, a picker, said, 'You're being tracked by a computer the entire time you're there. You don't get reported or written up by managers, you get written up by an algorithm.' Another worker said, 'You're keenly aware there is an algorithm keeping track of you, making sure, you keep going as fast as you can, because if there is too much time elapsed between items, the computer will know this, will write you up, and you will get fired.'[51]

Workers in these types of roles are already lowly paid, and where exploitation of this nature occurs, it raises the question as to whether this is discrimination perpetrated on those seen as inferior.

49 Kelley, J. (2021) https://forbes.com/sites/jackkelly/2021/10/25/a-hard-hitting-investigative-report-into-amazon-shows-that-workers-needs-were-neglected-in-favor-of-getting-goods-delivered-quickly. October 25th.

50 Sainato, M. (2020) I'm not a robot: Amazon workers condemn unsafe, grueling conditions at warehouse. *The Guardian*, February 5th.

51 Ibid.

Employees of Amazon are referred to as 'Amazonians' by company officials. This may be designed to make them feel a part of a bigger whole, even something wonderful. Others may find it chilling, even dystopian.

In justifying these practices Jeff Bezos, founder and executive chair of Amazon, is quoted as saying that productivity measures, such as tracking workers' every move, were needed to be taken as workers were 'inherently lazy' and that the company was engaged in 'a march to mediocrity'.[52] Jeff Bezos's apparent contempt and reported treatment of people under his care is truly unfathomable.

Here we see the conflict between the aims of company owners, or managers acting on their behalf, and those working within the company on a day-to-day basis. This problem of 'lack of agency' is a common one and can be seen throughout history.

In other examples of poor business behaviour, a number of Australian businesses have been accused of abusing customer and societal trust:

- AMP Insurance, continuing to charge fees on life insurance policies after their clients had died
- Qantas continuing to sell seats after flights had been cancelled
- PricewaterhouseCoopers (PwC) embroiled in a major conflict of interest scandal involving the alleged leaking of confidential tax information, gained through their contracts with government, to global commercial clients.

There appears to be an underlying willingness to either break the law or 'sail very close to the wind', betraying their customer base in the process. It begs the question as to why business leaders would take these legal and reputational risks?

---

52 Kay, G. (2021) https://businessinsider.com/amazon-polices-based-jeff-bezos-belief-all-workers-are-lazy-2021-6. June 16th.

The answer would seem to lie in the risk/reward equation. It is likely that the managers don't expect to get caught, or if they do get caught, they don't expect to be prosecuted. Also, that the financial gain will outweigh any financial penalty imposed on the company.

If the CEO is chasing a significant personal bonus, then surely there is a conflict of interest here, potentially affecting their decision-making. It raises the question as to whether boards are incentivising CEOs appropriately.

Shareholders need to understand that when the company that they are part owners of engages in illegal or immoral behaviour the managers will at some point be caught. This will rebound on shareholders via fines imposed by regulators and potentially even class actions by former employees or customers, resulting in reputational damage which will negatively impact future revenue and see the share price fall.

Recently there has been push-back against the mining industry based on concerns about global warming, windfall profits, the commodities being viewed by many as national resources, and the perceived abuse of power in connection with the degradation of regional farming land and infringement on the rights of Indigenous communities.

Yet the industry contributes significant amounts to the Australian government's tax base. In the 2021-22 financial year the big miners paid one fifth of the total taxation paid by all large companies in Australia. This still doesn't answer the question as to whether this was enough, relative to the resources mined, particularly considering booming international commodity prices. However, the contribution is undeniably significant.

Poor treatment of Indigenous communities is an issue that must be addressed. In Australia, free, prior and informed consent (FPIC) as regards Indigenous rights and protections for cultural heritage are being called for by investors. This concept has not moved into legislation at this point; however, existing international human rights standards are well known to the global miners.

The highest profile case of irresponsible corporate behaviour within the mining sector in Australia concerned the deliberate destruction of an Indigenous cultural heritage site. This was the destruction of the 40,000-year-old Juukan Gorge rock shelters by global mining giant Rio Tinto in 2020.

These shelters were areas of high archaeological significance and sacred to First Nations people of the Pilbara Region of Western Australia. This was a gross abuse of their rights, their culture and the environment, demonstrating huge disrespect for Indigenous people.[53]

Rio met the legal and regulatory requirements necessary to blow up Juukan Gorge, but the decision was simply wrong. In such cases a compliance mentality must be replaced with the consideration of far broader consequences, and the setting of far higher standards and levels of accountability, to avoid tragedies of this magnitude occurring.

In the case of companies mining raw materials such as iron ore, it is doubtful that they feel the full effects of reputational damage or consumer backlash that a business to consumer company, such as a clothing brand or supplier of products on supermarket shelves, may experience. We would hope, however, that our companies are not only making decisions based on the avoidance of potential negative monetary impacts for themselves but on the important cultural and environmental impacts of their actions also.

Ross Gittins, writing in the *Sydney Morning Herald*, ponders why chief executives have been so confident their misdeeds would go undiscovered or unpunished. He concludes that it is because for a long time, it was true. He speaks of their 'Brahminisation', a reference to believing that they are of a higher caste worthy of remuneration far more than others and of special treatment. He writes:

---

53 Wahlquist, C. & Allam, L. (2020) Juukan Gorge inquiry, Rio Tinto's decision to blow up indigenous rock shelters inexcusable. *The Guardian*, December 9th.

Their Brahminisation has reached the point where they think they can break the law with impunity. They're confident that corporate watchdogs and competition and consumer watchdogs won't come after them – or won't be able to afford the lawyers they can.[54]

Given Alan Joyce departed Qantas in 2023 with a final payment amounting to millions of dollars while the airline was still facing investigation by regulators, and almost certainly a class action from dismissed workers, Gittins is probably correct. His solution: 'That's why penalties for business lawbreaking need to be very high. I think going to jail – even for just a few months – would be a highly effective deterrent.'[55]

When boards or senior executives inflict harm on society, or show little regard for their people or customers, it rarely ends well and there are inevitably negative consequences for the business and its leaders.

In early 2021 Jean-Sebastien Jacques 'stepped down' as CEO of Rio Tinto in Australia following the company's destruction of Juukan Gorge the year before. Richard Goyder, the Chair of the Qantas board, announced that he would 'retire early' sometime prior to the 2024 annual general meeting (AGM) of shareholders.

There was also fallout following the scandal at PwC Australia with financial advisory managing partner Peter Callega and chief strategy, risk and reputation officer Sean Gregory both departing in 2023. The business overall was affected as well and in March of 2024 PwC announced that it would make 329 staff roles redundant and that 37 partners would take early retirement. This represented about 5 per cent of their Australian workforce.

---

54   Gittins, R. (2023) Big business should serve us not enslave us. *Sydney Morning Herald*, September 13th.

55   Gittins, R. (2023) Corporate lawbreakers should be jailed. Imagine what their spouses would say. *Sydney Morning Herald*, September 20th.

One thing that has long concerned taxpayers in many countries is the issue of large corporations, particularly multi-nationals, potentially with US or European head offices, often paying no tax, or low levels of taxation – thereby avoiding making a contribution to the country from which they are drawing their profits. This lowers the tax base of the local country, while the company prioritises head office profits and overseas shareholders.

Their tax avoidance strategies are in most cases legal, yet the morality of their strategies is questionable, and yet we still see the government rewarding these firms and their advisers, with multi-million dollar government contracts. Surely denying them access to government contracts until they wind back these practices would provide some incentive to stop finding their way around tax laws and instead contribute their fair share to the running of the country.

Bad Businesses or Bad Leaders?

Criticism of companies tends to be directed at the perceived excessive drive for profits, at high levels of executive remuneration, and at perceived disregard for the outcomes for all stakeholders when decisions are made by the company exclusively in their own best interests.

However, as Joel Bakan reminds us, 'companies don't make decisions, managers do,'[56] and it is the behaviour of these decision-makers that should be the focus of scrutiny.

Dutch Professor of Leadership Development Manfred Kets De Vries talks of 'alexithymic behaviour' to describe those leaders cut off from feelings. He further describes the narcissistic behaviour of many leaders as contributing to the 'abuse of power', leading to 'organisational decay and loss of reality'.[57] As the stewards of good governance,

---

56 Kets De Vries, M. F. R. (1991) *Organizations on the Couch*. Jossey-Bass, San Francisco, CA.

57 Ibid.

company boards must be alert to this type of behaviour and for its existence in their own ranks.

In many cases poor decision-making from global business leaders is fuelled by a blind obsession with company growth. There are numerous examples of where this has eventually proven detrimental to the organisation, resulting in restrictions being placed on the company by regulators, often following push-back from those negatively affected. One wonders if to some extent 'capitalism is eating itself' due to poor leadership decisions.

Business does not have to continue down this path of growth at all costs. In an interesting move, New Zealand business consultancy Heliocene, founded by Jennifer Wilkins, announced that from 2024 the focus of their work would be in helping organisations prepare for a post-growth future. There is even a masters degree now in Degrowth, Ecology, Economics and Policy offered by Barcelona University.

In one move designed to restrict growth, New York City has brought in new restrictive legislation on rentals via platforms such as Airbnb which should return much of this rental stock to the market for longer term rentals. Many other jurisdictions are contemplating similar legislation. Did Airbnb simply push the envelope too far?[58]

Restrictions have also been placed on services such as Uber following its aggressive global expansion. Taxi drivers rioted in the streets of Paris in 2015 protesting against UberPOP, which offered trips at lower prices than taxis and other services offered by Uber. Authorities determined that this service was illegal and shut it down, but not before traditional licenced operators had lost between 30% and 40% of their income over the preceding two years.

By 2022 Uber was forced to significantly change its business model in Europe and instead of being the nemesis of the taxi industry, partner with it, by offering its app as a mechanism to book a taxi.

---

58 Sachs, A. (2023) What New York City's new Airbnb rules mean for travelers. *The Washington Post*, September 6th.

This model came into force in France, Belgium and Italy and Uber begrudgingly then extended this to Greece and Israel as a means of getting around restrictive local laws. As with Airbnb, did Uber go too far in its quest for global dominance of the taxi and private vehicle hire (PVH) industry?[59]

Another aspect of Uber's operation that comes in for criticism with consumers is Uber's use of surge pricing, a term rapidly being replaced in the travel industry with the somewhat sanitised term 'dynamic pricing'. This is where the price for a particular journey increases with demand. In defence of Uber, it is very transparent about this and when logging on via the Uber app a customer will be shown the degree of the increase, 2X, 3X etc, prior to making any booking.

In one of the more extreme examples of this in December 2014, during a hostage crisis in the Sydney CBD, one person, desperate to flee the city, reportedly paid hundreds of dollars for a trip to their home in the suburb of Bankstown, a trip of some 18 kilometres (11 miles).

Uber will say that users who are not needing to travel urgently have the option of waiting until peak demand subsides and then travel at a lower cost. Also, that drivers will often head over to areas where surge pricing is occurring thereby changing the demand/supply equation that the algorithm operates on, bringing prices down.

Commercially this seems a reasonable way to operate, and ride share companies are certainly not the only industries to use surge pricing. This is now standard practice in other forms of travel with airlines and hotels increasing prices during periods of peak demand.

However, what people are less comfortable with is the suggestion that the Uber app can monitor the charge level of the battery in your phone, with surge pricing being activated not by high demand for vehicles in a particular area but by an increased desire on the user's part

---

59   BBC. France cracks down on Uber service after protests. https://bbc.com/
      news/world-europe-33267581

to get to their destination. Uber has stated that it can detect battery information in order to determine whether to have its app go into power-saving mode but deny using this for variable pricing purposes.

In a 2016 interview, Uber's former Head of Economic Research, Keith Chen, stated that the business had discovered that users with lower battery levels were more open to surge pricing. However, Mr Chen denied that the firm had used the knowledge from their research to explicitly hike pricing for these users. However, it raises questions then as to why Uber was monitoring battery life at all.[60]

In all cases, senior executives are making these strategic decisions to further company growth and increase profits. Often, they are 'faceless men'; however, in some cases the public's ire, demise of a brand and subsequent loss of business are slated home to one high-profile person within the organisation, generally the CEO or Chair.

In an Australian context there is no clearer example of this than in the case of Alan Joyce, CEO of Qantas Airways, who many blame for the airline's loss of reputation while at the same time receiving a multi-million-dollar payment on his way out.

In several unkind references, Joyce has been referred to as the most hated man in Australia. This reference followed the departure of Philip Lowe, the Governor of the Reserve Bank of Australia, who previously held this ignominious title. In his case, he had presided over 12 interest rate rises in 13 months.

While many would not hold him directly responsible for the economic situation that prompted these increases, he had publicly indicated that he did not expect rates to increase. This emboldened those seeking to enter the home market, with the result that many of these people found themselves suffering from mortgage stress as monthly repayments escalated.

---

60 NDTV (14/04/2023). Uber accused of increasing prices when battery is low. https://ndtv.com/world-news/uber-accused-of-increasing-prices-when-users-phone-battery-is-low-report-3947694

In the case of both Qantas and the Reserve Bank, it will now be up to women to rebuild the tarnished reputations of those institutions.[61] In the case of Vanessa Hudson, the new CEO of Qantas, her compensation for undertaking the mammoth task of rebuilding public confidence in the airline came with a base salary 25 per cent below that of her predecessor.

Michelle Bullock, the Governor of the Reserve Bank, has a huge job to rebuild public confidence. It was expected that she would bring a fresh perspective and a new leadership style. However, her comment that most Australians were 'doing fine' around the concerning cost of living increases appeared to do little other than reinforce the perception that our large institutions really are out of touch with the average person.

These are not the first women brought in to clear up a mess left by their male predecessors. Whereas the term 'glass ceiling' describes the barrier to women ascending to senior leadership positions, the term 'glass cliff' has now been coined in reference to a woman, or member of a minority group, in charge in challenging circumstances where the risk of failure is high.

Key Takeaways

- Big isn't necessarily better.
- Bad business equates to bad leadership.
- Profits before people is not a sustainable strategy.
- Executive remuneration tied to short-term results creates a conflict of interest.
- Indigenous communities and their culture must be treated with respect by business.

---

61 Priestly, A. (2023) https://womensagenda.com.au/latest/eds-blog/women-take-over-as-alan-joyce-brings-retirement-forward-and-philip-lowe-chairs-final-board-meeting. September 6th.

Books Referenced

- Bakan, Joel, *The Corporation: The Pathological Pursuit of Profit and Power* (2004)
- Dunphy, Dexter, Griffiths, Andrew & Benn, Suzzanne, *Organizational Change for Corporate Sustainability* (2003)
- Garten, J. E., *The Mind of the CEO* (2001)
- Gelles, David, *The Man Who Broke Capitalism: How Jack Welch Gutted the Heartland and Crushed the Soul of Corporate America – and How to Undo His Legacy* (2022)
- Kets De Vries, Manfred F. R., *Organizations on the Couch* (1991)
- Komroff, Manual, *The Travels of Marco Polo* (1926)
- Micklethwait, John & Wooldridge, Adrian, *The Company: A Short History of a Revolutionary Idea* (2003)
- Schumacker, Ernst F., *Small Is Beautiful: A Study of Economics as if People Mattered* (2011)
- Weber, Max, *The Protestant Ethic and the Spirit of Capitalism* (1905)
- Weber, Max, *Churches and Sects in North America* (1906)
- Welch, Jack, *Jack: What I've Learnt Leading a Great Company and Great People* (2001)

CHAPTER 2

The Changing Face of Business

Consumer Advocacy

It was the egregious behaviour of some corporations which caused the consumer movement of the late 1960s to expand so rapidly. Social reformers moved from civil rights, where considerable gains had been made, and took on the big corporations.

One person unafraid to take on the powerful forces of the corporate world was champion of the consumer Ralph Nader. The son of Lebanese immigrants, he built on the earlier work of activists such as Upton Sinclair. Sinclair was a social activist and author of *The Jungle* (1906) and established and ran a not-for-profit organisation that met the largest US companies head on.[1]

Over decades Nader functioned as advocate for the interests of consumers. He tackled the issue of industrial pollution of the nation's rivers and lakes, as well as consumer credit laws. The battles that 'Nader's Raiders' fought over the years with industry are now legendary. These included wins for the consumer over the automobile industry, pharmaceutical and medical companies, and government bodies such as the Nuclear Regulatory Agency.

He even bankrolled other critics of industry, people such as director Michael Moore, by funding his first film, *Roger and Me*, which told of

---

1   Nader, R. (2000) *The Jungle*. https://nader.org/2000/09/07/the-jungle-2000/

the futile attempts by Moore to interview the then CEO of General Motors, Roger Smith.[2]

Nader was opposed to the introduction of the Model Penal Code of 1962, adopted by most US states. It followed Anglo-Welsh principles and held that a corporation could not be charged with an offence. The issue is what is known as 'mens rea', a Latin term meaning 'guilty mind'.

It concerns criminal intent and corporate criminal liability, and relates to the problem of how an entity, namely the corporation, could intend to, or knowingly, commit a crime, as opposed to whether there had been any actual criminal behaviour.[3]

Nader wrote to the senate, stating:

I and other leaders in the consumer movement hope you will oppose any efforts to make it easier for corporations and corporate executives to avoid prosecution for their crimes by changing the mens rea standard.[4]

This has now been partly resolved by holding the directors, or senior management of a corporation, liable for the acts of its employees. This principle has now been embodied in legislation across most Western countries.

It has been said that capitalism itself is inherently criminogenic because of the pressures put on managers to produce profits which in turn leads to dysfunctional corporate behaviour.[5] To fail to meet the profit expectations set by the board or the demands of stock market analysts and funds managers can result in the significant loss of

---

2   Moore, M. (1989) Roger & Me. https://documentary.org/feature/michael-moores-roger-me-1989

3   Minkes, J. & Minkes, A. (2000) The Criminology of the Corporation. *Journal of General Management*, 26 (2).

4   https://nader.org/2015/11/18/letter-to-representative-john-conyers/

5   Minkes, J. & Minkes, A. (2000) The Criminology of the Corporation. *Journal of General Management*, 26 (2).

reputation for senior executives, with potentially significant negative career ramifications.

Personal reputation and standing in the wider business community is valued greatly and its loss through scandals made public may well be the greatest punishment for some.

Of course, most CEOs are decent people and responsible managers of their businesses and we have recently seen good behaviour rewarded through the movement of capital into ethical investment funds. Many people want to be sure that the companies they are part owners of, through the purchase of shares, are generating profits through responsible and sustainable business practices. Never have those with superannuation or pension savings taken such a granular interest in which companies are making up their investment portfolios.

One of the drivers of change is that militant investors are attending annual general meetings of shareholders and applying 'the blow torch to the belly' of the boards of companies in which they own shares. They are asking the tough questions and at times voting against directors' bonuses and compensation increases. This often reaches the attention of media outlets as well. The Australasian Centre for Corporate Responsibility (ACCR), a shareholder advocacy organisation, is highly active in this area.

Corporate Social Responsibility

Corporate social responsibility (CSR) is a commitment to improve community wellbeing that lies outside legal frameworks and as such are discretionary business practices. It will generally involve the contribution of company resources, such as funds and staff time, to various programs. It involves a commitment to contribute to local communities and society at large to improve their quality of life, and is based on a principle of sustainable economic development.[6]

---

6   Corporate Social Responsibility (2006) *World Business Council for Sustainable Development*. Geneva, Switzerland.

Dr Simon Longstaff of The Ethics Centre suggests that the term CSR may be too narrow to encompass the full range of responsibilities incumbent on business:

> *One possible criticism of the use of the word 'social' as a qualifier is that it may draw attention away from the obligations of corporations to non-humans – such as other creatures and the natural environment more generally.*[7]

One incident that had a defining impact on the attitude of the Australian public towards corporate giving was the Indian Ocean tsunami that hit Southeast Asia on Boxing Day in 2004 which killed over 220,000 people. There were widespread demands for companies to direct funds to our neighbours to alleviate suffering and aid in the rebuilding of these societies.

The countries affected, such as Thailand where people regularly holidayed, and India and Sri Lanka, who played cricket against Australia, were regarded with great affection by many Australians. We felt connected to them which no doubt engendered a greater sense of empathy.

A discussion as to whether an obligation exists to give to those less fortunate than ourselves divides people. We see a huge range of attitudes and behaviours as regards charitable giving. Professor of Ethics at Princeton, Peter Singer, has an interesting perspective – 'Where world poverty is concerned 'giving to charity' is neither charitable nor generous; it is no more than our duty and not giving would be wrong.'[8]

As regards corporate giving, he presented an interesting perspective in his article 'The Competitive Edge of Doing Good' in which he

---

7   Longstaff, S. (2021) The Ethical Foundations of Responsible Management. MBA course material. https://unsw.edu.au/news/2021/10/leading-the-way-in-responsible-and-sustainable-management

8   Tracey, D. (2003) *Giving It Away: In Praise of Philanthropy*. Scribe Publications, Melbourne.

highlights the benefits of moving from giving away a tiny percentage of profit, an approach adopted by a number of organisations, to potentially giving away 100 per cent.[9]

He cites Newman's Own, founded by actor Paul Newman, who since 1982 has donated over $US600 million to charitable causes, and Laughing Man Coffee founded by actor Hugh Jackman.

Humanitix, a ticketing agency whose slogan is Tickets For Good, Not Greed, was founded by Australians Adam McCurdie and Joshua Ross in 2016. It's a great example of a business that not only has a world-class online booking platform, but also differentiates itself from competitors by donating 100 per cent of its profits to highly effective charities.

In 2022, in a somewhat extraordinary move, Yvon Chouinard, founder of outdoor clothing manufacturer Patagonia, and his wife and two adult children effectively gave the company away. They placed Patagonia into a not-for-profit trust where funds generated by the business would be used to combat climate change. The brand had become virtually synonymous with sustainability in the corporate world. Chouinard said, 'Hopefully this will influence a new form of capitalism that doesn't end up with a few rich people and a bunch of poor people.'[10]

While most companies will not go as far as those cited, operating a company in a manner that exceeds mere legal requirements is a widespread public expectation of business. In fact it has been for some time, with Henry Ford saying 'a business that makes nothing but money is a poor business.' Companies have also come to understand that being in step with public opinion on this matter brings potential benefits for them also.[11]

---

9   Singer, P. (2024) https://project-syndicate.org/commentary/donating-all-profits-can-be-good-for-business-by-peter-singer-2024-02

10 Gelles, D. (2022) Billionaire No More: Patagonia Founder Gives Away the Company. *New York Times*, September 21st.

11 Brachlianoff, E. (2016) https://huffingtonpost.co.uk/estelle-brachlianoff/a-business-that-makes-not_b_10958310.html. July 13th.

In this scenario the corporation may not be motivated by pure altruism and may embark on a strategy of community giving as a way of enhancing its own reputation with the resultant commercial benefits. Some people are still not comfortable with the concept of the giver receiving a benefit, even if the company is not intentionally seeking one, whereas others simply see this as a 'shared value' model. A kind of 'enlightened self-interest'.

Some boards are still opposed to the concept of corporate giving, beyond a tokenistic level, and will reference the Corporations Act (2001) which regulates the formation and operation of companies and the duties of its officers. It states, 'As the director of a mutual company you must exercise your powers and duties in good faith, in the best interests of the company and for a proper purpose.'

What is often overlooked is that despite the behaviour of directors now being legislated, how this requirement is enacted is nevertheless subjective. The directors need to determine if an action is indeed in the best interests of the company of which they are the stewards.

One refrain from senior executives is that they'd like to do good things for society, but the law (The Corporations Act) doesn't permit them to do so. In other words, they have made a judgement call that doing something that benefits society is counter to the interests of the company and its owners, the shareholders. Presumably, this is because in their minds it would lessen shareholder dividends. This is increasingly being seen as a very shortsighted and ill-informed view.

If we turn the argument on its head for a moment and assume that there are significant benefits, including financial, for organisations that genuinely implement practices that do contribute positively to society, then wouldn't a failure to implement these be in violation of the requirement to act in the best interests of the company under the Corporations Act?

However, some see corporate social responsibility as a kind of political ideology that wants private interests to be subsumed by public interests, and that corporations should not be used to resolve societal problems.

However, there is a little-known quote from Milton Friedman that showed that he had a more pragmatic position than many supporters of his most famous public comments are prepared to acknowledge:

> *It may well be in the long-term interests of a corporation to devote resources to providing amenities to its community or to improving its government. That may make it easier to attract desirable employees, it may reduce the wage bill ... and have other desirable effects.*[12]

Business and Human Rights

The term slavery is often used in a historical context as something eradicated with the civil war in the US or as a result of acts of parliament in the UK in the 1800s. Yet it continues today and the use of slave labour, now known as 'modern slavery', is one of the most egregious forms of exploitation in contemporary society.

It continues because we allow it to. A high percentage of those in forced labour are in corporate supply chains manufacturing the products that we all use in our daily lives. Every time we as individuals and organisations across all sectors purchase any manufactured product or engage with any service provider without considering if exploitation is present in the provision of that product or service, we are accepting the continuation of this practice.

A research study, titled *The Global Estimates of Modern Slavery* (2022), undertaken by the International Labour Organisation and

12 https://corpgov.law.harvard.edu/2020/09/30/the-enduring-wisdom-of-milton-friedman/

NGO Walk Free, suggests that there are nearly 50 million people globally who live in modern slavery today.[13]

There are more slaves in the world today than at any other point in history. It means there are many more slaves in the world today than the entire number that were transported out of Africa on slave ships in the 400 years before the British Parliament made the slave trade illegal in the 1850s. No age group or gender are exempt. The research shows that 54 per cent of people trapped in slavery are women and girls.

Walk Free, founded by Andrew, Nicola and Grace Forrest, is working to end the scourge of modern slavery. To quote Andrew Forrest, 'It is forgivable to feel overwhelmed by the scale of the task in ending modern slavery, but it is unforgivable to do nothing.'[14]

Andrew Forrest is the Chair of Fortescue Metals Group, the third largest mining company in Australia, and it is encouraging to see such a prominent corporate figure engaging in such an important social cause.

The term slavery is used when a person is not only subjected to exploitation but has no ability to leave the place of work that they are trapped in, resulting in complete loss of agency. It will be characterised by coercion, and often violence.

They may be in this situation because they were kidnapped and sold into slavery, sometimes even by their own family who are often so burdened by debt and so desperate that they would be driven to do so.

Another common route into bondage is through having been deceived by recruitment agents trawling through impoverished countries. This is exacerbated following the devastation of natural disasters.

The method is a simple one. People are offered a job in another wealthier country. They are told that that all immigration and travel

---

13 Global Estimates of Modern Slavery (2022) International Labour Organisation. https://ilo.org/global/topics/forced-labour/publications/ WCMS_854733/lang--en/index.htm

14 *The Australian* (2016) Slavery the curse that has never gone away. December 16th.

arrangements will be taken care of and that they will have good working conditions, be paid good wages and be able to send money home each month. They are told that if they are willing to sign a contract, say for two years, they will earn enough to set their family up for life, have their own home and provide a good education for their children.

However, a quite different situation to the one promised awaits them. Firstly, there are high fees payable to the recruitment agency who arranged their immigration and travel, so the person has now incurred a debt, usually an exorbitant amount at extremely high interest rates. This will be deducted from their monthly pay. Then there are the employer fees. Fees for sub-standard accommodation and food, and in some cases even rent charged for space taken up in a company refrigerator. With these deductions, they will retain nothing and earn no salary at all.

They are in a foreign country where they can't speak the language and have no understanding of local laws or their rights. Their passport has been taken from them, and they are told that if they attempt to leave, the local police will arrest and imprison them. Threats are often also made against their life, or even their family's lives back in their home country, if they don't fulfill the contract they signed.

In 2023 reports surfaced that workers who had been brought from Nepal to work in Amazon dispatch centres in Riyadh, the Saudi capital, were desperate to return home after claiming that they had been deceived by the recruitment company and were experiencing appalling working conditions. Then unexpectedly Amazon abruptly terminated their employment.

They were thousands of miles from home with a debt to the recruitment company hanging over their heads and no income. When they approached the recruitment firm that held their contracts, they were told they either had to remain in Riyadh, and the company would seek to place them in other companies, or have an exit fee of $US1,300 as a penalty for breaking their contact added to their debt. This added up to a fortune for these people.[15] Regrettably these types of situations are all too common.

Due to the Rana Plaza fire in Bangladesh in 2013, the exploitation of workers gained some prominence. Although not technically slavery, what occurred was exploitation resulting in mass loss of life. Workers had protested outside the factory complaining that the building in which they were working was unsafe. They were herded back into the nine-storey building, which subsequently collapsed, killing 1,134 people in one of the deadliest industrial disasters in history.[16]

These employers were making garments for some of world's most famous fashion labels. There was, and still is, an insatiable appetite in the West for 'fast fashion', the phenomenon of buying cheap clothes multiple times a year, only wearing them a few times and then shopping again for more items. Meanwhile the minimum wage for garment workers in Bangladesh has been around $A25 per week since 2018 and even discussions to increase this by 50 per cent would still leave workers, mostly women, earning less than a liveable wage.

More recently Chinese garment manufacturer Shein (pronounced She In) has been heavily criticised for encouraging 'extreme fast fashion' with its 'one-time wear' philosophy. An item of clothing in Australia can cost as little as $20 and social media, aided by some influencers, has been swamped by posts extolling the virtues of being able to buy more clothes so cheaply.

Many factories manufacture for the big global brands, and contracts are highly competitive with lowest price and fastest turnaround paramount components of whether a contract is secured or not. This places enormous stress on these manufacturers in developing nations, and in turn on workers.

---

15 Acharya, P. & Hudson, M. (2023) Revealed: Amazon linked to trafficking of workers in Saudi Arabia. *The Guardian*, October 11th.

16 Young, S. (2020) https://www.independent.co.uk/life-style/fashion/rana-plaza-factory-disaster-anniversary-what-happened-fashion-a9478126.html. April 23rd.

However, there are positive initiatives seeking to improve the lives of garment workers. One of these is the Fashion Impact Fund, a women-led training program for women in the garment industry looking to achieve employment, education and inclusion.

Human rights abuses are not limited to the supply chains of garment manufacturers. In 2023 slave labour, including child slavery, was found at coffee plantations in Minas Gerais in Brazil, an area where Starbucks, Dunkin Donuts and McDonald's, among others, source their beans. A total of 39 estates were inspected, and 159 workers were rescued from slavery, including many teenagers.

A report titled *Behind Starbucks Coffee*, published by Reporter Brasil, states, 'Starbucks … is unable to guarantee that the coffee sold at its stores is not associated with serious labour and human rights crimes.'[17] Starbucks, a company that reported a net profit of $US3.2 billion in 2022, can surely do better than this.

The Australian government, and other governments around the world, have been working to address this problem through legislation and multi-sector consultation. Following the lead of the British government, they created the Australian Modern Slavery Act (2018) to compel companies with a turnover of greater than $100 million per year to report annually on their efforts to eliminate slavery from their own operations and supply chains.

Australia's largest state, New South Wales, is the first to appoint an Anti-slavery Commissioner. Initially Professor Jennifer Burn, founder of Anti-slavery Australia, was appointed as the interim commissioner and then in 2022 Dr James Cockayne was given a permanent role within the Department of Communities and Justice with a contractual term of five years.

The focus of the Anti-slavery Commissioner is to advocate for greater action to eliminate modern slavery, raise community

---

17   Freitas, H. & Dallabrida, P. (2023) Behind Starbucks Coffee. *The Reporter*, Brasil, November 14th.

awareness, oversee NSW public procurement to remove products produced through modern slavery from state and local government supply chains, and also to identify and provide support for victims of modern slavery.

Despite the efforts of governments, modern slavery appears to continue unabated. It is now up to the corporate sector to take a pro-active leadership role in eradicating slavery from their supply chains and overall operations.

If much of the corporate world continues to turn a blind eye and fails to act on human rights abuses within their operations or remains focused on minimal compliance rather than showing real leadership on such an important issue, then it is doubtful that significant progress will be made.

The critical role of business to step up for there to be real impact on ending modern slavery is highlighted by Justine Nolan and Martin Boersman in their book *Addressing Modern Slavery*.[18] The big question is, what will it take for more companies to throw their massive resources, knowledge and power behind the elimination of modern slavery?

Justine Nolan also highlights the role that governments can play:

> *Through the tender process governments can lead by example prioritising companies that are doing the right thing, while stopping non-compliant companies from even bidding. They can ban goods made with forced labour from even entering the country.*[19]

The companies who value their reputations need to appreciate that this is not an appeal to altruism, or to exercising their discretionary

---

18 Nolan, J. & Boersman, M. (2019) *Addressing Modern Slavery*. NewSouth Books, Sydney.

19 Nolan, J. (2024) Australian Human Rights Institute, YouTube post March 6th.

power to have greater positive social impact. It is a request to stop contributing to the enslavement of nearly 50 million people in order to lower the cost of manufacturing the goods they sell, or those they use in their businesses. They must see the resources that they need to allocate to eliminate human rights abuses within their value chain as being another cost of doing business like any other cost.

In 1791 William Wilberforce, considered by many to be the father of the anti-slavery movement, said in a speech to the British Parliament outlining the extent of the slave trade and the human misery that it was causing, 'Having heard all of this you may choose to look the other way, but you can never again say you did not know.'[20]

This speech was delivered over 200 years ago, yet unbelievably we are still having this conversation. There have been multiple studies based on rigorous research and countless articles written about one of the most pressing social problems of our time, however, we must now transform knowledge into action.

The role of the company director today is extremely complex, involving decisions on a vast range of challenges. It is unwise to try and tackle everything all at once, to 'boil the ocean', and they can't be experts at every aspect of the company's business. However, as the stewards of our corporations, they need to have a minimum viable understanding of major issues in order to at least ask insightful questions of the executive team. This must then be followed up by asking for evidence of action.

As regards the elimination of modern slavery, every board must commit to doing whatever is necessary to stop a business model that is based on human misery and despair where the most vulnerable people in our society are being exploited.

This exploitation of workers in order to produce cheaper and cheaper goods must be replaced by a model where the payment of

---

20   A Biography of William Wilberforce (2011) https://bbc.co.uk/religion/religions/christianity/people/williamwilberforce_1.shtml. May 7th.

a living wage, good working conditions, freedom of association and individual agency are the norm.

Environmental, Social & Governance (ESG)

Investors are increasingly becoming aware of issues such as modern slavery and environmental impact. More and more data and increased resources are becoming available that give us insight into the companies we invest in and their social and environmental credentials. One such organisation providing this is Altiorem, founded by Pablo Berutti, which is an excellent not-for-profit library giving access to resources to help people understand the role that the finance sector is playing in addressing sustainability challenges.

The Australian Council of Superannuation Investors (ACSI), established in 2001 and led by CEO Louise Davidson, is another organisation driving high ESG standards by engaging in research and providing knowledge to its members who consist of some of the largest asset owners in Australia.

Fund managers wishing to establish portfolios of sustainable companies now have access to detailed research through organisations such as Morningstar's Sustainalytics, MSCI and others. This allows for the analysis of ESG credentials as well as comparisons of corporate sustainability performance.

Traditionally within the 'S' (social aspect) of ESG, measuring and tracking impact has been seen as complex, however, the availability of data and new providers entering the market has made this easier and these platforms and tools are being embraced increasingly by large companies.[21]

Publicly listed companies are starting to sit up and take notice. Investment decisions are now being made not only on the highest rate

---

21 HSM Advisory (2023) https://hsm-advisory.com/insights/creating-a-sustainable-future

of return but on a combination of dividends and the reputation of the company for acting in a manner that conforms to society's new expectations. As regards societal contracts between the corporation and the community, a significant shift has started to occur.

However, an important issue not to be overlooked is that the three aspects of ESG need to be connected and embedded into the fabric of the organisation. These considerations cannot be 'outsourced' by senior leadership to one internal department in a 'box ticking' exercise that meets minimum standards only.

One setback to driving higher corporate standards has been the issue of 'greenwashing', whereby companies overstate their ESG credentials resulting in investor and regulatory backlash. More than simply putting some spin on marketing statements about products or services, it can be considered as false, misleading and deceptive conduct.

There are companies who need to spend less time 'virtue signalling' as regards their ESG credentials and more time working to progress legitimate ESG initiatives within their business models.

It has been revealed that ExxonMobil executives, while publicly acknowledging the link between fossil fuel emissions and climate change, had tried to undermine scientific studies verifying this. This became known during New York's attorney general's investigation into ExxonMobil announced in 2015.[22]

A disturbing report, published in *Scientific American*, references the efforts of petroleum companies to influence public opinion on the validity of climate change, using a clear strategy to obfuscate rather than bring clarity. The report states that there's a quote in material from petroleum companies that says, 'Victory will be achieved when the average person is uncertain about climate science.'[23]

---

22 Noor, D. (2023) New files shed light on ExxonMobil's efforts to undermine climate science. *The Guardian*, September 15th.

23 Shannon, H. (2015) https://scientificamerican.com/article/exxon-knew-about-climate-change-almost-40-years-ago. October 25th.

In general, mining and energy companies which have huge investments in their operations are showing no sign of backing off their fossil-fuel-based business models. In fact, in late 2023, ExxonMobil bought giant US shale company Pioneer Natural Resources for $US60 billion, further tying their future profits to fossil fuels.

In a world-first Federal Court case, Santos (South Australia Northern Territory Oil Search) is the latest company to be held to account. The case was brought to court by the Environmental Defenders Office, an NGO that engages in public interest litigation. Santos was ordered to provide written statements to the court over its claims natural gas is 'clean fuel' and its claim that it has a credible pathway to net zero emissions by 2040.[24]

An Australian study examined the top 500 companies on the Australian Stock Exchange, the ASX, over the past 15 years. Disturbingly, their report published in 2023 revealed that some companies were changing prior years' data to show progress, sometimes triggering executive bonuses.

It was found that 55 per cent tied a percentage of their CEO's bonus to ESG metrics and that this group were twice as likely to have adjusted past ESG performance, particularly around social issues such as gender equality and workplace safety. Although this practice occurred in a range of sectors it was most prevalent in the financial and materials (mining, chemical, construction and forest products) sectors.[25]

Brynn O'Brien, the Executive Director of the Australian Centre for Corporate Responsibility, the driving force behind the Santos case, shares her rules to live by as regards honest and transparent ESG reporting:

---

24 Environmental Defenders Office (2021) https://edo.org.au/2021/08/26/ world-first-federal-court-case-over-santos-clean-energy-net-zero-claims. August 21st.

25 https://businessnewsaustralia.com/articles/how-australian-companies-can-fudge-their-numbers-to-show-social-and-environmental-progress.html

- Don't lie.
- Don't exaggerate (your positive impact).
- Give a complete picture (as far as possible, and be transparent about areas of uncertainty).[26]

The fundamental questions asked of companies by the regulator, the Australian Securities and Investment Commission (ASIC), in assessing misleading or deceptive conduct, are more than reasonable. They are:

- What did you say you would do?
- Did you do what you said you would do?

Greater scrutiny is leading to some organisations becoming reluctant to publish ESG data or go public with their ESG initiatives, for fear of being accused of greenwashing. Some are even retreating from their sustainability agendas, slowing progress in this area. This has become known as 'green hushing'.[27] However, it is vital that we still have an aspirational light on the hill to inspire higher standards.

The importance of developing legitimate ESG initiatives and strategies must continue. Despite some push-back, four of the top 10 LinkedIn Jobs on the Rise in 2024 relate to ESG. It is important that ESG in these jobs must not be turned into data collection and reporting roles to match the compliance expectations of regulators, while meaningful action is relegated to the backburner.[28]

Companies need to remember that investors and regulators want to see responsible businesses undertake tangible initiatives, and that the company will benefit when they do. There should be no reticence

---

26 O'Brien, B. (2023) LinkedIn post (September).

27 Good On You (2023) Green hushing is a new buzzword for lingering problem. Fashion's dangerous lack of transparency. https://goodonyou.eco. September 20th.

28 Sekol, M. (2024) *The Plagues of an ESG Career.* https://esgadvocate.substack. com

in making these initiatives public – the issue is that companies simply have to report them honestly.

We should be wary when we see scare campaigns by commentators, either driven by a cynical view of all business, or worse still, from those with vested interests in slowing the adoption of ESG initiatives. In this case, these scare tactics are a kind of distraction or conjurer's trick to derail the efforts of those boards who may otherwise intend to increase their focus on important ESG agendas.

Regulators will continue to demand further action concerning transparency, and in 2024 will introduce legislation that will require superannuation funds to declare climate-related financial risks in their portfolios. However, there is uncertainty as to whether they have put in place the mechanisms to report accurately on these risks.

'Social washing' is another term that has come into being, and there is evidence that the hijacking of the 'responsible business' agenda is on the increase with many companies trumpeting their goodness with only hollow gestures to back it up.

'CEO activism' is another phenomenon being challenged, whereby CEOs of companies are taking public positions on social issues. This is welcomed by some, but viewed cynically by others, who challenge the right of the CEO to take the role of a political self-appointee on behalf of the entire company, and even ascribe a sinister motive to such actions.

Professor Carl Rhodes, Dean of UTS Business School, is the author of *Woke Capitalism: How Corporate Morality is Sabotaging Democracy*, and highlights what could be called the commodification of social causes by the capitalist sector in their attempt to enhance their reputation rather than in order to engage in genuine social change.

He discusses the role of the CEO in such initiatives and cautions us to be mindful that '... instead of trying to fix the failures of democracy CEO activism reflects a trend towards a new corporate plutocracy, which could also be described as government by the wealthy.'[29] There is no denying the power and influence of today's corporate giants.

Carl Rhodes has reviewed historian Hannah Forsyth's 2023 book, *Virtue Capitalists: The Rise and Fall of the Professional Class in the Anglophile World (1870–2008)*. His article is entitled 'Critics of woke capitalism want to return to a time when money was the only value. But it never existed.'[30]

He highlights that we have seen a rise in criticism of companies who are seen as having lost their way in their adoption of an agenda that embraces the principles of ESG. 'Many conservative pundits angrily denounce "the woke" for failing to follow what they (the critics) see as the real purpose of capitalism,' yet he says that Hannah Forsyth's work reminds us that capitalism has always had a relationship with virtue (albeit at times a troubled one).

This is ultimately balanced with the disappointing perspective that 'the reality of today's woke corporations serves to re-legitimise capitalism, while leaving its exploitative nature unaltered.'[31] This only goes to underline the importance of authenticity and genuineness when any company embarks on initiatives to produce positive social change.

29 Rhodes, C. (2022) *Woke Capitalism: How Corporate Morality is Sabotaging Democracy*. Bristol University Press, UK.

30 Forsyth, H. (2023) *Virtue Capitalists: The Rise and Fall of the Professional Class in the Anglophile World (1870–2008)*. Cambridge University Press.

31 Rhodes, C. (2024) Critics of woke capitalism want to return to a time when money was the only value. But it never existed. *The Conversation*, February 26th.

Key Takeaways

- Consumer advocacy has brought about positive change.
- Modern slavery still proliferates in corporate supply chains.
- Shareholder primacy is being replaced by stakeholder primacy.
- The rise of ESG is contributing to the raising of corporate standards.

Books Referenced

- Forsyth, Hannah, *Virtue Capitalists: The Rise and Fall of the Professional Class in the Anglophile World (1870–2008)* (2023)
- Nader, Ralph, *The Jungle* (2000)
- Nolan, Justine & Boersman, Martijn, *Addressing Modern Slavery* (2019)
- Rhodes, Carl, *Woke Capitalism: How Corporate Morality is Sabotaging Democracy* (2022)
- Tracey, Denis, *Giving It Away: In Praise of Philanthropy* (2003)

CHAPTER 3

Challenges

Continuing Concerns

Many companies will inevitably have negative environmental impacts causing damage to the physical environment, through greenhouse gas emissions. These could be either directly generated, or via Scope 3 emissions, yet could be offset with positive environmental initiatives such as paying another organisation to plant trees. This would result in the company's carbon neutral operation.

This approach has been widely criticised as a company's avoidance of the fundamental issue of reducing their own emissions. Buying carbon credits while your business continues to pollute is not a legitimate path to a clean conscience.

A dark secret lies at the heart of many of these commercial schemes to facilitate carbon neutrality for polluting organisations. The issue at hand is that vast tracks of land are often planted out with a single species of tree, often unnatural to that environment. This favouring of monoculture, over biodiversity, is a poor substitute for natural habitat and often provides modest climate benefits.[1]

Additionally, in the race to create more and more hydropower dams, sustainable forestry schemes and agriculture projects to sell

---

1   Greenfield, P. (2023) Tree planting schemes threaten tropical diversity, experts claim. *The Guardian*, October 4th.

more carbon offsets there are instances of the rights of Indigenous communities being violated.

Regrettably, rather than strengthening these protections, draft legislation introduced in 2019 at the UN's COP 25 removed the requirement for parties to 'respect, promote and consider their respective obligations on human rights'.

Here, yet again we see expediency underpinned by the narrow vision of decision-makers demonstrating a lack of capacity to deal adequately with business issues that overlap with environmental and social issues. When companies in wealthier nations purchase carbon credits they need to consider if these schemes have a detrimental effect on those people of poorer nations.

The lesson for businesses with a genuine desire to minimise harm caused by these operations and contribute positively to the environment is to do thorough due diligence on any carbon offset schemes proposed to them.

When oil companies run pipelines through local Indigenous communities without their consent, we have seen high profile protests. When similar abuse by companies occurs in the name of creating a carbon offset scheme to sell credits, then these actions appear to illicit little condemnation.[2]

A far better approach in the sequestration of carbon is to prioritise the restoration of native forests delivering a broad range of benefits well over and above simply carbon capture. This is another case where governments need to intervene to curb commercial practices that are not in the overall best interests of society.

To their credit, Nestlé, the largest food producer in the world, which operates in 189 countries, has changed tack. Rather than becoming net zero, including through investing in carbon offsets,

---

2   Timperley, J. (2019) https:/climatechangenews.com/2019/12/09/carbon-offsets-patchy-human-rights-record-now-un-talks-erode-safeguards/. December 9th.

Nestlé is now focused on reducing actual emissions for its brands with a goal of being net zero by 2050. This is no small task given that only 5 per cent of its greenhouse gas emissions come from its own operation and 95 per cent from its value chain, including independent growers.

It has stated that, 'Our net zero roadmap does not rely on offsets. We focus on greenhouse gas emissions reductions and removals within our value chain to reach our net zero ambition.'[3]

One area where public discontent does exist with corporations, and at times whole industries, is when initiatives to have positive social or environmental impact are perceived as inauthentic and disingenuous. People do not like inauthentic leadership.

Criticism is often on the basis that the corporation is simply doing good in some areas as a form of appeasement for the damage that it is inflicting on society in other parts of its business.[4] One thing is certain – doing good does not offset doing harm.

No amount of charitable giving can offset poor corporate behaviour such as allowing a poor internal culture to exist, or the poor treatment or exploitation of workers in a company's supply chain. Whereas in the environmental sphere there is the option, albeit perhaps questionable, of buying carbon credits to erase negative environmental impacts, there simply are no carbon offsets in the world of human rights.

This naive and disingenuous approach has led to criticism of companies participating in CSR and ESG initiatives. This has become a popular pastime for some writers. They claim that businesses today are guilty of adopting personas of being good corporate citizens working in the interests of society while simultaneously engaging in self-serving behaviour.

---

3   Nestlé. Our Road to Net Zero. https://www.nestle.com/sustainability/climate-change

4   Kouzmin, A., Hase, S., Sankaran, S. & Kakabadse, N. (2006) Je Regrette: Toward Marshalling Remorse in Knowledge Transfer. *International Journal of Knowledge, Culture & Change Management*, Vol.5(1).

There will always be the contradiction of some good and some bad, or less than optimal, practices coexisting in an organisation. Parnell Palme McGuiness highlights the challenge in her delightfully titled article, 'The problem with moral yoga is that it is difficult to hold the pose' – if we enjoy engaging in 'contradiction spotting' we need look no further than into our own lives as we too are fallible.[5]

One contributor to poor behaviour and poor decision-making at the top is the lack of diversity within senior executive ranks and on company boards. Human beings tend to group together with people like themselves. With regard to board composition, we see a preponderance of groups of people who have arrived via similar career paths, or at the very least are members of the same socio-economic group.

This can result in a distinct lack of diversity of backgrounds and lived experience, and result in cohorts who think similarly and who are often removed from their customer base, or in the case of governments, their constituency. For some years now, many ASX listed companies have been dominated by directors who are described as 'pale, male and stale'.

Human beings are often suspicious of people who are not like them, they may even subconsciously fear them, and they certainly judge them. This can result in discrimination in multiple ways and cruelty towards others who are different.

'Intersectionality' adding to discrimination is only now being fully acknowledged. This is where there is an interconnectedness of social categorisations such as race, gender and class at the same time, all overlapping and increasing the likelihood of discrimination and oppression and adversely shaping the lived reality of many people.

The distrust of others may manifest as racism in some organisations whereby people from non-Anglo backgrounds may find it difficult to

---

5   Palme McGuinness, P. (2024) The problem with moral yoga is that it's almost impossible to hold the pose. *Sydney Morning Herald*, January 21st.

progress in their careers, yet most companies would see such cruelty and discrimination as 'out there', not 'in here'.

A stark example of this was demonstrated in the 2023 Australian National University, Crawford School of Public Policy study, which showed that people from English-speaking backgrounds were 70 per cent more likely to be promoted to executive positions in the Federal Public Service.[6]

Managing Expectations

Societal contracts between the corporations and the community have always existed in some subtle form but they are now centre stage with a significant shift having occurred. Lynn Sharp Paine, author of *Value Shift*, notes that expectations for corporate behaviour are constantly evolving.[7] She suggests that conduct that may have been ethically acceptable in one era, can, as expectations rise, be deemed not to be so in another.

The concept of stakeholders, or interested parties, beyond simply the business owners, has emerged and is now commonplace. In corporate terms a stakeholder can be anyone who is materially concerned with the welfare of the company.

A publicly listed company may have stakeholders as diverse as employees, shareholders, customers, suppliers, subcontractors, the stock exchange, government regulators and the community at large, all capable of working together for the overall good of society. We can do more together than we can do alone, so if we honour the needs of all stakeholders, we can assist each other in a true spirit of partnership and for the benefit of society at large.

---

6   https://taxpolicy.crawford.anu.edu.au/sites/default/files/publication/
    taxstudies_crawford_anu_edu_au/2023-10/complete_wp_breunig_hansell_
    win_oct_2023.pdf
7   Paine, L. S. (2002) *Value Shift*. McGraw-Hill, Columbus, Ohio.

In *The Spirit of Conscious Capitalism*, authors Michel Dion and Moses Pava write:

> *Just as all other professions in our society have purposes besides maximizing profits – doctors heal the sick, teachers help educate people, architects design buildings, and lawyers promote justice – so too should business, this is what conscious capitalism is all about.*[8]

R. Edward Freeman is considered the father of Stakeholder Theory and published his seminal work *Strategic Management: A Stakeholder Approach* in 1984.[9] He saw business not as a single entity but as a system connected to multiple stakeholders, with the purpose of creating value for all stakeholders.

Notably this connects capitalism with ethics and redraws the framework through which business operates. He states that we should not forget that 'businesses are deeply human organisations'[10] and business success should not be defined by its ability to satisfy shareholders alone but all stakeholders who have a stake in the business. He believes the skill of today's executive is to do this without trade-offs. He posits that great companies endure even in tough times through their alignment with stakeholders that operate within the company's ecosphere.

Geopolitical instability, climate change and the current experience of rampant inflation producing cost of living increases has led to a weakening of the social fabric and deep division. We see a lack of faith in societal institutions triggered by this economic anxiety,

---

8   Dion, M. & Pava, M. (2022) *The Spirit of Conscious Capitalism*. Springer, New York.

9   Freeman, R. E. (1984) *Strategic Management: a Stakeholder Approach*. Cambridge University Press, UK.

10 Ibid.

disinformation, mass-class divide and a failure of leadership. This has brought us to where we are today, deeply and dangerously polarised. Trust in our leaders and in our institutions has never been more important.

Trust will always be a vital component of driving social change. Michele Levine, CEO of research firm Roy Morgan, enunciates the importance of trust:

> *It's distrust where society's deepest fears, pain and betrayal surface – and that's because distrust embodies the fundamental vulnerabilities, past betrayals, and concerns that can erode the foundational bonds and shared beliefs that unite a community.*[11]

This applies equally in the corporate world, and Roy Morgan's 2023 research demonstrated that people were 'distressed at the moral blindness of corporate Australia' and that they have never been more distrusting of business.

The research came after massive data breaches at telco Optus and insurer Medibank, Rio Tinto's destruction of Juukan Gorge in 2020 from which its reputation had still not recovered, revelations of PricewaterhouseCooper's abuse of information gained during government advisory work, and the refusal of the huge retailer Harvey Norman to repay federal government JobKeeper subsidies gained during the Covid pandemic, despite posting record profits in following years.

Alan Joyce's attempts to deflect blame for the poor performance of Qantas onto the airline's passengers didn't help. He stated that it wasn't due to the airline suffering operational issues that was creating

---

11 Hutchens, G. (2023) Voters are distressed by the moral blindness of corporate Australia, says Roy Morgan. https://abc.net.au/news/2023-09-03/australians-distressed-by-moral-blindess-of-corporate-australia/102807234. September 3rd.

long delays, but as a result of their passengers no longer being 'travel fit'. He claimed they had forgotten how to check in and pass through security, following several years of not having travelled during Covid.

Another aspect of corporate behaviour that erodes trust is the corporate apology upon being caught out, following unlawful or immoral practices. We have seen Qantas Chair Richard Goyder apologise for what he termed 'operational matters', such as the illegal sacking of workers and the sale of non-existent flights. The apology should have been for his, and the board's, poor governance of the company that allowed this to take place.

The 2023 Qantas AGM at the end of the airline's 'annus horribilis' (horrible year) was seen by many as Goyder's opportunity to show contrition and send a clear message that the company had learnt from its experiences and had turned the corner of cultural change. Staggeringly, when one shareholder asked a question concerning the huge final payment made to the outgoing CEO, Alan Joyce, Goyder instructed the organisers to turn off the microphone being used by the shareholder. Actions such as this add a whole new meaning to the term 'tone deaf'.[12]

Optus is Australia's second largest telco. It is owned by Singaporean firm Singtel, which in turn is majority-owned by Temasek, the investment arm of the Singapore government. In 2022, 9.8 million customer records were stolen, damaging the company's reputation.

Generally speaking, most members of the public understand that no company is perfect. However, what customers do expect is that when the company that they deal with lets them down the Chair or CEO will come straight out and personally speak to them. Optus didn't do this and were rightly pilloried as a result.

There is an old saying, 'never let a good crisis go to waste'. In other words, learn from it, show some humility and do better next time.

---

12 Maxworthy, C. (2023) Qantas turned off my microphone at the AGM. *Australian Financial Review*, November 8th.

It was generally assumed that this lesson would carry though to any future crisis that Optus may experience.

However, 2023 proved to be another year that Optus would rather forget. In November Optus's 10 million clients woke to the realisation that their internet and mobile services were offline. This had occurred due to a system outage at 4am. Non-Optus users, who sought to interact with businesses reliant on Optus, were of course also affected.

Optus responded with a short post, apologising and stating they knew there was a problem and that they were looking into it. Of course, their customers were unable to access this message on their devices linked to the Optus network. Among their customers were 400,000 businesses as well as the critical infrastructure being used by hospitals, schools and transport systems who were significantly impacted.

It wasn't until nearly seven hours after the outage had commenced that the CEO did her first radio interview; using WhatsApp due to no mobile connection being available. The federal government's Minister for Communications, Michelle Rowland, had been fielding calls from media since 5am. Whatever disaster recovery plan Optus had in place had failed.

What Optus customers wanted during this outage was for the CEO to come out and appear on morning TV news shows that customers could still access, and participate in radio interviews, personally apologise and offer whatever explanation might be possible at that early stage of diagnosing the problem. This didn't happen, and arguably her lack of willingness to speak publicly in a timely manner was considered by many to be as egregious as the inconvenience of the outage itself.

During her interview, far from acknowledging that communication could have been better and showing contrition, the CEO defended the brief written statement as being adequate. She indicated that people were not upset with her lack of communication, but with the fact that she had not been able to tell them what they wanted to hear (presumably what went wrong and when would it be fixed).

She made a public statement about how 10 million people were feeling, surely a risky proposition. She also justified her lack of response in part by saying that it was a complex matter that 'couldn't be covered in a sound bite'. This misses the point entirely. Communication isn't only about content – it's about connectedness to people, empathy and accountability.

Her inability to 'read the room' would suggest that no lesson had been learnt from the data security breach and resultant PR disaster the year before. Optus is a communications company, yet they demonstrated that they were unable to understand the fundamentals of communication in a crisis; that is, to respond quickly and communicate often. The CEO departed the company two weeks later.

Rupert Murdoch, who stepped down from his longstanding role as chair of global media empire News Corp and Fox in 2023, is generally credited as writing the playbook on how to survive public scrutiny following a scandal. When News Limited employees were caught in the illegal phone hacking scandal in the UK in 2011, he proclaimed that this was the 'most humble day of my life' and the news cycle simply moved on with no demonstrable consequences for Murdoch.

It is a pity to see something as simple as a genuine apology compromised in many instances by lack of authenticity. As *Sydney Morning Herald* journalist Malcolm Knox stated, 'An apology is no longer an assumption of responsibility. It is often the opposite; a get-out-of-jail-free card.'[13]

Beyond the corporate sphere trust in the media is also down, which may not be due entirely to how media barons themselves are viewed by the public but is perhaps in part due to the proliferation of misinformation abounding across multiple media platforms. 'Fake news' is an expression that has now slipped into common usage.

---

13 Knox, M. (2023) Everyone is saying sorry. If only they actually meant it. *Sydney Morning Herald*, September 30th.

Elon Musk, following his purchase of Twitter, now X, has been heavily criticised for allowing misinformation to proliferate on this social media platform, including that generated by automated bot accounts.[14]

These are automated software applications imitating human behaviour and performing tasks such as internet posts at rapid speed. They can have a powerful influence on attitudes gained via exposure to social media sites.

Ed Coper is the CEO of values-based communications agency Populares and author of *Facts & Other Lies: Welcome to the Disinformation Age*.[15] He provides some answers as to how powerful our addiction to social media can be given the content and images appeal more to emotion than logic. He states that:

> *Social media equally presents another confronting imbalance: it favours the spread of misinformation over factual information. This is largely due to the truth being mundane while misinformation is both gripping and deliberately spread by those on a mission to game the algorithm. Narratives in the social media age are easily manipulated … and lies easily weaponised.*[16]

Our decisions and values and who we align with have all changed in the digital era. Ed Coper uses the example of how if we lived in a street where everyone else held a certain view, we might be more inclined to think through our own position and perhaps align with the group. Now we can simply ignore those in our immediate environment

---

14 Milmo, D. (2023) X criticised for enabling spread of Israel Hamas disinformation. *The Guardian*, October 10th.

15 Coper, E. (2022) *Facts & Other Lies: Welcome to the Disinformation Age*. Allen & Unwin, Sydney.

16 Ibid.

and easily find thousands on the internet who agree with us and who we can now form an allegiance with.

We are less concerned with the truth these days and more with satisfying our emotions, often choosing to ignore that the information with which we align has been generated by a powerful army of bots all acting in alignment to further a specific agenda.

No wonder people are feeling confused and cynical. The answer would seem to be to align not with internet chatter but with our own values, that have most likely stood us in good stead throughout our lives and certainly at times of making important decisions.

Concerning the PwC scandal, the company admitted to having betrayed the public's trust and committed to an inquiry headed by former Telstra CEO Ziggy Switkowski. He found PwC Australia's culture and governance practices were so weak they led to integrity failures.

This example demonstrated an organisation that prized revenues and growth over ethics, values and purpose, with a whatever it takes culture that made heroes out of partners who raked in the most money.

If you were at the top, you were called a 'rainmaker'. The biggest rainmakers who brought in the most money was referred to as 'untouchables', to whom the rules didn't always apply. Switkowski found the culture was 'collegial in the sense that dissent wasn't welcome.'[17] There may be lessons for other organisations in his key findings:

1. Excessive power conferred on the CEO.
2. A disproportionate focus on revenue growth.
3. Unclear responsibilities and accountabilities.
4. A lack of independence and external voices on the governance board.

---

17 Rhodes, C. (2023) Beyond the PwC scandal, there's a growing case for a royal commission into Australia's ruthless corporate greed. *The Conversation*, https://theconversation.com/beyond-the-pwc-scandal-theres-a-growing-case-for-a-royal-commission-into-australias-ruthless-corporate-greed-214474. September 28th.

It must be remembered that there are many fine people who work at PwC who were not in any way involved in this egregious behaviour. The betrayal of public trust by some senior partners at PwC was as much a betrayal of their own people.

The government demonstrated its concern as regards the consulting sector when in March 2023 it convened the *Inquiry into Management and Assurance of Integrity by Consulting Services*.

The events that occurred have in some people's minds cast a shadow over the whole professional services sector, and by implication, the people who work in it. This would be unfair. The vast majority of people working within these firms are no doubt people of integrity.

It is time for the whole corporate sector to value trust as a distinct asset, like any other asset sitting on its balance sheet. The public's trust will be highest in those companies who treat all stakeholders with integrity and honesty. Those who care for the wellbeing of their people, are honest and transparent with their customers and contribute positively to society.

Investor–Driven Change

Governance is, of course, one of the pillars of ESG. This is the domain of obeying laws, as well as compliance with internal company policies. Strong governance is designed to limit illegal or unethical or immoral behaviour from leaders which would otherwise harm a company's stakeholders and inevitably damage the company's reputation.

The VW emissions scandal of 2015 by the German car manufacturer was a classic case of governance failure. A range of models had software installed in diesel engines that could detect when they were being tested. This software then moved the vehicle into a lower power and performance setting resulting in lower carbon dioxide emission levels. This method of cheating regulators was detected by the Environmental Protection Agency in the US.

No company should need threats from regulators to conduct their business in an honest and responsible manner. Contributing positively to people and planet should be enough. If this isn't enough for any board or CEO, then look no further than the changing investor landscape.

BlackRock, through its managed funds, is the world's largest asset owner with $8.5 trillion under management. It is often criticised for its market power and alleged ability to distort markets, with another common criticism being its willingness to supply fossil fuel companies with a steady stream of capital and to invest in companies engaged in rampant deforestation – thereby funding the climate crisis.

However, its founder and CEO, Larry Fink, has talked about the changing landscape regarding investor expectations. This concerns a desire to see more responsible business practices, as well as pragmatic investors who want to see data on the link between ESG and company performance.

BlackRock asked all companies it invests in to report against the Sustainability Accounting Standards Board (SASB), noting this resulted in an increase of 363 per cent in disclosures in just one year. This is an example of how one powerful financial services business can shift priorities in a range of other sectors. Fink sees opportunities for investors and states, 'Decarbonising the global economy is going to create the greatest investment opportunity of our lifetime.'[18]

Daniel Simons, in his 2023 article 'Why climate tech is where the smart money is now', also sees positive investment opportunities in addressing climate change.[19] This turns a cost into an investment:

18 Fink, L. (2022) https://blackrock.com/corporate/investor-relations/larry-fink-ceo-letter

19 Simons, D. (2023) Why climate tech is where the smart money is right now. https://startupdaily.net/advice/investing/why-climate-tech-is-where-the-smart-money-is-right-now. August 29th.

*An entire ecosystem of investors, financiers, super
funds, VCs, private equity, family offices, banks,
high net worth individuals, sovereign wealth funds,
governments and even corporates are scrambling
to shift funds into climate solutions in the race to
decarbonise and build resilience.*[20]

So, taking a more responsible position as regards all three aspects of ESG is not only the responsible thing to do, but also the smart thing to do.

Climate Change

No book on business is complete without a section devoted to climate change. The impact by business is that great. Our corporate leaders must appreciate the ramifications of their decisions on the planet and never lose sight of the interdependence of all things within the world in which we live. This applies to the significant impact by business on our changing climate.

There will also be instances where some visionary corporate leaders will at times be ahead of regulators and even investor sentiment, as regards their commitment to environmental and social issues, which may draw criticism from some quarters. This is where courage is required by business leaders. The very nature of a leader means you are out front, and at times this can be a lonely place to be.

Energy company British Petroleum (BP) experienced this when it embarked on an image makeover with its slogan 'Beyond Petroleum' (a play on BP) as it moved into cleaner fuels and investment in solar power. More cynical market observers dubbed it BP 'Beyond Profit', indicating that in some quarters the concept of making profits, while

---

20 Ibid.

taking a longer-term view of the market and incorporating environmental responsibility, was not clearly understood.[21]

Issues such as human-induced global climate change must be addressed by business as well as governments as a matter of urgency. The goal set at the 2015 Paris Agreement was to limit global warming rises to 1.5 degrees Centigrade (2.7 degrees Fahrenheit). Global warming is directly linked to CO2 emissions.

In order to achieve and maintain this, creating a state of net zero carbon emissions by 2050 is the strategy set by the Intergovernmental Panel on Climate Change (IPCC), which has become the internationally agreed upon goal. The important word here is 'net'.[22]

While targets have also been set at the UN Climate Change Conference (COP) as regards reaching net zero CO2 by 2050 this does not mean that there will be zero carbon emissions. It is a state created by the greenhouse gases going into the atmosphere being balanced by their removal out of the atmosphere.

We need our best minds confronting the challenge of global warming. One weakness, in meetings such as COP, is that the same gender imbalance that afflicts the upper echelons of the corporate world is evidenced again at such events. Of 140 world leaders attending COP28 in 2023, only 15 were women, albeit up from six women at last year's summit.

COP29 will take place in Azerbaijan in November of 2024, and at the start of that year the members of the 28-member organising committee were announced. Staggeringly, there was not a single woman on the committee.

After sustained pressure the government of Azerbaijan announced that they were adding 12 women to the committee (plus one additional man). As Victoria McKenzie-McHarg, Strategic Director of

---

21 Laszlo, C. (2005) *The Sustainable Company: How to Create Lasting Value Through Social and Environmental Performance*. Island Press, Washington.

22 University of Oxford (2023) What Is Net Zero. https://netzeroclimate.org/what-is-net-zero-2/

Women's Environmental Leadership Australia, said, 'When you have more women at the decision-making table, you get better environmental outcomes.'[23] This applies equally to the boardroom table as it does to the civil society or political one.

Progress is being made however, and one point made at the Just Energy Transition Partnerships event at the COP28 talks was that we should remain optimistic as we *are* capable of making progress while at the same time ensuring a fair and just transition to a cleaner world for all affected parties.[24]

Slowness of action is hard to fathom considering reports such as the American Institute of Biological Science's *2023 State of the Climate Report: Entering Uncharted Territory*.[25] This study has been endorsed by 15,000 scientists globally and highlights the harm that we are doing to the planet and states that the earth's 'vital signs are worse than at any time in human history,' and further that 'life on planet earth is under siege.'[26]

They quote statistics that in 2023 we had the highest global air temperature and ocean temperatures, and that earth was probably the hottest it had been in 100,000 years. The average global temperature was 1.3 degrees Celsius above pre-industrial levels, according to Climate Central scientists.

In late 2023 the earth's average temperature was recorded for two days at levels that were 2 degrees above pre-industrial revolution levels, an era prior to the use of fossil fuels.[27] It was also determined

23 McKenzie-McHarg, V. (2023) Byron Writers Festival, Byron Bay. August 12th.

24 https://ihrb.org/events/cop28-official-side-event-unpacking-progress-from-south-africa-and-indonesia-on-the-j-in-jetp

25 Ripple, W., Wolf, C., et al (2023) The 2023 State of the Climate Report: Entering Uncharted Territory. *Bio Science*, American Institute of Biological Sciences, October 24th.

26 Ibid.

27 Copernicus, (2023) https://climate.copernicus.eu/global-temperature-exceeds-2degc-above-pre-industrial-average-17-november

that there is a 66 per cent chance that we will reach the 1.5 degree increase in 2027 with the upward trend line producing unimaginable consequences.[28]

Adding further to the imperative to take action, an article published in April 2024 in *Nature* states that the economic impact of climate change will be six times greater than the cost of action to limit global heating to 2 degrees, and that without significant action it is estimated that average incomes will fall by one fifth due to the impact of climate change.[29]

The 'carbon budget' is the term given to the maximum amount of carbon that we can emit and still reach the goal set at the Paris Agreement. At current levels of emissions, it is estimated that the budget will have been entirely exhausted within the next six years.[30]

The UN's *Emissions Gap Report 2023* predicts that the world will warm by 2.9 degrees this century, underlining the fact that far greater action to mitigate global warming is crucial.[31]

Due to the current lack of action by governments and business, and also individuals unwilling to modify their lifestyle choices, this goal of limiting global warming to 1.5 degrees is most likely already out of reach. The current trend can be reversed, but it will require genuine commitment.

Mining and energy companies are some of our largest corporations, and fossil fuels are undoubtedly a major contributor to global warming. Forecasts are that coal production is expected to increase up until 2030 and oil and gas production to 2050 and beyond.

---

28 Outlook India (2023) https://www.outlookindia.com/international/
    un-predicts-warmest-ever-period-between-2023-2027-news-287063

29 Kotz, M., Levermann, A. & Wenz, L. (2024) The economic commitment of
    climate change, *Nature*.

30 https://theguardian.com/environment/2023/oct/30/climate-crisis-carbon-
    emissions-budget

31 UN Emissions Gap Report 2023. https://unep.org/resources/emissions-gap-
    report-2023

As profitability drives business decisions, and as long as we have an insatiable thirst for oil and gas products to support our lifestyles, and oil and gas companies believe that they can weather the storm of adverse public opinion, then production will continue.

In a sign of growing push-back on some practices within this sector, the UK high court has ruled that thousands of villagers in Nigeria can bring legal claims against Shell for the disastrous impacts of oil spills in the Niger Delta. This effectively enshrines the human right to a clean environment.

Shell claimed it had made reparations already and spent eight years attempting to convince the courts that there was no further case to answer. Perhaps this money could have been spent in a more humane manner and in reassessing its exploration and extraction practices.

We have been warned that not achieving the goal of remaining below 1.5 degrees would risk the earth's population being exposed to increased storms, rising sea levels, severe heatwaves, wildfires on an unprecedented scale and devastating droughts with the subsequent catastrophic impacts on other forms of life.

A prescient warning for our species comes in the form of a break-through in early 2024 in the field of palaeontology. For years scientists had been puzzled by why our largest relative had vanished. The three-metre tall, 300-kilogram heavy primate Gigantopithecus Blacki had become extinct some two million years ago. Macquarie University researchers, through the use of luminescence dating, have now deter-mined that 'Giganto' had failed to adapt to climate change'.[32]

Canadian American John Vaillant is just one author who is asking us to wake up and make changes to our lifestyles. His book *Fire Weather: A True Story From A Hotter World* tells the story of the horrendous wildfires that struck Alberta in 2016.[33]

---

32 Dalton, A. (2024) We now know what killed human's largest relative – and it's eerie. *Sydney Morning Herald*, January 11th.

33 Vaillant, J. (2023) *Fire Weather: A True Story From A Hotter World*. Penguin Random House, New York.

He discusses the conundrum of our dependency on fossil fuels, and our unwillingness to disrupt the status quo which has created comfortable lives for most of us, while at the same time we are aware we are condemning the world to a potentially catastrophic future. He says we need to have honest conversations, and that one of these is around the fact that:

> *… you can't have profits and happy shareholders and*
> *believe that the things that are making them happy*
> *and profitable don't have real impacts on the physics and*
> *chemistry of this earth in ways that make it burn worse*
> *and more intensely than it ever has in human history.*[34]

One imperative in demanding a reduction in carbon emissions is that the impact of climate change disproportionately affects people in certain nations, often with poorer economic situations. This restricts their government's ability to affect outcomes, and therefore their citizens are more vulnerable.

Research combining the work of the Stockholm Environment Institute and Oxfam through its *Climate Equality: A Planet for the 99%* report published in late 2023 highlights that the richest 1 per cent in the world are responsible for more carbon emissions than the poorest 66 per cent, with the impact falling largely on the poorest and most vulnerable.[35] This is often referred to as the 'climate chasm' or 'the great carbon divide'.

Rising sea levels affecting Pacific Island nations is just one example of this. This is where climate change overlaps with human rights considerations; that is the E, environmental considerations, and the S, social

---

34 Creamer, E. (2023) John Vaillant wins Baillie Gifford nonfiction prize with highly relevant work on wildfires. *The Guardian*, November 17th.

35 Oxfam (2023). https://policy-practice.oxfam.org/resources/climate-equality-a-planet-for-the-99-621551/

sustainability, of ESG intersect. A focus on one without the other will increase risk for the business and boards need to understand this.

You may remember images of the foreign minister of Tuvalu addressing the UN's climate conference in Glasgow in 2022, standing in the sea in thigh-deep water to get the world's attention.

Reinforcing the reality of Australia's impact on its neighbours in late 2023, Australia's prime minister Anthony Albanese announced that Australia would grant visas for 10 per cent of the residents of the Pacific micro-state of Tuvalu, effective over a four-year period. This is a part of the progressive evacuation of the entire population of 11,200 people.

Australia was also one of a hundred nations across the globe in committing to a tripling of renewable energy capacity by the end of the decade. This was seen as a significant achievement at COP28.

The Australian Climate Accountability Project, through the Australian Human Rights Institute at UNSW, is undertaking new research into the harm generated in Australian communities by climate change.[36] The project is led by Gillian Moon, and my daughter Nina Cooke has worked as a researcher on the project.

One focus area is Australia's massive and growing exports of oil and gas. This highlights that although Australia has a relatively small population, and hence, we may believe that we contribute very little to global warming, this is not the case. We are, in effect, exporting emissions.

In its report *Children Displaced in a Changing Climate*, UNICEF has documented that between 2016 and 2021 43.1 million children have been displaced due to weather-related disasters including floods, storms, drought and wildfires. This is the equivalent of 20,000 per day and the situation is projected to get worse.[37]

---

36 https://humanrights.unsw.edu.au/research/australian-climate-accountability-project
37 UNICEF (2023) Children Displaced in a Changing Climate. https://www.unicef.org/reports/children-displaced-changing-climate. October.

We need a far great effort from all our institutions including businesses to minimise their impact on the planet. We must stop the excesses of the modern world that inflict this suffering on children. There is no kindness present here.

There is also a gender element to the climate crisis. A report by the UNFPA (United Nations Population Fund) shows that women and girls are particularly vulnerable to negative impacts. The report studied the climate action plans of 119 countries regarding specific reference to women and found only 38 include any form of planning for continuing access to contraception, maternal and newborn health services. Reference to the potential of increased violence against women is only mentioned in 15 of the national plans studied.

Companies must review their policy frameworks to ensure that they are addressing their impact on the environment broadly, affecting all members of society. However, specific focus also needs to be on potential climate change risks for their own workers. One example of this concerns additional breaks for workers in an ever-warming world.

Once again, the poorest are the most vulnerable. Someone working in a factory with intolerable temperatures or performing outside manual labour, may not take the breaks they need to rest or rehydrate if they feel it may put their job at risk.

This same consideration also needs to apply to those incarcerated. Governments need to act with a duty of care; however, so too do corporations, with the number of detainees in prisons that are privately run by profit-making corporations now reaching 10 per cent of the total prison population in the US.

Extreme heat is killing people in prison. Temperatures in some South and Southwestern prisons in the US have reached 115 degrees Fahrenheit or 46 degrees Celsius. Some of those incarcerated are children and some are in solitary confinement. These government agencies and private companies need to demonstrate compassion for the people under their care, irrespective of why the individual may have been sentenced.[38]

Eliminating Exploitation

It is incumbent on every business leader to first obey the law in respect of all aspects of their business, and not to seek ways around the law in order to exploit workers. Regrettably there are too many instances of this, with sham contracts for workers and various other forms of exploitation.

There are social deficits such as the abysmal pay and conditions experienced by millions of workers in countries across Asia and other parts of the world. Greater short-term profits can be generated when you don't pay workers a living wage, but can anyone seriously suggest that this can be justified in any way?

Boards who choose to turn away and pretend they are unaware of the human misery that their companies are causing are culpable, and even if solely motivated by the pursuit of short-term profits, must surely realise that they are sowing the seeds of deep and sustained reputational damage for the brand that they are stewards of. Mahatma Gandhi's comment is relevant here, 'There is enough for everybody's need, but not enough for everybody's greed.'[39]

This is not only the domain of those working in manufacturing, retail, transport or agricultural sectors. We have also seen exploitation in white collar environments such as the legal profession with unpaid work routinely expected, particularly of young people, if they are to keep their job or to progress their careers.

Working arrangements are changing rapidly and the term 'gig

38 Weill-Greenberg, E. & Wing, N. (2023) Extreme heat is killing people in prison, what's being done about it? *The Appeal.* https://theappeal.org/heat-prison-deaths-air-conditioning/. August 29th.

39 Badiner, A. H. (Ed.) (2002) *Mindfulness in the Marketplace: Compassionate Responses to Consumerism.* Parallax Press, Berkley, CA.

economy' has moved into common usage. It refers to part-time or temporary positions and the term is borrowed from the music industry where musicians refer to performing a 'gig'.

When many saw this phenomenon becoming widespread, there was a feeling of nervousness around who the winner and who the loser might be. Business no longer had to pay leave entitlements, offer workers compensation insurance or provide any security of tenure or notice periods or redundancy payments in the event of the role no longer being required. In return, the person taking up one of these newly styled roles received far greater flexibility.

They were billed as offering workers an exciting new opportunity to be the master of their own destiny with more agency than ever before. Often characterised by picking up short-term tasks via digital platforms there was little meaningful ongoing contact with another human being in the company and no-one personally responsible for their wellbeing.

In the worst cases of abuse, delivery drivers have earnt well below what their compensation would have been where they were an employee under previous systems, with the arrangement resulting in some working extreme hours to cover living costs. Regrettably, lives have been lost which some have attributed to the extreme workload.

Many delivery drivers working in the gig economy are overseas students on visas which limit the number of hours of work they can undertake in a month. They may well be exceeding this, driven by financial pressures, and hence reluctant to speak up about poor conditions for fear their breach of visa conditions will be reported or detected and the visa cancelled.

In the case of Uber Eats in Australia, the plight of drivers is contrasted against a backdrop of the company achieving revenue of $2.6 billion and profit of $1.2 billion in 2022. Following adverse media reports, Uber Eats has now moved to put in place support packages for drivers injured on the job or for families of drivers who have lost their lives.

In 2023 legislation was drafted to provide protections; however, this drew criticism from business lobby groups arguing that this would drive up business costs, force some businesses to close altogether and result in massive job losses and damage to the economy.

Viewed through a moral lens, this argument could be rephrased – we have built a business model on exploitation; if you no longer allow this exploitation to continue our costs will rise, and trading conditions will become more difficult. There is no basis for this argument to be deemed reasonable, and arguments of this nature by business should never stop reforms to protect the wellbeing of exploited workers.

Exploitation is not limited to those in the gig economy. In 2022 in one of the higher profile cases of the underpayment of employees, or 'wage theft', the franchised convenience store network 7-Eleven was found in some cases to be paying as little as $10 per hour, while the legislated minimum wage sat at $21.[40] Many of the workers were overseas students. Pay slips recorded significantly reduced hours with the employee told to clock off but immediately return to their job with the second number of hours not recorded.

Compensation amounting to $173 million was paid to 4,000 employees and far stricter internal monitoring systems implemented to lessen the likelihood of reoccurrence. Notwithstanding the often-quoted complexity of legislation concerning wages, it remains incumbent on those running our companies to decide to do whatever is necessary to pay people correctly and fairly. The government also perhaps has a role to play in the simplification of legislation governing various wage rates.

Aldi, the German supermarket chain, is another business that has fallen foul of the courts. Aldi had a long-standing practice of requiring staff to commence their shift 15 minutes earlier than its official

---

40   Clayton, R. (2020) 7 Eleven Owners pay back $173 million to employees. https://abc.net.au/news/2020-10-30/7-11-pays-back-$176-million-worth-of-backpay-super-to-staff/12831176. October 30th.

start time, which had affected some 4,000 workers. Aldi originally disputed this claim; however, the federal court made a judgement against Aldi, with the judge stating there had been 'a clear implied direction' to employees.

In late 2023 a class action was commenced by the SDA, the union representing retail and warehousing workers, seeking compensation.[41] McDonald's is facing a $100 million class action alleging that it asked staff to work one hour each shift for free.

Bubble tea franchise Chatime was another high-profile retailer in which the government's workplace regulator, the Fair Work Ombudsman, determined that there had been significant under-payment of staff.[42]

Beyond exploitation is the issue of modern slavery which must be eradicated from corporate supply chains. The public should have con-fidence that the purchases they make were not produced by slaves or people working in slave-like conditions.

The term 'supply chain', sometimes termed 'value chain', refers to the operations of the companies that a business buys things from either to resell or use in your business. This is Tier 1, and the tiers below this refer to your direct suppliers' own suppliers, be it finished goods, componentry or raw materials. A look into one of Australia's largest companies, Wesfarmers, gives us some understanding of the complexity, with their website stating:

41 Lawyerly (2023) https://lawyerly.com.au/aldi-faces-150m-underpayments-class-action/. October 28th.

42 Ferguson, A. (2023) Chatime faces huge fines for exploiting the wages of Australian employees, or it may be just the tip of the iceberg. https://www.abc.net.au/news/2023-08-28/chatime-wage-underpayment-one-in-long-list-of-scandals/102777492. August 28th.

Across the Group, we have relationships with nearly 26,000 suppliers. Our businesses directly source products for resale from about 12,000 third-party suppliers in more than 40 countries. Our major product sourcing locations include Australia, Bangladesh, China, Europe, India, and Indonesia.

Our supply chains are often complex with multiple tiers, sometimes across multiple countries, supplying diverse products to our divisions. We do not own the sites and factories where products are manufactured but engage suppliers to manufacture own–brand goods for us and other suppliers.[43]

The size and complexity of modern slavery in corporate supply chains is undeniable, we only have to look at the millions trapped in various forms of forced labour to know that. Those organisations that are demonstrating concern for these people and making genuine commitments, and allocating significant resources, should be applauded.

The Australian Modern Slavery Act (2018) requires all boards of Australian companies with an annual turnover of more than $100 million to sign their organisation's Modern Slavery Statement, which is submitted to government on an annual basis. For company directors to state, 'I didn't know there were risks in our supply chain' or 'I didn't know what I was signing' is inexcusable. The information on the ethical sourcing risks that every company faces is readily available; it is our responsibility to read it.

---

43 Wesfarmers (2023) Sustainability our priorities ethical sourcing and human rights. https://wesfarmers.com.au/sustainability/fy2022/our-priorities/ethical-sourcing-and-human-rights

Regrettably, there are still many who are not focused on the millions of victims in the world today, but merely on producing the next modern slavery statement which is sufficient to comply with current legislation. Risk statements on company websites will generally focus on 'risk to company' but rarely on 'risk to workers' as a result of company practices. There could be no greater act of kindness than freeing these victims and allowing them to return home to their families.

Sourcing goods and services ethically isn't just about de-risking corporate supply chains – it is about the agency, the liberty and the lives of each person trapped in any form of forced labour. When asked why they think many companies are still only doing the minimum required under the Act, the answer is often that boards and senior executives are just too removed from this and just don't realise what is happening in their supply chains.

If this is the case, it is a poor excuse that does not live up to the standards of leadership that we have a right to expect. Boards need to widen their lens from reducing risk for the company to reducing risk to workers in their supply chains.

In order to strengthen the Act, Professor John McMillan led a review in 2023.[44] One recommendation was that the reporting threshold be lowered to an annual turnover of $50 million, thereby extending the obligation to report to a greater number of company boards. His work led to the *Modern Slavery Amendment Bill 2023* which was passed by the Senate in May of 2024 and established the role of a National Australian Anti-slavery Commissioner.

Some believe that directors have too many ESG issues on their plate and point to the focus of directors being on issues that are more top of mind for their customers and clients, which may directly affect the company's reputation and short-term commercial performance.

---

44 Report of the statutory review of the Modern Slavery Act 2018 (Cth) | Attorney-General's Department (ag.gov.au)

Notably the company's environmental impact through issues such as carbon emissions, plastic packaging and waste. Still, 'I was attending to other ESG issues' is a poor excuse for not doing everything possible to eliminate human rights abuses from any responsible business.

It begs the following questions of every company director – when do you think you will have time to eliminate slavery from your business? How long are you planning to leave people in your supply chain trapped in modern slavery for, another year, another 10 years?

If you hold senior office in any organisation in this land, and you are not doing everything within your power to eliminate slavery from that organisation, then it raises concerns as to your suitability to hold that office. Boards would do well to contemplate these three questions:

1. Are we doing enough to eliminate slavery from our organisation?
2. Could we be doing more?
3. How much longer are we willing to generate profits by exploiting vulnerable workers trapped in forced labour in our supply chain?

Good Tech Bad Tech

A clear example of the challenges we are facing in ensuring ethical business concerns the enormous advances in technology that we are experiencing. Technology brings with it considerable inherent challenges along with the fact that advances in technology can be used for both good and bad purposes.

We see this when tech is used in order to hack corporate systems and individuals' accounts, while tech is also used by those charged with defending company data. Millions of attacks on corporate servers are a daily reality already, however we can expect these to increase.

There is a cat and mouse game being played out globally whereby attacks are growing in frequency and effectiveness, as good tech seeks to keep up. Companies will often employ 'white hat' hackers who seek to stress test corporate systems looking for ways in. If weaknesses are found, the client will then strengthen these.

It is a never-ending battle with the odds stacked against the 'good guys' given that hackers may launch millions of attacks and only need to be occasionally successful to reap their rewards; whereas those responding to these attacks have to be successful 100 per cent of the time, otherwise they are deemed to have failed.

Some of the biggest companies in the world by market capitalisation, such as Amazon, Alphabet and Meta, are representative of the explosion of internet usage and collection of data. Over 50 per cent of the world's population are now regularly accessing the internet. We contribute data on ourselves every day through collection devices such as our phones, GPS systems in our cars, smart appliances in our homes, and smart speakers with voice activated assistants such as Alexa, Siri and Google Assistant.

This has given rise to the rapid growth of data centres in Australia and across the globe. In 2018 the Australian Energy Council calculated that data centres accounted for 4 per cent of all energy consumption in Australia and estimates globally are as high as 10 per cent.[45]

Researchers stated in their paper 'Trends in Data Centre Energy Consumption under the European Code of Conduct for Data Centre Energy Efficiency', published in 2017 in the MDPI journal *Energies*, that they estimated that data centres would grow to the point where they consumed a fifth of all the world's energy by 2025.[46]

Every document that we save to the cloud, every social media post, every swipe and every entry made into an online search engine involves the use of servers within a data centre somewhere, and every touchpoint generates more data that is stored. The effect is cumulative, adding to the exponential growth of data being stored.

---

45 Lovell, J. (2018) *Big Data: a big energy challenge*. Australian Energy Council.
46 Avgerinou, M., et al (2017) Trends in Data Centre Energy Consumption under the European Code of Conduct for Data Centre Energy Efficiency. *MDPI Journal Energies*, September.

The phasing out of cash in favour of digital transactions along with the rise of cryptocurrencies and blockchain NFT's (non-fungible tokens) only add to the explosion of data storage, as do higher definition cameras in our phones.

All this data storage comes at a cost to the environment via the huge power consumption requirements, rivalling that consumed by small nations, and water consumption to cool servers, at a time when we are experiencing drought conditions in many regions due to climate change. This is just one of the trade-offs of making our corporate and personal lives in developed nations more efficient and comfortable.

Much of our discarded tech, as we upgrade to the latest models, ends up as landfill in developing nations, with chemicals leaching into the environment causing contamination with half-lives, the time it takes to break down, of hundreds of years. Out of sight, out of mind. The discussion of 'forever chemicals' has now become mainstream.

Despite tech transforming our lives, and notwithstanding its potential for good, tech can also cause harm. If directed towards the agendas that have plagued some traditional businesses, namely short-termism, or in some cases greed or even corrupt conduct, then unfortunately the potential for harm is now far greater than ever before.

As consumers we are easy to manipulate and now with 'big data' it is easier than ever before, with targeted advertising based on millions of data points. Some would say this is just clever personalised marketing; others that we are witnessing the complete moral disintegration of corporate values.

Wearable tech, the fitness trackers that many of us have on our wrists, is coming under scrutiny. The marketing involves an appeal to better health, and we are incited to take responsibility for our own health and wellbeing. Those that wear these devices are demonstrating a willingness to face even uncomfortable truths about their levels of fitness or dietary preferences. Yet some will say that there is a dark side.

It may surprise many to know that the underlying technology, including many of the patents involved in these devices, are also found in criminal detention ankle bracelets, the monitors used for house arrest. Both devices transfer massive amounts of data about us, back to the distributor of the equipment for their use. It is unlikely that we have any understanding of who this data might be shared with and for what purpose.

It is not just consumers who are embracing wearables though, it is companies as well. Some, such as Amazon, are in many cases compelling their factory workers to fit a belt or other device to monitor their performance and transmit data back to the company's server.[47]

These systems are an adaptation of technology that has been developed to enhance athletic performance and are sold based on having the potential to create 'industrial warriors'. No wonder the term 'a brave new world' is being used by commentators, acknowledging Aldous Huxley's dystopian work of fiction published in 1932.[48]

Sophisticated spyware is now a huge part of the intelligence gathering and military tech industries with programs such as Pegasus's extensive data collection capabilities that infiltrate both Android and IOS devices. Apart from an invasion of our own personal privacy, it has been claimed that some governments have deployed Pegasus to monitor human rights activists within their countries.

It should be stated that the technology does have the capacity to allow law enforcement agencies to track and potentially apprehend and prosecute criminals engaging in terrorism, or activities such as money laundering as well as individuals preying on children online. This is 'tech for good'; however, in these situations governments must balance surveillance capabilities used to protect citizens with privacy and civil liberty issues.

While tech companies such as Google, Amazon, Facebook and others have made themselves indispensable and trade on the undeniable

---

47 Suneel Jethani, (2023) Invisible Strings panel, Byron Writers Festival, Byron Bay, August 12th.

48 Huxley, A. (1932) *Brave New World*. Penguin, London.

benefits they bring us, they are also wary themselves of the likelihood of increased regulatory restrictions. This has resulted in them investing huge sums of money in PR and lobbying efforts to minimise any attempts to limit their growth and influence.

The ever-increasing power and control that some global tech companies now have over us, in the new digital world that we live in, is highlighted in the work *The Age of Surveillance Capitalism* by Shoshana Zuboff.[49] Her groundbreaking book, published in 2019, posits that we are now no longer the customer of digital companies but their raw material whereby they monitor our every move and harvest our data for sale to the highest bidder.

Coles and Woolworths, Australia's two largest supermarket chains, which for many years were among its most trusted brands, have come in for criticism over their market power and treatment of suppliers. However, criticism has also extended to their move to self-service checkout systems. Following some initial concerns, mostly around job losses and the reduction in staff numbers, this new way of paying for items has been accepted by the majority of people as providing faster checkout times.

However, now a new dimension has been added to this technology, namely customer surveillance technology, which videos the scanning of items and partially includes the customer's image.

This involves the use of artificial intelligence to detect when items are not being scanned correctly. This is largely in response to multi-million-dollar stock losses by both supermarkets caused by theft or incorrectly scanned items. While it is understandable that these businesses would seek to stem these losses, nevertheless privacy concerns have been raised.

Chair of the Australian Privacy Foundation, David Vaile, has said that whenever a business uses CCTV to monitor customers biometric

---

49 Zuboff, S. (2019) *The Age of Surveillance Capitalism: The Fight for a Human Future at the Frontier of Power.* Profile Books, London.

data could potentially be used by third parties for other purposes to identify customers by facial and iris recognition and even gait and voice recognition.[50]

When the tide turns against a brand it is cause for concern, as it is well known that consumer distrust is a more powerful determinant of buyer behaviour than trust is and can quickly undermine previous brand loyalty. Some entire industries, due to the products they sell, may be considered as incapable of engendering trust or embodying an ethos of being kind to people and planet.

The gambling industry, massively enabled by digital technology, also raises questions as to whether, by its very nature, it contributes positively to society. It is a legal form of entertainment, enjoyed by many, however, one that inflicts major societal damage.

Investigations by regulators into Crown and Star casinos would suggest the industry is not capable of self-regulating to avoid societal harm. In the absence of moral leadership on boards and at executive levels, it is falling to governments to intervene to restrain the ambitions of this industry, which appears at times to be willing to operate outside the law.

There has been a proliferation of gambling adds, often during live sporting events, inciting us to download the betting organisation's apps in order to have the ability to gamble in the palm of our hands. Children are watching these ads and anecdotally there are reports of young children using the terminology of the gambling industry in playground conversations with friends.

It is just another example of capitalism not being able to restrain itself in its quest for a greater share of consumer spending, in order to produce higher returns for investors. Seemingly blind to the reality that this may ultimately lead to self-destruction once regulators step in.

---

50 Shultz, A. (2013) Up to 70 cameras watch you buy groceries. What happens to that footage? *Sydney Morning Herald*, August 27th.

Vaping is an insidious new trend under scrutiny. This personal use technology heats nicotine creating a vapor that is then breathed into the lungs. A single disposable e-cigarette can contain as much nicotine as 50 traditional cigarettes. This dispels the myth that vaping is a path away from cigarettes to a nicotine-free future. There are no similarities between this product and methadone used in lowering dependency in heroin users.

Research has shown damaging effects on both physical and mental health. Vapes have been found to contain up to 200 dangerous chemicals including acrolein used in weed killers, arsenic found in rat poison and xylene found in paint stripper.[51] Children have been aggressively targeted by these companies with flavours such as chocolate milk, candy floss and cola ice. It is tragic that the public must be ever vigilant to the dubious actions of businesses engaging in profit making at the expense of individual and societal health.

Tobacco giant Philip Morris International (PMI) has been lobbying to stop WHO (the World Health Organization) and various governments from cracking down on vaping, seeking to protect a market which for them produced over $US10 billion in revenue in 2022.

The targets of these industries are often among the most vulnerable members of society – those with addictions who are easy prey as well as children. In an internal message to staff the vice-president of external affairs at PMI has described attempts by governments to protect the health of their citizens as a 'prohibitionist attack'.[52]

At the end of the day, it may just be that the regulators have to act almost as quasi company directors. So when no director has a strong enough moral compass to speak up at the board table, then reasonable business principles are imposed by others from outside with the power

---

51   Vic Health (2023) Everything we know so far about vaping. https://vichealth. vic.gov.au/our-health/everything-we-know-so-far-about-vaping

52   Marsh, S. (2023) Philip Morris lobbying to stop WHO attack on vapes and similar products. *The Guardian*, October 13th.

to do so. They are saving the company from itself and its own moral blindness.

Robotics has brought us great advances in many areas but is far from perfect. In November of 2023 there was an industrial accident at a distribution centre in South Korea, in which a robot accidentally crushed a worker seemingly mistaking him for a package that the robot was assigned to pick up and transport. Other accidents in which workers have been seriously injured have also been reported.[53]

However, technology has underpinned much of society's advances, making our lives more comfortable and efficient, and has been responsible for much of the standard of living that many of us enjoy today. It is employed in every sector and a functioning society as we know it today is unimaginable without the utilisation of the latest technologies.

Technology is of course used in confronting many of society's most pressing problems enabling meaningful gains to be made in tackling the measurement of carbon emissions, biodiversity loss, producing advances in agriculture, the level of global modern slavery and the tracing of victims of human trafficking.

Notwithstanding the huge benefits that technology brings us there is nevertheless somewhat of a cloud that hangs over its all-encompassing deployment. Economist and former Finance Minister in the Greek government, Yanis Varoufakis, describes this as 'technofeudalism'.

He expresses concerns around the power that the global tech barons, such as Zuckerberg, Musk and Bezos, possess, and describes the power of the algorithms that they have created and the knowledge they collect about us as having, in a sense, enslaved us.

He speaks of 'cloud capital' and describes us as having become 'cloud serfs'. His solution is for governments to legislate for greater accountability of those who own the algorithms so that they serve

---

53   *Agence France Press* (2023) Industrial robot crushes man to death in South Korean distribution centre. November 9th.

society or the collective interest, not just those of the big tech firms and their shareholders.

His book, *Technofeudalism: What Killed Capitalism*, sounds yet another warning to capitalism that its obsession with growth, market share, power and control of its customers may well ultimately be its undoing.[54] In this case the answer to the question posed by the title of the book is, of course, that capitalism killed itself.

Kindness, fairness and compassion ahead of greed, exploitation and excessive consumption are the keys to mankind thriving.

Artificial Intelligence

One of the biggest advances from tech companies is in the field of artificial intelligence (AI). Despite its recent upwards trajectory AI has been 'hiding in plain sight' for decades, and it has been responsible for serving up recommendations on our streaming platforms and determining what we see on social media for years.

AI is simulating human intelligence, learning from experience and therefore replacing the need for the human themselves. Its power is in its adaptability to respond to us on an individual basis according to perceived needs.

One of the most rapidly adopted AI systems is ChatGPT (Chat Generative Pre-trained Transformer), released in 2022 by OpenAI. It can respond to users' requests on almost any subject and at extremely high speed. As regards usage in the corporate sector, if the goal of automating business processes is to increase efficiency and eliminate cost, then this is rapidly being achieved.

History tells us that technological developments are being embraced at a more rapid pace than ever before. Economist Ross Gittins provides a useful timeline – 'It took the telephone 75 years to

54 Varoufakis, Y. (2023) *Technofeudalism: What Killed Capitalism*. Vintage Publishing, London.

reach 100 million users, whereas the mobile phone took 16 years, and the web took 7.... ChatGPT took just 2 months.'[55] Threads, Meta's competitor to Twitter, now X, achieved 100 million subscribers in five days.

McKinsey research published as 'The Economic Potential of Generative AI: The Next Productivity Frontier' indicates that generative AI (Gen AI) stands to add up to $4.4 trillion to the global economy, annually.[56] AI is now essential to business. As an example, Telstra receives over one billion data points on the operating performance of its network every day. It is simply not possible for human beings to analyse that much data.

In February of 2024, Nvidia, which makes the chips critical to training and operating AI systems, became the third most valuable company in the US by market capitalisation, which reached $US2 trillion. Only Apple and Microsoft were ahead.

While there are economic gains due to enhanced productivity, as with other technological advances there are ethical and moral considerations that must be faced, and our challenge is to harness the benefits while minimising the risks. One of these moral dilemmas starts with the information that is fed into AI to train the various systems to respond to user requests.

Many authors are only now becoming aware that their works have been incorporated into AI systems and are labelling it as 'outright theft'.[57] Is this misappropriation of intellectual property without

55 Gittins, R. (2023) AI will make or break us, probably a bit of both. *Sydney Morning Herald*, September 22nd.

56 McKinsey (2023) The Economic Potential of Generative AI: The Next Productivity Frontier. https://mckinsey.com/capabilities/mckinsey-digital/ our-insights/the-economic-potential-of-generative-ai-the-next-productivity-frontier. June.

57 Heath, N. (2023) Australian authors' works feature in Books3 dataset of pirated e-books used to train generative AI. *Sydney Morning Herald*, September 30th.

permission or the right of the purchaser of a book to use its contents for this purpose? Surely the licensing of authors' work would have been a reasonable option for AI developers, however, this would have come at a cost.

The longer-term concern is not that AI systems will simply be more knowledgeable due to absorbing the content of multiple authors, but that the systems are learning to write in certain styles, and within genres, thereby potentially replacing the very authors whose work trained them, albeit without the consent of the author.

The Screen Actors Guild is another group that has raised concerns on behalf of actors regarding the accelerated use of AI among members of the Alliance of Motion Picture and Television Producers. Extras are now being asked by studios to sign a contract on their first day that will permit their image to be scanned for future use, at the discretion of the studio. In many cases this may negate the requirement for the studio to extend any work beyond that one day to these actors.

Photographers are not immune either from the intrusion of AI. Swedish artist Annika Nordenskiöld won the world's first artificial intelligence art award at the Ballarat International Foto Biennale with a life-like image of twin sisters cuddling an octopus, which she created using computer prompts. She said, 'I understand the fear of AI and find it somewhat healthy. But I see it more like a colleague I am working with.'[58]

She recently held an exhibition of her work in Stockholm aptly named *We Don't Exist*. Quite, as none of the people, places or things she 'photographed' do exist. The images are all generated by prompts entered into AI systems. The issue may be seen as an assault on artists themselves, however there are wide-ranging media and societal implications also.

---

58 Pitt, H. (2023) World's first AI award ignites debate about what is photography. *Sydney Morning Herald*, October 8th.

How do we discriminate between something that exists versus an AI generated image of something that does not exist? In an example of tech for good, Google has now developed a tool which will watermark AI images to assist with this.

Without doubt, legislators will need to stay on top of its application to avoid harm. In the above case there are complex legal issues to be resolved, not to mention how to legislate across international boundaries. Universities have their own challenges detecting and regulating student use of AI to complete assignments and assessable work.

It is not possible to ignore or even resist AI; however, the most positive outcomes for society will be achieved through its responsible application. Can we trust the corporate world with the power of AI? Would Amazon, for instance, rather sell books and receive a margin on the sale price or 'write' books with AI and keep 100 per cent of the profits?

Some experts in the field hold deep concerns. Eliezer Yudkowsky, head of research at the Machine Intelligence Research Institute, said, 'We have no idea what we're doing …. We don't know how to align the machine with human values.'[59]

Sam Altman, well before becoming CEO of OpenAI, wrote in 2016 that a pandemic, nuclear war and AI 'that attacks us' were all potential disasters that we may face.[60]

Altman along with Demis Hassabis, the CEO of Google Deep Mind, and hundreds of other experts signed a statement in 2023 warning of the risks of AI. The following statement was posted on the website of the Centre for AI Safety – 'Mitigating the risk of extinction from AI should be a global priority alongside other societal risks such as pandemics and nuclear war.'[61]

---

59 Yudkowski, E. (2023) Pausing AI Developments Isn't Enough. We Need to Shut it All Down. https://time.com/6266923/ai-eliezer-yudkowsky-open-letter-not-enough. March 23rd.

60 Kelly, S. (2023) When OpenAI's CEO was sacked I thought it was corporate trivia. Here's why it's not. *Sydney Morning Herald*, November 27th.

61 https://www.safe.ai/statement-on-ai-risk

Mark Zuckerberg has caused concern with his announcement of Meta's intention to build a powerful AI system on a par with human levels of intelligence. He said Meta would make these 'open source' therefore open to anyone outside the company, thereby making it impossible to ensure that AI was being used responsibly.

Professor Toby Walsh, author of *Machines Behaving Badly: The Morality of AI*, asks several questions that we will need to come to grips with: 'Can we build moral machines? Is Alexa racist? Can robots have rights? What happens if a self-driving car kills someone? What limitations should we put on the use of facial recognition?'[62]

In his latest book *Faking It: Artificial Intelligence in a Human World* he further addresses these questions and states:

> *... at the heart of AI is a fundamental deceit: its goal is to imitate human intelligence. Although AIs like ChatGPT are powerful and convincing, they are fakes. They lack true understanding, sentience, consciousness and common sense, the very traits that make our human intelligence so special.*[63]

Walsh states, 'It can be used to influence what we buy, who gets shortlisted for a job and even how we vote.' As Australia ranks second-last out of 14 leading economies on its deployment of Gen AI, there is likely to be an accelerated take-up very soon. A Deloitte report, *Generative AI ready or not here we come*, states that due to 'AI: a quarter of Australia's economy faces significant and imminent disruption'.[64]

---

62 Walsh, T. (2022) *Machines Behaving Badly: The Morality of AI*. La Trobe University.

63 Walsh, T. (2023) *Faking It: Artificial Intelligence in a Human World*. La Trobe University Press, Melbourne.

64 O'Mahony, J., Nuttall, K. & Scotis, S. (2022) Generation AI: Ready or not here we come. *Deloitte Access Economics*, https://deloitte.com/au/en/services/consulting/analysis/generation-ai-ready-or-not. September.

Ed Santow, former Human Rights Commissioner and now Industry Professor – Responsible Technology at the University of Technology, comments on the preparedness of companies to enter the new world of AI, 'Companies are in the early stages of a long journey. Many have started to take action to understand the social and human rights implications of their use of AI, but they generally haven't been good at taking meaningful action.'

Discussions now often centre on the topic of job losses and which professions will be most affected. AI now writes, paints, composes and makes decisions. If you watched the Australian Open Tennis in 2023 or 2024 you may have noticed that players no longer dispute line calls. This is because there were no humans making the decisions, and hence no room for human error or push-back from competitors.

The line call was made by AI (having replaced Sony's Hawkeye system) and even conveyed to the players in an Australian accent. This system will be adopted for all ATP (Association of Tennis Professionals) events from 2025.

AI is now widely deployed in call centres where it performs its purpose efficiently and courteously but can only respond to a situation using the rules and policies that it has learnt, while accessing individual customer history on which to make a final decision. Would a human being have made a different decision in certain situations perhaps regarding a person in a vulnerable situation? The big questions are – can we build compassion and empathy into AI? Will the world be a happier place with artificial intelligence in it?

Encouragingly, a McKinsey report indicates that we will start to see developments within the world of gen AI in two important areas, namely 'social emotional reasoning' and 'social emotional sensing'. It is important that ethical codes and moral sensitivity can be incorporated into our automated decision-making systems of the future. We cannot trade off fairness and other moral considerations in the name of increased productivity and economic growth.

Some of the positive applications for AI are clearing the backlog in the judicial system. However, differences to laws or even language used in different jurisdictions must be taken into account and limit the universal applicability of AI systems. There are benefits in the health care sector also such as reducing wait times for medical consultations, and in mitigating staff shortages in the aged care sector, a problem becoming even more prevalent with our aging population.

However, there have already been instances in the US of wrongful arrests based on flaws in AI-driven facial recognition systems; interestingly this has always occurred with African Americans. How comfortable would you be if you were arrested based on AI or even sentenced to prison by AI systems?

With an increasing move towards the privatisation of prisons in the US where profits are driven by prisoner numbers, could we rely on business to responsibly employ AI if it was used to make decisions around sentencing or parole applications?

The argument for the deployment of AI in this way is that we would get consistent decisions removing any bias from judicial decisions. Yet we know that there are inherent biases built into any software system. That is the unconscious bias of the developers. AI is trained to simulate the behaviour that already exists and hence we are potentially building in existing prejudices and preferences that are unfair and prejudicial.

We have seen this in HR systems designed to review CVs for job applications, allowing the hiring manager to only review shortlisted applicants. In combatting one common inbuilt bias that discriminates against women, some companies are now employing 'gender decoding' systems to highlight where their policies and job advertisements are displaying bias.

AI may be tasked with matching applications to a job description, yet it is unlikely that AI can learn to assess the 'whole person' beyond matching skills and experience to job specifications. We have already seen discrimination against women, people of various ethnic backgrounds and older workers with software-based screening systems.

There is a high level of trust in our health care professionals. People will share the most intimate details of their lives with their doctor, or in the case of mental health support with their counsellor. Part of the healing process is the warmth and kindness and empathy that one feels from a supportive health care professional. Is this replicable with AI?

Some people turn to religious leaders for advice. Would we feel as supported or nurtured by this connection if the human dimension were replaced by computer science? AI in the confessional? AI will only ever be a tool, never a sentient being, however, the question of sentience will be asked more and more as technology emulating humans advances.

In 2023, Melbourne's Monash University created the 'DishBrain', a semi-biological computer chip with some 800,000 human and mouse brain cells lab-grown into its electrodes. Demonstrating something like sentience, it learned to play *Pong* within five minutes.[65]

We now have autonomous AI which essentially has trained AI to reproduce itself but with ever-increasing abilities. If there is a high degree of autonomy here as regards what the future AI systems will look like, then can we be sure that they will serve humanity and align with our moral and ethical standards through which we now operate within the world?

It is likely that practicalities of life will be tended to; however, in sensitive situations such as aged care the issue remains as to whether software can truly provide the same level of nurturing as human contact. What about childcare? Would you want your newborn to be cared for by an AI-enabled robot?

As thought-provoking as many of these issues that surround the adoption of AI may be, they pale into insignificance when we shift our attention to the more macro topic of national security.

---

65 Blain, L. (2023) Computer chip with built-in human brain tissue gets military funding. *New Atlas*, https://newatlas.com/computers/human-brain-chip-ai. July 21st.

A number of experts have painted the picture of a world in which future wars will not be fought by human beings but by competing AI systems. The attacking state agency will seek to wreak havoc on critical national infrastructure while the defending state agency seeks to repel these attacks. This may well be the case already in aspects of the Middle East conflict.

Future wars are painted as being a situation where competing software systems are making their own decisions every second with the capacity to undertake warfare at lightning speed and with potentially devastating consequences.

In a sign that our world's leaders are taking the potential threats from AI seriously, in December of 2023 the European Parliament and EU member states agreed to the world's most comprehensive laws to govern AI.

This was a marathon sitting whereby 100 people spent nearly three days in a room to reach a consensus on the use of AI with ramifications for the world's largest social media platforms and search engines.

Key Takeaways

- Lack of diversity is a contributor to poor decision-making.
- In response to a crisis, communicate early and often.
- Trust is a vital component of driving change.
- We should always look at the human impact of the decisions we make.
- Technology has changed our lives, but it must be used for the good of humanity.
- We must learn to manage the challenges that AI brings.

Books Referenced

- Badiner, Alan Hunt, *Mindfulness in the Marketplace: Compassionate Responses to Consumerism* (2002)
- Coper, Ed, *Facts & Other Lies: Welcome to the Disinformation Age* (2022)
- Dion, Michel & Pava, Moses, *The Spirit of Conscious Capitalism* (2022)
- Freeman, R. Edward, *Strategic Management: A Stakeholder Approach* (1984)
- Huxley, Aldous, *Brave New World* (1932)
- Laszlo, Chris, *The Sustainable Company: How to Create Lasting Value Through Social and Environmental Performance* (2005)
- Paine, Lynn S., *Value Shift* (2002)
- Rhodes, Carl, *Woke Capitalism: How Corporate Morality is Sabotaging Democracy* (2022)
- Vaillant, John, *Fire Weather: A True Story From A Hotter World* (2023)
- Varoufakis, Yanis, *Technofeudalism: What Killed Capitalism* (2023)
- Walsh, Toby, *Machines Behaving Badly: The Morality of AI* (2022)
- Walsh, Toby, *Faking It: Artificial Intelligence in a Human World* (2023)
- Zuboff, Shoshana, *The Age of Surveillance Capitalism: The Fight for a Human Future at the Frontier of Power* (2019)

PART 2

A New Paradigm

The most interesting intersections lie between heart and soul, between passion and values, and between what we believe and feel, and what we say and do.

P. Karoff & J. Maddox
The World We Want – New Dimensions in Philanthropy and Social Change

CHAPTER 4

It Makes Sense to be Kind

Doing Good and Doing Well

Change starts at the top and it is vitally important that senior executives are role models of the highest order to ensure responsible business practices and kindness are the norm across the organisation. The perception of a business is often a reflection of its most senior people. However, there can be a disconnect between how some managers believe they are perceived as a leader, and how they are actually being perceived.

Hall & Partners, which describes itself as 'an insight agency obsessed with how marketing influences people, brands and culture', has undertaken a global study on kindness in the workplace, titled *The Kindness in Leadership Report*.[1] Across the 1,500 respondents, it found only '1 in 3 people agreed with the statement that their boss was kind and 1 in 4 people considered the leader of the organisation to be unkind.' We can do a lot better.

Regrettably, when moving into managerial positions some people will default to mechanistic role types and take shortcuts in order to achieve outcomes, but at the expense of their people. In the case of

---

1 Hall & Partners (2019) The Power of Kindness. Kind Leaders Shaping the Future. https://issuu.com/hall_and_partners/docs/kindness_in_leadership_final. November 6th.

newer managers, this may be the result of inexperience. For more experienced managers, shortsightedness or a lack of understanding of the true nature of what motivates people is their blind spot.

It exists when the vision of a manager is a narrow one that fails to consider the benefits of building a business based on treating people well, on good values and on consideration for all stakeholders. The negative commercial repercussions can be considerable as it is also likely to be perceived that if people are treated poorly within a company, then that company may well be exhibiting the same behaviour externally to customers and society more broadly.

Fortunately, we are seeing attitudes shifting with many businesses demonstrating a greater concern for the wellbeing of their people, and understanding that kindness is generally reciprocated so everyone wins.

These days a responsible business has no choice but to act in a manner that respects all members of its ecosystem. The health and wellbeing of a business, along with that of society and nature, have become inextricably entwined.

In building a corporate culture that respects people, it is reasonable to ask whether this is incompatible with commercial aims. However, it is increasingly the experience of business that to do so enables a business to advance its standing in the community and as such attract talent into the business.

There is no incompatibility between the display of finer qualities and a focus on profit. Kindness is one of the greatest contributors to culture and building positive cultures is one of the most powerful contributors to profit.

Fairness and equity are fundamental to creating kind work environments. The opposite of these characteristics can regrettably manifest in multiple ways, however an all-too common one is the entrenched discrimination against women overlooked for senior roles and promotions during their careers.

Liz Broderick, former Australian Sex Discrimination Commissioner and founder of Champions of Change Coalition, said,

'When workplaces actively support women and build a culture of respect, they change lives. It's going to take all of us – every single one of us – to build a more gender equal world.'[2]

It is imperative for long-term success that every business widens its vision to include all stakeholders affected by the business. We are now seeing progressive businesses incorporate the families of their people in their ecosphere of stakeholders and develop policies and take actions that reduce the tension between work and family responsibilities.

Caring for one's own people is a critical part of the Social aspect of ESG. The Gallup organisation's research into the impact of higher levels of employee engagement showed that those organisations with high engagement scores demonstrated '17 per cent greater productivity, 20 per cent increase in sales and 21 per cent higher profitability.'

Gallup observe that, 'Engaged employees are more present and productive; they are more attuned to the needs of customers; and they are more observant of standards, processes and systems.'[3]

By fostering a compassionate workplace, companies can attract and retain top talent, reducing turnover, recruitment costs and the productivity lag when a new employee joins the organisation.

ESG programs should be viewed by boards as more than simply reputation-building or risk-mitigation initiatives but as enablers of superior commercial performance. A report in *The Accounting Review* states, 'A strong ESG proposition correlates with higher equity returns from both a tilt and momentum perspective.'[4]

Global consultancy firm McKinsey succinctly states that 'when governing authorities trust corporate actors, they are more likely to award them the access, approvals and licences that afford fresh

---

2   Broderick, L. (2023) https://championsofchangecoalition.org/

3   Harter, J. & Mann, A. https://www.gallup.com/workplace/231602/right-culture-not-employee-satisfaction.aspx. Gallup Workplace.

4   Mozaffar, K., Serafeim, G. & Yoon, A. (2016) Corporate Sustainability: first evidence on materiality. *The Accounting Review*, Nov. Vol. 91, No. 6.

opportunities for growth.'[5] A focus on an ESG agenda is a major benefit to business and McKinsey lists five ways in which ESG creates value, all resulting in being a source of competitive advantage:

1. Revenue growth. Superior ESG performance helps companies to access new markets and expand into existing ones, plus it is a strong driver of consumer preference.
2. Cost reduction. This includes raw material costs by identifying the true cost of water and carbon, which its report showed could affect operating profits by as much as 60 per cent.
3. Reduced regulatory and legal interventions.
4. Employee productivity uplift.
5. Investment and asset optimisation. Capital will be allocated to more sustainable opportunities.

Business is a pragmatic beast, constantly seeking to follow trends that are linked to greater commercial success, and customers are increasingly seeking out businesses that align with their values.

In a world where consumers are more conscious of the social and environmental impact of their purchases, a corporation in tune with stakeholder expectations can differentiate itself from its competition. When demonstrating a commitment to kindness towards people and planet, companies can build trust and loyalty with their customers, leading to enhanced brand reputation and increased sales.

This principle should also be extended to all stakeholders including suppliers. They play a vital role for every company, however they are often viewed in an almost combative way as adversaries to be beaten down with demands for ever lower pricing, unrealistic terms and conditions, and penalties for non-compliance. This constitutes the creation of a master-servant relationship, based on threats and even coercion.

---

5 Henisz, W., Koller, T. & Nuttall, R. (2019) Five Ways that ESG Creates Value. *McKinsey Quarterly*, November.

When a business enters a commercial arrangement for the supply of goods and services with a partnership mentality, there will be considerable benefits for both buyer and seller. Reciprocal trust and goodwill are more likely to achieve a successful outcome than any legal contract has ever been able to do.

Yvon Chouinard, the founder of Patagonia, Inc., based in Ventura, California, details the journey of his company in his book *Let My People Go Surfing*.[6] The title is drawn from Chouinard's philosophy that you hire good people, give them autonomy, albeit with account-ability, and then let them get on with their work. If the surf is good, then on those days that's where you'll find them.

Patagonia's overarching philosophy as regards the business as a whole is to leave the environment better than you found it, and this has underpinned great commercial success for the organisation.

Contrast this approach to the latest trend of workplace surveillance being implemented by some companies. This has gained particular prominence with the increase of working from home, during and post the Covid pandemic. This includes key-stroke monitoring, mouse tracking, periodic screenshots of a worker's computer and even the use of a computer's webcam to view the employee.

Far from demonstrating trust these practices will instil fear in people, erode trust and work against building cultures that create a sense of belonging. A company may have a legal right to install software for this purpose on the equipment that they own, but this is where mere compliance with the law must give way to moral and ethical considerations and a deeper understanding of the impact of company policies on people.

Treating people kindly is one of the key elements that separate leaders from managers. Trust is the glue that unites a company with its stakeholders and is a prerequisite for employees buying into any major changes that a company may seek to implement. Chouinard wrote his

---

6   Chouinard, Y. (2018) *Let My People Go Surfing*. Penguin, London.

book as much as a handbook for employees to better understand the company's ethos, as it was to inform a broader audience.

He clearly understands the importance of people trusting and feeling connected to the company they work in and buying into a bigger vision. As author Stephen Covey has said, 'Change happens at the speed of trust.'[7]

Once people-centric policies have been implemented, it is incumbent on every leader of every organisation to monitor their decision-making to ensure they are staying true to the highest ideals of their business and not compromising these. This will sustain the culture you are seeking which will underpin commercial success.

Not everyone is comfortable with the concept of business kindness being linked to greater profits. The view is that business should find room in its heart for kindness driven by a purely altruistic motive, not one seeking a return on investment from the good things that it is doing.

There would be widespread cynicism with any company developing a set of values purely as a marketing tool, yet genuine adherence to positive values is going to inevitably benefit a business. The principle of reciprocity of benefits is not necessarily ensured if one does so for marketing purposes. It is important to consider that you can do the right thing, for the wrong reasons.

The distinction here is between motive and consequence. When a company authentically seeks to do good because it is consistent with what they stand for, and then discovers that this inspires their people and creates greater alignment with their customers and societal expectations, then this is a positive outcome for all.

It is important for companies to consider that when they develop their social impact plans and remember that when they communicate their social purpose, they are entering a field of corporate communications that requires considerable thought and sensitivity.

---

7   Covey, S. (2006) *The Speed of Trust: the one thing that changes everything.*
    Free Press, Simon & Schuster, New York.

Profit and Purpose

Increasingly these two terms are no longer being seen as opposing concepts, rather a symbiotic relationship exists between them. The previous view of having to choose had failed to acknowledge the potential for synergy and benefits exchanged between the two, and has given way to the understanding that a virtuous circle is created between the two.

Incorporating purpose into one's business increases commercial performance while the increase in profit generates the capacity to have greater positive social impact. Profit and purpose nourish each other. This can also be expressed as 'values create value'.

Adopting the concept of a virtuous circle existing between profit and purpose, business can be conducted with a focus on both simultaneously. Josephine Wolanski expresses the concept of business serving humanity beautifully when she says, 'The purpose of capital is to be in service to life. The more capital, the more service.'[8]

The role of the leader in driving change and building a culture that incorporates purpose is critical. However, not everyone will necessarily be supportive, and it is challenging to seek to understand opposing views and potentially incorporate the thinking of others into their decision-making. The juggling act is to keep an open door and an open mind, while staying true to their values and beliefs.

In a world where some still struggle with the link between economic success and societal wellbeing, your greatest ally will be tangible results. Over time, even your harshest critics will start to see that your approach has enhanced the company's reputation, attracted new clients or customers in the consumer world, earnt you the accolade of being an employer of choice for new talent, and that these have in turn become the building blocks of enhanced financial performance.

---

8   Wolanski, J. (2024) https://nrcf.org.au

We know from research studies that when companies incorporate positive social initiatives into their businesses they will reap the benefits, particularly in regard to being favoured by some consumers. The 2019 Millennial Survey by Deloitte Global produced the following results:

- 36 per cent said a company's commitment to social issues motivated them to become a customer or deepen their relationship with the organisation
- 38 per cent of millennials and Gen Zs have stopped or lessened a business relationship because of a company's poor ethical behaviour.[9]

The status quo in corporations is giving way to a culture that embodies purpose, and an ethos of ensuring positive social impact.

For strategy to incorporate purpose is an extraordinary breakthrough in a world that was previously known for cut-throat practices, led by people big on bravado but low on empathy. Success through kindness to others in society was not a concept commonly contemplated in decades past, and using terms such as 'compassionate' to describe a corporation was unimaginable.

In 2006 three college friends, Andrew Kassoy, Bart Houlahan and Jay Coen Gilbert, founded B Labs and with it established the B Corp certification program. They shared a hope for a better way to do business: better for workers, better for communities, better for planet.

They have now certified over 5,000 companies as having met the criteria for certification. This program has contributed significantly to businesses embracing the ethos of becoming a force for good.

One such organisation is Intrepid Travel, founded by Darrell Wade and Geoff Manchester, which is the world's largest travel B Corp,

---

9   Deloitte Brand Voice (2020) Why doing good is good for business. https://forbes.com/sites/deloitte/2020/01/21/why-doing-good-is-good-for-business/?sh=6746a1146b29. January 21st.

who have developed a reputation for caring for people and planet as they conduct their adventure business. Their aim is to create positive change through the joy of travel.

This concept of business for good is further echoed by Professor Rebecca Henderson in her book *Reimagining Capitalism in a World on Fire*.[10] She talks of reforming capitalism to align it with global imperatives such as pressing environmental and social issues faced by the world today and argues strongly that capitalism can indeed be a force for good. Such a focus reduces risk and hence is also likely to bring the benefit of attracting capital for the sustained growth of the organisation.

Doughnut Economics Action Lab (DEAL) is another. In her best-selling book, *Doughnut Economics*, Kate Raworth invites us to embrace a different way of thinking about economics in the 21st century.[11] Within this system of economics, the circular shape of the doughnut represents an ecosphere that replaces the goal of endless GDP growth with a regenerative economic mode. She writes:

> *The Doughnut consists of two concentric rings: a social foundation, to ensure that no one is left falling short on life's essentials, and an ecological ceiling, to ensure that humanity does not collectively overshoot the planetary boundaries that protect Earth's life-supporting systems.*[12]

In a tribute to Raworth, British environmentalist George Monbiot described her as being 'the John Maynard Keynes of the 21st century.'

10 Henderson, R. (2020) *Reimagining Capitalism in a World on Fire*. Public Affairs Books, North America.

11 Raworth, K. (2018) *Doughnut Economics, Seven Ways to Think Like a 21st-Century Economist*. Random House, London.

12 Ibid.

Advocates of purpose-led businesses will advise that the corporation must reframe its mission such that profit is not an end but rather an enabler of achieving its purpose. Hubert Joly, the former Chair & CEO of US online retailer Best Buy, captures this concept beautifully in his book, *The Heart of Business: Leadership Principles for the Next Era of Capitalism*.[13] He advocates for placing people and purpose at the centre of business and the reinvention of capitalism to ensure a sustainable future.

With this philosophy, he orchestrated a spectacular turnaround in business performance and said back in 2012, 'everyone thought we were going to die'. However, under his guidance eight years later, Best Buy was transformed as Joly and his team rebuilt the company into one of the nation's favourite employers, vastly increased customer satisfaction and dramatically grew Best Buy's stock price.

The Appeal, a non-profit newsagency, is a US women-led media company that is a great example of a purpose-driven organisation empowering its people. Their mission is to shine a light on injustices within the US criminal legal system and they have developed what they call a 'care-centred company culture' with policies that truly focus on the mental health, wellbeing and empowerment of staff and contractors.[14]

The pillars of their reform are:

- democratic decision-making
- redefining leadership
- prioritising physical and mental care for journalists
- building a transparent and equitable compensation model

13 Joly, H. (2021) *The Heart of Business: Leadership Principles for the Next Era of Capitalism*. Harvard Business Review Press, Boston MA.

14 Francis Chan, T. & Green, M. (2023) We've created a democratic, worker-led, care-centred newsroom. Reynolds Journalism Institute. https://rjionline. org/news/weve-created-a-democratic-worker-led-care-centered-newsroom. August 2nd.

- implementing best practices for remote newsrooms
- working with a board of directors that guides and supports, rather than dictates.

This is not always so easy to sell in large shareholder-driven companies, where boards may have more traditional positions. Even in this world it is vital that short-termism must not be allowed to creep into management thinking, whereby values are compromised in the name of a quick financial win. The link between being a profitable and purposeful organisation, and honouring both, must not be lost.

Pragmatism is often required to get others on board and get your ideas over the line. If the board of a large corporation, or the fund managers who influence its stock price, are more comfortable with certain language being used in these discussions then adopting that language would seem to be sensible. An evangelical crusade, albeit well intentioned, may not be the best approach. Sometimes incremental steps are also required, as is compromise – 'don't let the perfect get in the way of the good.'

The very definition of business success itself is also being redefined. You no longer have to be the biggest and most dominant player to be seen as successful. Many smaller companies, renowned for their values while still making good profits, are admired and seen as successful by the public and even peers.

The first step is for each individual company to clearly define what purpose means to them. This ensures it is authentic and not simply a cookie-cutter approach. Ideally everyone in the company should be involved in formulating the company's values rather than it being a top-down approach. Team members could perhaps be invited to vote, or some other similar mechanism used. This respects the views of the people working there and increases the likelihood of purpose being widely embedded in day-to-day business practices.

The values adopted by any organisation also need to outlive the leader who was instrumental in establishing them. CEOs come and go, and values cannot be dependent on one person. When it is not clear to others why the leader is undertaking certain new cultural or policy initiatives, it is not possible for people to fully embrace these or to support the transformation that you are seeking.

Once the purpose and values have been agreed upon, these must be embedded in the fabric of the organisation. There then needs to be regular messaging across the company so your values are widely known and stay top of mind, and terms such as respect, compassion, empathy and kindness slip into common usage. Clarity of intent and reinforcing the reason you are building a company that honours and embeds purpose is essential, as is constant reinforcement.

A set of values that appears in frames on company walls, without being lived every day, will not serve the company well and will be viewed as inauthentic and tokenistic. To avoid this, the most senior people in the company need to be seen to always act in a virtuous manner consistent with the company's stated values.

One aspect of embedding values is that the company needs to move quickly to investigate any complaints such as bullying or harassment or discrimination. Sex Discrimination Commissioner Kate Jenkins's report, *Respect@Work*, for the Australian Human Rights Commission is important to read as it provides valuable insights that should be implemented by every organisation.[15]

A company cannot legitimately say that they value diversity, and they respect all cultures while overlooking people from diverse cultural backgrounds or LGBTIQA+ people for promotion.

Gender Equality

Companies need to initiate genuine action on eliminating gender discrimination from their workplaces. You can't say you stand for gender equality and not have gender diversity in leadership positions.

---

15 https://humanrights.gov.au/our-work/sex-discrimination/publications/ respectwork-sexual-harassment-national-inquiry-report-2020

It is quite reasonable to suggest that with more women in senior roles corporate environments will be created in which sexual harassment is less likely to proliferate. In many cases women bring greater sensitivity into the corporate world, including greater awareness of the value of including minority groups in the redesign of corporate environments and in decision-making processes in general.

It is abhorrent that there are still people who think that to engage in unwelcome behaviour of a sexual nature is acceptable. No one should ever be subjected to a situation which will inevitably lead to psychological, emotional and potentially physical harm.

There is no denying that there is a huge amount of work to do in the area of financial inequality. There must be wage parity to ensure fairness and equity. We must not accept the continuing income divide between men and women.

In late February of 2024, The Workplace Gender Equality Agency (WGEA) made its data collected over the last decade available online to the public. Now anyone could enter the name of a company into a search field on the WGEA website https://wgea.gov.au/data-statistics/data-explorer.[16] The data showed that 50 per cent of companies had a gender pay gap (disadvantaging women) of 9.1 per cent or more.

The median gender pay gap in Australia is 14.5 per cent, which equates to women on average earning $11,542 per year less than men. Some of the higher median gender pay gaps that stood out were Jetstar at 53.5 per cent, 'meaning that for every $1 a male worker earns at the company, women earn on average 46.5 cents.'[17]

Others in the airline sector were Virgin at 41.7 per cent and Qantas at 39.3 per cent. Banking, finance and insurance sectors also demonstrated very large gender pay gaps – Commonwealth Bank 29.8 per cent, IAG 27.5 per cent, Westpac 27 per cent and Suncorp 20.5 per cent.

---

16 https://wgea.gov.au/data-statistics/data-explorer
17 https://www.abc.net.au/news/2024-02-27/australia-gender-pay-data-revealed-for-first-time/103487530

Salary inequality, of course, flows through to all aspects of a person's life. A study published in late 2023 concerning emergency savings that people had been able to put aside showed that the average amount for Australian men was $A17,832 while for women the significantly lower figure of $A6,859.[18]

There is also a gender element to the accumulation of superannuation, with women aged between 50 and 54 having an average of 32 per cent less than men, and women between 60 and 64 having 23 per cent less. 'Super' is a good indicator of the considerable division of wealth in Australia. The top 20 per cent retire with an average balance of $500,000 while the bottom with an average balance of $66,000.[19]

The government needs to legislate for company super on parental leave, but boards don't need to wait until they are forced to do so and should consider voluntarily implementing this within their organisations. This addresses the loss of super when women are out of the workforce following childbirth.

In a positive indication that times are changing, some professional services companies are ahead of the curve on this issue. They're providing longer periods of parental leave and also paying super on this leave – KPMG, Deloitte, Accenture, PwC, Allens, Clayton Utz and Grant Thornton are among them.

The inequity that we are seeing would likely be addressed more rapidly if there were more women at the top of our large companies. When women do achieve senior executive roles, they need to be remunerated with salary packages equivalent to their male counterparts.

However, getting there is not easy, with women often facing discrimination in regard to career advancement. Of course, none of this

18 Wallis, S. & Godfrey, J. (2023) Savings Account Statistics 2023. Finder.com October 30th.

19 https://abc.net.au/news/2024-01-03/wealth-inequality-increases-with-superannuation-driving-it/103233320

discussion addresses the big issue of women being the gender overwhelmingly engaged in unpaid work.

While systemic change is required, there are those working to assist women build the skills through which to overcome the disadvantage currently present in many workplaces.

One such person is diversity, equity and inclusion consultant Michele Redfern, who has created the Advancing Women Formula which comprises modules whereby a woman can develop higher-level skills across three focus areas, namely, Business Intelligence (BI), Emotional Intelligence (EI) and Social Intelligence (SI).[20]

The importance of such programs is underlined by the fact that as of late 2023, 48 of the 50 highest paid Australian CEOs were men. Interestingly, one of the two women, Shemara Wikramanayake, Managing Director and CEO of Macquarie Bank, has the distinction of being the highest paid CEO in the Australian corporate sector, irrespective of gender.

The ultimate challenge is to fix the system, to eliminate the systemic barriers that still exist to women's advancement. Catherine Fox highlights this in her book *Stop Fixing Women*.[21] In Australia, there has been a reduction in the pay gap over recent years; however, it has been sitting stubbornly at 22.8 per cent since the 2021/22 financial year.

One initiative that may help is new legislation to be introduced in 2024 that will force companies with over 100 employees to make public their pay gaps. As happened in the UK when this level of transparency came in to force, it is likely that larger ASX listed companies will seek to close the gap more rapidly if they value their corporate reputations. There is little doubt that transparency drives accountability. Larger companies have already been moving more quickly than

20 https://michelleredfern.com/blog/speak-up-and-actually-stand-out-10-proven-leadership-skills-to-foster

21 Fox, C. (2017) *Stop Fixing Women*. NewSouth Books, Sydney.

smaller ones, with a 5.3 per cent change in the three years leading up to 2022 versus 0.4 per cent.[22]

Estimates as to how long equality between men and women will take vary greatly. The World Economic Forum states that it will take another 132 years to close the global gender pay gap. The pay gap is, of course, only one measure of the unfairness experienced by women and according to the UN Women's most recent report, at the current rate of progress, it will take 286 years for the world to achieve true gender equality.[23]

These alarming timeframes should not discourage us but embolden us to do more, and at a faster pace. Some do see a way forward and lay down a challenge to governments. Jodie Heymann, distinguished professor at UCLA and co-author of *Equality Within Our Lifetimes: How Laws and Policies Can Close – or Widen – Gender Gaps in Economies Worldwide*, says that gender inequality:

> *… costs national economies trillions of dollars annually. Yet the global gender gaps in employment, pay and leadership aren't simply the result of historic discrimination, cultural bias or individual choices – they're driven directly by laws and policies that derive from and reinforce gender stereotypes.*[24]

She, along with many others, proposes that an overhaul of legislation by governments globally is required. Ideally, we would have seen

---

22 Clun, R. (2023) Fixing the pay gap can be as simple as knowing how big it is. *Sydney Morning Herald*, October 5th.

23 Schnall, M. (2023) Gender Equality is Achievable in our Lifetime. *Forbes*, May 21st.

24 Heymann, J., Sprague, A. & Raub, A. (2023) *Equality Within Our Lifetimes: How Laws and Policies Can Close – or Widen – Gender Gaps in Economies Worldwide*. World Policy Analysis Centre, UCLA, Los Angeles.

business stepping up voluntarily, based on either it simply being the right thing to give all genders equal pay and equal opportunities, or based on realising that huge opportunities exist by utilising women in leadership roles.

One area where we have seen progress made is in Australian federal politics. In May 2022, seven women who became known as 'The Teals' due to the campaign colour adopted by the majority of candidates, ran successfully in the federal election. They ran on platforms of climate action, gender equality and greater political integrity and accountability.

Zali Stegall, in the northern Sydney electorate of Warringah, had run successfully in 2019 against former Prime Minister Tony Abbott in the previous federal election, on a platform of reforms including climate action and integrity in government, and the others emulated her achievement against incumbent Liberal (conservative) candidates.

These women ran on commonsense platforms that resonated with voters; however, in order to run had to remove themselves from the entrenched two-party system, where it is unlikely they would have achieved preselection to represent their party.

Cassandra Kelly, a highly respected international board director, member of the European Union Global Tech Panel, Chair Treasury Corporation of Victoria and co-founder of global corporate advisory firm Pottinger, emphasises that we must overcome complacency and be prepared to take bold action. On this, and other matters of social change, she says 'playing safe is unlikely to have an impact' and that 'we should be impatient for change', and further states:

We should be uncompromising in building a better version of ourselves and the future. We need to look up and out, bring in fresh perspectives and challenge the status quo. And we need to start now. It will take ALL of us![25]

---

25 Kelly, Cassandra, https://cassandrakelly.com

In a positive move to acknowledge the importance of addressing the inequality faced by women, in October 2023 the Nobel Prize for Economics was awarded to Harvard faculty member Professor Claudia Goldin.

Her research highlighted that the gap in pay rates, and participation in the labour market more broadly, is not simply down to the biological difference between a man and a woman but to the greater responsibility for caregiving and provision of unpaid household labour that falls to women to provide. She said, 'We are never going to have gender equality, or narrow the pay gap, until we have couple's equity.'[26]

In 2023 the federal government's Women's Economic Equality Taskforce chaired by Sam Mostyn handed down its final report.[27] One of the key recommendations was that the Australian Government must invest in policies and programs that recognise the economic importance and value of care work in Australia and help families to better share caring responsibilities.

Sam Mostyn stated, 'In the crudest terms, $128 billion is the value to the Australian economy that can be realised by purposefully removing the persistent and pervasive barriers to women's full and equal participation in economic activity.'[28]

Sam Mostyn has spent her life advocating for a fairer and more equitable society. The Prime Minister of Australia, Anthony Albanese, has announced that she would be appointed as only the second female Governor-General of Australia, effective July 1st, 2024. Displaying

---

26 Smith, M. (2023) Nobel Prize-winning Harvard economist Claudia Goldin: The gender pay gap will 'never' close unless this happens. Interview with CNBC. https://.cnbc.com/2023/10/10/nobel-prize-winner-claudia-goldin-the-gender-pay-gap-will-never-close-unless-this-happens.html. October 10th.

27 https://ministers.pmc.gov.au/gallagher/2023/womens-economic-equality-taskforce-reports-government

28 Wright, S. (2023) $128 billion – the cost of gender inequality in Australia. *Sydney Morning Herald*, October 22nd.

the humility that has characterised her life's work she said, 'I am ready to serve with integrity, compassion and respect.'

It is important to state that although this discussion has focused on the gender gap between male and female, discrimination occurs for all other gender groups as well, including transgender, gender neutral, non-binary and others.

Employee Wellbeing

Investing in employee wellbeing does not only benefit the individual but enhances the prosperity of the whole organisation along with providing a social dividend. Building a culture based on empathy, caring for team members and where kindness is the norm is foundational to business success. It is human nature to want to be treated well, treated with respect and to have others show interest in our wellbeing.

In his book *The Kindness Revolution*, social demographer Hugh Mackay talks about human beings as a social species dependant on each other on many levels including for their security, emotional wellbeing and sense of belonging.[29] This fosters cooperation and Mackay points to research that indicates there is, in fact, a centre in our brains that we can think of as a 'cooperative centre'. Coexisting in a cooperative manner is fundamental to our survival. Hence characteristics such as kindness, altruism, neighbourliness, mutual respect and tolerance of individual difference are crucial.

Historically, during particularly challenging times, we survived by supporting each other, not just focusing on our own needs. This included those courageous people who crossed frontiers to create new settlements and banded together in close-knit communities. They raised barns together and shared food obtained by hunting or foraging with neighbours.

---

29 Mackay, H. (2021) *The Kindness Revolution: how we can restore hope, rebuild trust and inspire optimism.* Allen & Unwin, Sydney.

Opportunities abound today in our modern workplaces to be neighbourly. We all play our part in the formation of culture in our workplaces. Every interaction with others, every smile or acknowledgement, or conversely any unkind remark, acts of ostracising others or bullying in the workplace all contribute to who that company is.

Family Friendly Workplaces (FFW) is a program developed by Emma Walsh, founder and CEO of Parents at Work, that advocates for policies which reduce the tension between work and family. It has a threefold approach of providing:

- education for interested organisations
- benchmarking through which an organisation can assess its own HR policies
- certification that highlights that organisation as being an employer of choice.

It advocates that families are a part of the company's broader ecosphere, and policies need to take their needs into account. Considerations may include flexibility to support the needs of families with young children, but also responsibilities for aging parents.

In May of 2024, Family Friendly Workplaces released its comprehensive research National Working Families Survey, which provides practical and tangible recommendations to aid the implementation of progressive policies that leave the people within these organisations in no doubt that the company they work for genuinely cares for them and that this ethos of caring extends to their families.

It also advocates for employers to support their employees facing fertility issues. It has entered an exclusive arrangement with Genea Fertility whereby FFW member organisations will have access to Genea's Corporate Fertility support program.

While legislation is increasingly defining workplace practices in areas such as parental leave, domestic violence leave and flexible work arrangements, we are increasingly seeing companies taking a proactive position exceeding legislated requirements as regards their own internal policies. This denotes an encouraging breadth of awareness from our corporate leaders.

In what perhaps could be called 'beyond parental leave', Australia's oldest listed property trust, GPT, has introduced a groundbreaking policy to support employees returning from parental leave with up to $10,000 in support for childcare fees.

Cultural sensitivity is another important area, given it is likely that in a company of any size there will be people from multiple countries and most religions. To create an inclusive environment, leaders should consult with their People and Culture areas, department heads or directly with team members themselves to understand different requirements and do their best to accommodate these. These may include fasting and feasting days.

At the Melbourne launch of Family Friendly Workplaces, Rana Hussain, who launched consultancy firm Good Human in 2023, spoke of the importance of cultural sensitivity. She made the point that in Australia, our workplaces are becoming increasingly culturally diverse. She cited the example of religious festivals and the observance of special days that require a time commitment from practitioners and often days of cooking in preparation. How wonderful would it be if all workplaces went beyond simply holding an annual diversity day and kept these cultural practices top of mind throughout the year, and managers asked if there was anything they could do to support during those times.

Imagine being a person of Muslim faith, having your manager approach you to ask if there was anything they could do to support you during Ramadhan? Or a person of Hindu faith looking forward to the whole family coming together to celebrate Diwali, and being asked if you would like to leave a little earlier that day to prepare for that evening's meal.

Sensitivity towards people of all ethnic groups, including First Nations people, is vitally important in building positive cultures.

Investing in the development of our people is another demonstration of kindness from a company. A little piece of business wisdom that pops up on social media platforms such as LinkedIn from time to time is framed as a conversation between a HR manager and a CFO. The HR manager is looking for increased funding in the forthcoming budget for staff learning and development. The CFO responds by saying, 'What if we spend this money on them and they leave?' to which the HR manager replies, 'What if we don't, and they stay?'

Beyond the company's policy framework, however, are the day-to-day interactions between managers and their people. One of the most important things you can do is to get to know people, show interest in them and ask how you can better support them. This applies equally to exchanges between peers, others at your level in the organisation or those working in more junior roles, without a reporting line to you.

Opportunities exist for acts of kindness across all our workplaces. How often do people start a new job and feel isolated and alone? How often do they go for a coffee or lunch on their own, while watching work colleagues heading off in a group? Loneliness can exist in the middle of the office just as easily as it can in a person's personal life.

If the nobility of being kind in our workplaces isn't sufficient motivation for companies to create these positive cultures, then perhaps the realisation that it will bring enhanced results may create greater interest.

However, we shouldn't need to go looking for positive commercial outcomes for organisations to want to build kind cultures. People simply being the best human beings they can be, bringing their best self and whole self to work and being kind to others, will produce its own reward for everyone.

One of the most challenging situations faced by a managing director practising a philosophy of kind leadership is the issue of roles being made redundant. Sometimes circumstances in business change and these flow through to changes in the organisational structure and hence the roles that people currently occupy disappear. In some cases, explicit instructions may come from a global head office to reduce headcount as part of a global restructure.

There are some situations where a person is happy to leave, with a redundancy payment landing in their bank account; however, the loss of a job is devastating for the majority of people. One possible method of avoiding redundancies is to cut costs in other areas before taking people's jobs away.

It is the obligation of every employer to ensure that changes concerning people are implemented in as sensitive a manner as possible. Measures that are more heart-based can include offering voluntary redundancy across the company so those who leave have volunteered to do so, and others whose jobs were due to be removed are able to stay. Retraining people for new roles that may be required in the future rather than recruiting externally is another, as is offering reduced hours to lower total labour costs.

Regrettably redundancy will at times be used as a mechanism for avoiding what may be perceived as a difficult discussion concerning poor performance. A kind leader, however, will have those conversations, as a means of supporting team members and hopefully improving performance.

Despite what action is taken, the fundamental rule should always be that people are treated with respect and compassion at this difficult time. It is important to explain that it is the change in business circumstances that is creating the new structure and in no way is attributable to a performance issue on their part. They should be provided with adequate notice, time to hand over to others, thanked for their service and farewelled with dignity. The archaic practice of marching people out the door, justified by rhetoric that they might be a security risk and take data with them, has no place in a humane company.

It is important not to overlook the fact that even in a wealthy country someone can have a job but may still be among the 'working poor' or be among the 'working homeless'. As the cost of living rises, this will regrettably become more common. It does, however, present an opportunity for kind companies to seek ways to help which will create a far greater sense of belonging for those going through challenging times.

Social Impact

A natural extension of a strong internal culture is a desire to have impact across the community. This will often be the hallmark of our more enlightened leaders.

Carly Forina, the former global CEO of Hewlett Packard, had this to say on corporate social impact and the link with commercial outcomes:

> *For many years, community development goals were philanthropic activities that were seen as separate from business objectives, not fundamental to them. Doing well and doing good were seen as separate pursuits.*[30]

Jim Cantalupo, former global CEO of McDonald's, talks of the embedding and long-term focus required of business – 'Social responsibility is not just a program that begins and ends, it's an ongoing commitment.'[31]

This illustrates a considerable shift from the sentiments expressed in the 'hose-down-the-throat' quotation from the former CEO of McDonald's cited previously, and is one small example of how mainstream a stated commitment to CSR has become.

One powerful approach to foster success as a purpose-driven organisation is to partner with other organisations driven by the same motive. This concept can play out wonderfully well, where even competitors are willing to share knowledge they have gained in tackling complex social issues. This is known as working in a 'pre-competitive space'.

---

30 Kotler, P. & Lee, N. (2005) *Corporate Social Responsibility: Doing the Most Good for Your Company & Your Cause.* John Wiley, Hoboken, NJ.

31 Ibid.

An excellent example of this is Westpac Bank's Safer Children, Safer Communities program.[32] It was established to support the child safeguarding activities of a range of organisations with funds committed to date being in excess of $60 million. It was established after it was discovered that some of the bank's customers were transferring funds through the bank's overseas payments platform for the purpose of exploiting vulnerable children online. (I serve on an advisory roundtable, chaired by Dr Simon Longstaff.)

A team was established, led by Dr Kavitha Suthanthiraraj, reporting to the Chief Sustainability Officer, Siobhan Toohill. As the team's expertise grew, a decision was made not to use the knowledge gained to seek a commercial advantage, but to share this with other organisations to broaden the positive impact for children.

The team collaborated with experts from civil society, government and academia. The Westpac Group Chief Executive Officer, Peter King, is a great supporter of this work himself. After 11 years at Westpac Siobhan left in July of 2024, leaving behind an inspiring legacy.

The work has also been instrumental in the implementation of new internal policies to ensure that their operation did not cause harm in the future. The knowledge developed has been shared with competitors, via the Australian Banking Association. This is a great example of kind business epitomising true leadership.

Westpac has also provided seed funding for the creation of a new organisation, On Us: Australian Child Safeguarding Business Coalition. This is a cross-sector business-led initiative to drive action on child safeguarding across Australian businesses and improve outcomes for children and young people. The bank is a founding corporate member.

---

32 https://westpac.com.au/about-westpac/sustainability/our-positions-and-perspectives/safer-children-safer-communities/

Many businesses are unaware that they may be putting children at risk and have not fully investigated where this may be occurring in their business operations, despite societal expectations that they will. The Australian Childhood Foundation Consumer Poll showed that '88.5 per cent disagreed or strongly disagreed that Australian businesses already give enough consideration to how their organisations can impact on children.'[33]

The necessity to protect our children must rank among the highest priority for every business – it must not be seen as discretionary. 'Safety by design' principles need to be employed during the development of any new products or services to ensure that the safety and rights of users are placed at the heart of the design process.

Not all companies comply with this principle, and we see egregious breaches such as the recent determination against TikTok by the European Data Protection Commission, resulting in a fine of €345 million ($A570 million). TikTok was deemed to have broken EU data law in its handling of children's accounts, including failing to shield underage users' content from public view.[34]

Meta is another company which in 2024 came under scrutiny due to the revelations of Arturo Bejar, a whistleblower who had worked as a senior engineer at Instagram and Facebook, owned by Meta.

Molly Russell, a 14-year-old girl in the UK, regrettably took her own life in 2017, which triggered a coronial inquiry. The investigation determined that she had taken her own life after viewing material, including graphic videos related to suicide, self-harm, depression and anxiety.

At the inquiry her father said '… the algorithm means that you can't escape it, and it keeps recommending more (of the same) content.'

---

33 Australian Childhood Foundation Consumer Poll (2022). https://childhood.org

34 Milmo, D. (2023) TikTok fined €345m for breaking EU data law on children's accounts. *The Guardian*, September 15th.

Arturo Bejar claimed that his company already had the infrastructure to shield young people from harmful content, however, they had chosen not to use it.[35]

Australia's eSafety Commissioner Julie Inman-Grant has also said that Google was not using its own technology to detect known child abuse videos and the Commission issued a written warning to Google.

An investigation by *The Guardian* into online sex trafficking found that Meta is failing to report the extent of the online exploitation of children. The company's own documents reportedly show that about 100,000 children, largely girls, are sexually harassed on Facebook and Instagram every day.

In late 2023, Julie Inman-Grant fined social media platform X more than $A600,000 for failing to adequately explain what steps it was taking to fight live-streaming of child abuse.[36] It has been reported that in the months following the purchase of Twitter by Elon Musk the platform had significantly reduced its efforts to limit child abuse material.

Regulators have deemed the examples above to be breaches of child protection laws and companies who disregard the law must be brought to account. These global social media giants must stop putting the wellbeing of children at risk. They shouldn't need a law to tell them that – it is their moral duty to stop facilitating egregious acts perpetrated on vulnerable children.

Beyond simply complying with the law there are many opportunities for companies to have positive social impact of a discretionary nature as well as opportunities to take advocacy positions around certain specific important social causes.

---

35 Milmo, D. (2024) Meta has not done enough to safeguard children, whistleblower says. *The Guardian*, January 24th.

36 Baker, J. (2023) Heinous Crimes: Twitter fined $600,000 over child safety failures. *Sydney Morning Herald*, October 16th.

We have seen companies in Australia speaking out on important social issues, most notably on marriage equality for members of the LGBTIQA+ community, and the referendum to acknowledge First Nations people in the Australian constitution which included the establishment of an advisory body to parliament, known as The Voice.

Society is divided on whether a corporation taking a position on broader societal issues is appropriate or not. This is not surprising as views on the underlying issues themselves tend to be deeply polarising. Some see corporations as champions of helping to create a fairer, more just society, others that it is simply outside the provenance of business, rather it is poor governance and inappropriate for any chair or CEO.

One argument faced against taking a public position is that not everyone working within the company will agree. Of course, they won't. You can take any cross-section of society you like, on any issue, and you won't get complete agreement. This should not be the criteria for not speaking up.

If supporting the issue at hand aligns with the already explicitly stated tenets of the business, then to speak publicly is being consistent with those principles. If someone works within a company that has developed an Indigenous Reconciliation Action Plan (RAP) and has the Uluru Statement from the Heart prominently displayed in their offices, that person should not be surprised if their organisation comes out publicly in favour of an Indigenous voice to parliament. The company is simply being consistent with its stated principles.

Most people working within a company will feel a greater sense of pride in their company when the organisation takes a position on important matters. It is understandable that most managers will prefer to keep their head down and 'stay within their lane', and only ever speak publicly about their own products or services. However, it is difficult to define this as leadership. Sometimes courage requires that we 'stick our head up above the parapet' even if shots will be fired by some who disagree with our position or our motives.

Paul Polman is one leader who stands out for his courage to drive the change that he truly believed in. He was the global CEO of Anglo Dutch conglomerate Unilever, best known for its consumer brands such as Dove, Sunsilk, Rexona, Ponds, Lux and Lipton tea, and Ben & Jerry's, Magnum and Cornetto ice-creams. He held this role from 2009 until 2019 with a distinguished corporate career at senior executive levels prior to his appointment.

Writing in October of 2023, shortly after the outbreak of the Israeli/ Hamas conflict, and referencing numerous other conflict regions, he implored the world's corporate leaders to put their minds towards what their companies could do to help create a more peaceful world:

> *What is your company doing to support peace?*
> *'Nothing' is not good enough. Surely the time has come for us*
> *to stop accepting this idea that business can sit on the sidelines,*
> *as if peace is somebody else's problem? There is no thriving*
> *private sector in a world mired in violence and instability.*[37]

Partnerships

Businesses can be powerful generators of social value; however, there is considerable value in working in partnership with civil society, as they are each master of their own domains, with specific competencies not necessarily possessed by the other. Both sectors have built up considerable skill in operating effectively within their own spheres.

They are different beasts, one driven by profit motives and one by service delivery targeted at the alleviation of suffering and the building of capacity within the individuals and communities they serve. Typically, charitable organisations may lack resources and sometimes skills to deliver social change at scale.

---

37   Polman, P. (2023) LinkedIn post https://www.linkedin.com/posts/ paulpolman_i-am-sorry-to-say-it-but-today-the-world-activity-7117145113188839424-bTiA/. October 10th.

These two diverse groups have developed a range of skills, that if shared, can significantly benefit each other. Different people gravitate to different sectors and can enrich the work of others by bringing new and fresh perspectives and drawing on a diverse range of experiences. Some of the different skill sets and the benefits to partners are shown here:[38]

Corporate skill set	Benefit to partner
Strong commercial focus	Financial growth & stability
Managerial expertise	Knowledge, experience & pro bono help
Negotiating ability	Secure better outcomes
Marketing strategies	Facilitating growth of public awareness
Public relations strategies	Potentially valuable contacts
Strong networks	Tap into to secure increased support
Technology infrastructure	Share knowledge and infrastructure
Not-for-profit skill set	**Benefit to partner**
Strong societal focus	Growth of genuine respect
Tireless long-term focus	Ability to withstand downturns
Staff commitment	Discretionary effort & long-term loyalty
Marketing strategies	Ability to operate on shoestring budgets
Public relations strategies	Ability to attract prestige without spin
Strong networks	Valuable contacts in government & society
Strong core values	Viewed by others as trustworthy & dependable

---

38 Cooke, D. (2010) Redefining the epistemology of the corporate/not-for-profit engagement. *Australasian Journal of Business & Social Inquiry*, Vol. 8, https://works.bepress.com/david_cooke/

The corporate and not-for-profit sectors are working more closely together and in certain instances are now dependent on each other for maximum effectiveness. It is important to work at this relationship and discuss how this process of engagement might be enhanced to ensure its effectiveness for both parties. Twenty-two key elements are shown below with no ranking of importance being inferred by their order:

1. The role of the partnership leader is critical.
2. The choice of partners is important.
3. The choice of projects is important.
4. Be clear on one's motivation.
5. Genuine motivation is essential.
6. Understand what each other's needs are.
7. Agree on mutual goals, reconfirm regularly.
8. Make a long-term commitment.
9. A partnership mentality needs to be developed.
10. Cross-fertilisation of ideas should be fostered.
11. Have a mutually agreed exit strategy.
12. Balance of power must be maintained.
13. The provision of non-financial contributions such as core skills, influence and technology need to be valued.
14. Not-for-profits can adopt business skills from profit-makers.
15. Profit-makers can learn from the skills of not-for-profits.
16. Hiring executives with experience in the opposite sector.
17. The term 'investor' instead of 'donor' should be reinforced.
18. Ideally heart and mind, on both sides, should be integrated.
19. Include the voice of survivors with lived experience and remunerate them appropriately.
20. Consult widely with Indigenous groups on issues affecting their communities.
21. Trust each other and share your knowledge with others.
22. Social responsibility needs to be integrated into the fabric of the organisation.[39]

---

39 Ibid.

Some organisations have developed considerable expertise in working with the not-for-profit sector, and there is an ever-increasing willingness to share this with other companies, even competitors. This redefines what we normally consider to be the rules of engagement in the business world, where a company previously acted in an adversarial and at times even predatory manner.

Provided the motivation of business to work with the not-for-profit sector is a genuine desire to make a positive difference, doing so can elevate business to a new level and be transformative of a company's culture.

Lyn Swinburne, Founder and CEO of the Breast Cancer Network of Australia (BCNA), expressed this well – 'What is important is that it really has to come from a genuine place but that doesn't mean that that can't be a commercial place as well.'[40]

One of Australia's most respected community leaders, Tim Costello, has said that 'we cannot win a war on poverty in Australia, or beyond our shores, without the drive, innovation and problem-solving skills of businesses.'[41] This is an acknowledgement that corporates are the real generators of wealth. They create jobs, economic opportunities and markets.

This was very much the sentiment expressed by then UN Secretary General Kofi Annan, when he established the UN's Global Compact Network to further sustainability goals. He said that talking to governments will only get us so far, we need the world's businesses on board if we are to achieve our sustainability goals.

These same corporates, however, don't possess all the knowledge they need to operate in all circumstances. For example, it is unlikely that many companies have all the knowledge they need to work sensitively and effectively with Indigenous communities.

---

40 Swinburne, L. (2007) Research interview conducted by the author. Melbourne. September 20th.

41 Costello, T. (2007) *PwC Australian Foundation Annual Report: Why Bother?* PricewaterhouseCoopers, Melbourne.

Collaboration with local Indigenous groups in matters concerning them will prove extremely beneficial. This principle applies also in dealing with human rights abuses by the company and incorporating the expertise of people with lived experience in formulating action plans to mitigate, compensate and ensure no future harm.

Survivors of human trafficking and modern slavery can add immense value to any programs aimed at eliminating forced labour in corporate supply chains and in the design of schemes to compensate survivors.

Rani Hong is a survivor and a powerful anti-slavery advocate. At the age of seven, Rani was stolen from her mother and sold into the slave trade in India where she was starved and brutalised and forced to work in harsh conditions. She was then put up for international adoption, trafficked to Canada and now lives in Washington state.

She has founded Freedom Seal, a risk management company, to give organisations greater visibility of their supply chains in order to eliminate exploitation and abuse.

Moe Turaga is another survivor. He travelled from his home in Fiji to work in the agricultural sector in Australia, working from dawn until dusk in harsh conditions, and rather than being fairly remunerated he found himself in a situation of debt bondage. He now consults to organisations and speaks publicly on behalf of survivors.

In the situation where a company is seeking knowledge and assistance from those who have developed this expertise through personal experience, the utmost respect should be shown. They should never be used as pawns in a game of reputation building by organisations or individuals.

They should instead be treated as partners, and the position of the company in the relationship should never be seen as that of patron or benefactor. Those with lived expertise should be remunerated in the same way that any external consultant may be, rather than as being a charitable recipient of some kind of tokenistic honorarium.

A Culture of Curiosity

There will often be blockers to an organisation being its best self. Some cultures will accept poor behaviour; or accepted commercial practices may border on being unethical, albeit remain within the law. These situations may exist due to blind spots in decision-makers or in some cases by design.

A. C. Ping, a Fellow at the Queensland University of Technology (QUT), in his article 'Why good people do bad things in business' suggests, 'In reality we miss ethical cues due to perpetual blindness causing us to apply the wrong type of decision-making criteria.'[42]

Harvard psychologist Martha Stout in her book *The Sociopath Next Door* suggests that only 4 per cent of people could be considered as 'bad', with the overwhelming majority as 'good'.[43] Some will posit that a disproportionate number of the 4 per cent achieve senior positions, thereby having a disproportionate influence in society and regrettably often abusing their power.

In an article in *The Conversation* in 2021 entitled 'How to stop psychopaths and narcissists from winning positions of power', Steve Taylor stated that, 'It seems as though power attracts ruthless and narcissistic people with a severe lack of empathy and conscience.'[44] The article continues with, 'One of the human race's biggest problems has been that people who occupy positions of power are often incapable of using power in a responsible way.'

If we consider that a desire to dominate is associated with narcissism, and other psychopathic traits, it makes sense that people with

---

42 Ping, A. C. https://thepeoplespace.com/ideas/articles/why-good-people-do-bad-things-business

43 Stout, M. (2005) *The Sociopath Next Door*. Random House, London.

44 Taylor, S. (2021) How to stop psychopaths and narcissists from winning positions of power. *The Conversation*. https://theconversation.com/how-to-stop-psychopaths-and-narcissists-from-winning-positions-of-power-158183. April 8th.

these defective natures would seek power over others and a small percentage will make their way to the top.

There will be times when the person who leads your organisation will not embody the same values that you do. When you are working in an organisation and you feel uncomfortable about certain behaviours that you are witnessing or certain decisions being made, what should your response be?

It is easy to write about living one's values within the workplace and demonstrating courage and speaking up. However, the reality is that it is not that easy. In fact, it can be very difficult, and, in some cases, even result in dire consequences for the person who is seeking to improve the organisation in which they work.

This can be particularly difficult for a young person starting out in their career, or any person who would find themselves in a precarious financial position if they were to lose their job, and potentially remain unemployed for a period of time.

To have a quiet word with a colleague, particularly one that you trust and respect, in which you share your discomfort, may be the start of you contributing to positive change. If you feel it is appropriate to speak to your manager or to speak up in a meeting about something that is concerning you, it is advisable to consider carefully how best to do this in order to minimise personal risk. While not remaining silent, we need to develop skills that reduce the cost of courage.

One method that can be very effective is to show curiosity as to how a situation has developed or why a situation is permitted to continue. This will generally involve asking a question. This changes the dynamic from one of being critical about a situation that does not sit well with you, to one that demonstrates a desire to better understand. It is far less likely to illicit a defensive response, yet you have put the situation that concerns you on the table.

Let's say the cultural norm within your company that you want to change is the acceptance of sexist behaviour. Some potential questions might be:

- I wonder if there may be some people in the organisation who are uncomfortable with some of the jokes and banter that go on most days?
- How might we be able to find out if this is the case?
- How might we be able to tell if everyone in the organisation feels safe and respected? We often talk about the importance of a good culture; but how can we be sure that we've achieved it?
- How can we be sure that the culture that we are striving for has become embedded in the organisation?
- I wonder if we have got the bar set at the right level?

Curiosity is typically seen as being neutral but used in certain situations it can be a powerful instigator of reflection and an enabler of ethical change. Norwegian academic Soern Finn Menning describes curiosity as 'an ethical endeavour'.[45]

If you are criticised or scoffed at or even verbally attacked for your beliefs on how to lift up the company to a higher standard, don't react defensively. Simply seek to better understand the other person's position, then build your case from there. And always remember Michelle Obama's words, 'when they go low, we go high.'

In his important work, *Moral Courage*, Rushworth Kidder provides us with strategies or enablers to help us live our higher values and make it easier for us to speak up.[46] These start with things such as simply knowing our subject, starting any discussion with questions, listening to better understand our audience and presenting our points logically and incrementally. He advises that when seeking support for

---

45 Menning Finn, S. (2019) Why nurturing curiosity is an ethical endeavour: exploring practitioners' reflections on the importance of curiosity. *International Journal of Early Years Education*, Vol. 27 Issue 1. https://tandfonline.com/doi/abs/10.1080/09669760.2018.1547632

46 Kidder, R. M. (2006) *Moral Courage: Taking Action When Your Values Are Put to the Test*. William Morrow, New York.

ideas, look for allies or those with a shared purpose or values and look for win/win solutions where compromise is required.

There are frameworks and guidelines which may prove useful in helping every company become a kinder workplace more respectful of the needs of a diverse workforce. However, it still comes down to how individual people treat each other every day. We all have a role to play as regards how we treat those around us, and those with the most power to shape what the company stands for have a particular responsibility.

Sometimes the concept of speaking up won't be to challenge unethical thinking or poor behaviour but simply to introduce innovative ideas that are not being considered in a meeting. It is wise for any leader to be open to the ideas of others. This is the practice of inclusive leadership.

Key Takeaways

- ESG benchmarks are enablers of superior commercial performance.
- Short-termism must give way to strategies of sustained longer-term growth.
- Creating workplaces that respect everyone is vital in building positive cultures.
- Consider partnering with other sectors to leverage expertise.
- Profit and purpose nourish each other, creating a virtuous circle.
- Moral courage is required to live our higher values.

Books Referenced

- Chouinard, Yvon, *Let My People Go Surfing* (2018)
- Covey, Stephen, *The Speed of Trust: the one thing that changes everything* (2006)
- Henderson, Rebecca M., *Reimagining Capitalism in a World on Fire* (2020)
- Joly, Hubert, *The Heart of Business: Leadership Principles for the Next Era of Capitalism* (2021)
- Kidder, Rushworth M., *Moral Courage: Taking Action When Your Values Are Put to the Test* (2006)
- Kotler, Philip & Lee, Nancy, *Corporate Social Responsibility: Doing the Most Good for Your Company & Your Cause* (2005)
- Mackay, Hugh, *The Kindness Revolution: how we can restore hope, rebuild trust and inspire optimism* (2021)
- Raworth, Kate, *Doughnut Economics, Seven Ways to Think Like a 21st-Century Economist* (2018)
- Stout, Martha, *The Sociopath Next Door* (2005)

CHAPTER 5

Kind Leadership

The Power of Kindness

Kind leaders set the standard for others in the workplace through their own behaviour. Ambiguity needs to be removed and it must be clearly understood by everyone within the company that if you work in that company, it is expected that you will embrace the values and norms that the company has adopted and that are being exhibited by the leader and act in accordance with them. To contemplate doing otherwise would feel wrong and at odds with the culture of the whole organisation.

Most organisations will already be operational when moving to a more values-centred culture. This therefore involves an exercise in change management. Behavioural psychology would tell us that when you want to instil a change, making the ideal the new default is the most effective method. This is because people will generally fall in with the default rather than trying to change the status quo.

Creating a kinder culture should have broad appeal and kindness has an almost mystical power to transform any given moment and so cultural change may take place more quickly than perhaps other change management programs. The demonstrations of kindness don't have to be huge statements, but collectively can be a powerful force that drives positive change, and we are all capable of seizing these moments.

Acts of kindness are generally associated with individuals; however, they can just as easily play out in corporations. Many workplaces now encourage employees to 'bring your whole self to work'. Being fully accepted and included, and feeling a sense of belonging in an environment that thrives on diversity can increase the degree of happiness in people's work lives, and is fundamental to taking a kind approach to the management of people. This will also bring far greater satisfaction for the manager as well. In the words of Saint Francis of Assisi, 'For it is in giving that we receive.'

There is an old expression 'the tone starts at the top', so senior decision-makers have a disproportionate influence on culture. It is important to understand that behaviour at the top becomes contagious throughout any organisation. When you move into a staff management role, you now have people under your care and their wellbeing should be your highest priority.

Simple gestures such as saying good morning and asking how someone's weekend was or remembering a team member's child's name and asking how they are have the power to change the whole atmosphere within a company.

In the white paper The Power of Kindness: Kind Leaders Shaping the Future, Hall & Partners provides 10 simple yet powerful guidelines for kindness in the workplace:

1. Listen to others and value their views.
2. Communicate with a personal touch.
3. Celebrate and recognise.
4. Be honest.
5. Accommodate personal issues.
6. Treat others with respect.
7. Champion and encourage others.
8. Be inclusive.
9. Be humane.
10. Make kindness your philosophy.[1]

---

1 Hall & Partners (2019) The Power of Kindness. Kind Leaders Shaping the Future. https://issuu.com/hall_and_partners/docs/kindness_in_leadership_final. November 6th.

One of the key roles of a leader, mentioned above, is to acknowledge and reward exceptional service from team members. To be recognised by others, especially the most senior people in a company, can be truly uplifting. We only have to think of an occasion when the quality of our work or the extra effort we put in was acknowledged and appreciated, to know how powerful this can be.

Leaders will encourage others to express their ideas, even if counter to their own. They will break down silos and encourage collaboration and teamwork. They will be interested in people and look for ways to help them advance in life. These behaviours will engender a sense of belonging among those who work there. One study reported in the *Harvard Business Review* included this finding – 'We find that what leaders say and do makes up to a 70 per cent difference as to whether an individual reports feeling included.'[2]

Businesses led by emotionally intelligent leaders who appreciate this will also demonstrate stronger commercial metrics and long-term business success as 'the best and brightest' will gravitate to leaders and organisations which display these qualities. The opposite is also true – 'People don't leave companies, they leave managers.'[3]

Qualities of a Leader

A new language is entering leadership literature where progressive, more enlightened authors are willing to challenge traditional stereotypes. They share wisdom that, if adopted by the corporate sector, has the power to truly transform the way we do business.

Alison Cameron, an extraordinary guide, author and leader, is one of these and offers deep insights into the role of the leader through her work at the Leadership Retreat and in her book *Leadership for*

2   Bourke, J. & Titus, A. (2020) The Key to Inclusive Leadership Report. *Harvard Business Review*, March.

3   Goler, L., Gale, J., Harrington, B. & Grant, A. (2018) Why People Really Quit Their Jobs. *Harvard Business Review*, January.

the New Millenium. She states, 'At the dawn of the new millennium, humanity is being invited to create a more just, humane, and soulful existence for all people.'[4]

She shares, 'Leading and living from the heart is one of the most distinctive attributes of the New Millenium Leader.' She invites us to 'deconstruct conditioning and limiting beliefs in order to develop our extraordinary potential.' She celebrates the art of 'self-leadership' which leads to the development of self-knowledge, wisdom and heart.

Her descriptions of the qualities and attributes of true leadership are a refreshing departure from the stereotypical characteristics that we may have seen in days gone by. She lists these as Purpose, Patience, Love, Harmony, Truth, Commitment, Grace, Vitality, Humility, Passion, Self-knowledge, Wisdom and Heart.

Kirstin Ferguson, another highly respected leadership expert, public speaker and author of the best-selling book *Head & Heart, The Art of Modern Leadership*, expresses views that align with these.[5] She talks of four primary characteristics of this type of leadership – Humility, Self-awareness, Courage and Empathy.

She speaks of 'heart centred leadership' and captures the need for a new paradigm beautifully:

> *Listening with care and compassion to the stories and experiences of people who are very different to our lived experience, expands our world view and helps us develop an appreciation and understanding of the diversity of experiences and alternative ways of thinking about the world.*[6]

4   Cameron, A. (2020) *Leadership for the New Millennium*. Living Essence Publications, Currumbin QLD.

5   Ferguson, K. (2023) *Head & Heart, The Art of Modern Leadership*. Penguin Random House Australia, Melbourne.

6   Ibid.

Claire Summerer, who has facilitated numerous leadership programs across Australia, talks of the inter-relatedness of leadership and culture. She reminds us that it is the behaviour practised more so than the qualities possessed that is important:

Leadership is never practised in isolation. It is practised inside a system. You can be an amazing person with all the qualities of a leader and yet not practise them inside an organisation because the culture at play doesn't support those practices. Unless of course you are the CEO, in which case you have a unique opportunity to drive culture and instil the leadership practices you wish to see exhibited by everyone across the organisation.[7]

Jacinda Ardern, former Prime Minister of New Zealand, is another aligned to the idea of a new leadership model. She speaks of the detrimental impact of outdated notions of leadership, 'We've placed over time so much emphasis on notions of assertiveness and strength that we have assumed it means you can't have those other qualities of kindness and empathy.'[8]

It is time to challenge traditional stereotypes of what it means to be a strong leader and replace these with the view that the engagement of both heart and mind is the most powerful formula for a new style of leadership and redefined corporate strategy, which can be simply stated as, 'doing good is good for business'.[9]

---

7   Summerer, C. (2023) Email received October 13th.

8   Hammond, C. (2022) Does kindness get in the way of success? https://bbc.com/future/article/20221124-does-kindness-get-in-the-way-of-success. November 25th.

9   Deloitte Brand Voice (2020) Why doing good is good for business. https://forbes.com/sites/deloitte/2020/01/21/why-doing-good-is-good-for-business/?sh=6746a1146b29. January 21st.

Inclusive Leadership

Inclusive leaders value diversity, including the diversity of lived experience, as a means of creating richer cultures. Those who have experienced challenges in life, faced discrimination or even lived through traumatic experiences may well bring unique perspectives and their contribution should be valued. Today's managers should strive for diversity within their recruitment and promotion policies.

We should build inclusive cultures whereby people with diverse needs can flourish. By not recruiting against a stereotype, often influenced by unconscious bias, we build better organisations. This requires us to have the courage to look more broadly for the talented people we require.

Thankfully, we are not all the same, and if we can break free of our conventional paradigm and are open to tapping the rich pool of talent that diversity offers us, we will reap the rewards.

There are 'neurodiverse people' and 'highly sensitive people' who have an innate ability to pick up on the subtleties and nuances in situations, who can contribute in extraordinary ways. These people may well be undervalued as they may not fit into a stereotype, however their differences should be valued. They may be seen as speaking too assertively or being too quiet, or being overly sensitive or too reactionary to noise and stimulus, and hence be overlooked for more senior roles.[10]

Another pool that progressive leaders could consider hiring from are groups who may be awaiting visa or residency applications which could include asylum seekers. There will often be wonderful highly skilled people that may have been granted work rights, even if on a limited basis, who in many cases have fled persecution or war-ravaged regions and can add immeasurably to the talent pool of an organisation and to the richness of its culture.

Leaders can also seek new team members from the ranks of the currently unemployed, those who have fled domestic violence and

---

10 Aron, E. (2017) *The Highly Sensitive Person*. Thorsons, London.

those who are homeless. If their skills match those required for vacant roles, they will bring the bonus of loyalty and commitment that may far exceed that of the average person.

Australian tech entrepreneur Kylee Ingram has developed a powerful platform for diversity in decision-making called Wizer. Essentially the details of all members of an organisation are entered into a database. These include experience, education, personality type and so forth.

When project teams are formed, a question is entered into Wizer asking who would be the best people to form that team. Wizer will then construct the ideal team which will bring not only expertise but also diverse viewpoints, and even highlight if an external person should be added into the team for that project. Kylee Ingram states that, 'At Wizer we believe that diversity in decision making isn't just a moral imperative but a competitive advantage.'[11]

The value of drawing from the knowledge and views of different people from different backgrounds has been known for centuries. The Roman system of Direct Democracy involved Citizen Assemblies which convened not just to input to social challenges but to make important decisions concerning governing the state.

Lynn Carson, Research Director at the newDemocracy Foundation, has written an excellent article entitled 'Group Diversity Trumps Individual Ability' on the merits of 'deliberate diversity' to maximise decision-making outcomes.[12]

Inclusive leaders will also value diversity of opinion rather than the fastest route to agreement and be cautious of consensus if reached too quickly. 'Group think', or unchallenged decision-making in meetings, will not generally produce the best outcome.[13] Sycophantic agreement with the leader is often a precursor to this. Mark Twain offers advice

---

11 https://wizer.business/blog/diversity-in-decision-making-harnessing-talent-through-inclusivity

12 Carson, L. (2014) Group Diversity Trumps Individual Diversity. https://newdemocracy.com.au/2017/08/14/group-diversity-trumps-individual-ability/

13 Janis, I. L. (1982) *Groupthink: Psychological Studies of Policy Decisions and Fiascos*. Houghton Mifflin, Boston.

on avoiding group think – 'Whenever you find yourself on the side of the majority, it is time to pause and reflect'.[14]

Conscious Leadership

The characteristic most often related to 'conscious leadership' is the requirement for a leader to be 'present' when making decisions and aware of their impact on others.

'Conscious leadership is an emergent construct, which refers to leaders who have a deep commitment to making a lasting positive impact,' says Dr Tatiana Donato Trevisan.[15] She was the former Head of Sustainability at Walmart Brazil, who completed a PhD under the supervision of Professor Debbie Haski-Leventhal at Macquarie University, a champion for purpose-led business. It was titled *Elevating Consciousness in Business Leaders: Connecting Personal Development to Positive Impact* and focused on how to increase the number of leaders who use business for societal good.

She has emphasised the need of our time for leaders to move beyond the narrow day-to-day commercial imperatives of the business:

> *Against the backdrop of climate change, a global pandemic and emerging social issues, the need for leaders who use the power of business to solve societal challenges has become increasingly urgent.*[16]

One of the most prominent figures in the field of conscious leadership, and doing business differently, is Raj Sisodia, co-author (along with Wholefoods co-founder John Mackey) of *Conscious Capitalism.*

---

14 Twain, M. (1897) *Following the Equator.* American Publishing Company. Montclair, CA.

15 Donato Trevisan, T. (2022) *Elevating Consciousness in Business Leaders: Connecting Personal Development to Positive Impact.* PhD Dissertation, Macquarie University, Sydney.

16 Ibid.

This book spawned a global movement to transform the teaching and practice of business around the world.

He states that 'business and capitalism are inherently good'.[17] However, he also states that business leaders need to be consciously aware of the positive and negative impacts that they have on people and planet. Good business is about 'being awake to the consequences of business action.'[18]

The essence of this philosophy is stakeholder primacy, whereby organisations are aware of the value they can create for all stakeholders, including customers, employees, suppliers, investors, society and the environment.

Thinking and acting consciously is sometimes an abstract concept for people, a little like the now widely used expression 'mindfulness'. One of the best definitions I have seen for the concept of living consciously comes from Canadian American psychotherapist Nathaniel Branden, a contemporary of Russian American writer and philosopher Ayn Rand:

> *Living consciously is a state of being mentally active rather than passive. It is the ability to look at the world through fresh eyes. It is intelligence taking joy in its own function. Living consciously is seeking to be aware of everything that bears on our interests, actions, values, purposes and goals ... It is the quest to keep expanding our awareness and understanding, both of the world external to self and of the world within.*[19]

---

17 Sisodia, R. & Mackey, J. (2013) *Conscious Capitalism*. Harvard Business Press, Boston MA.

18 Ibid.

19 Branden, N. (2014) *The Conversation*. Conscious Capitalism: how to make the most of the kindness in business. https://theconversation.com/conscious-capitalism-how-to-make-the-most-of-the-kindness-in-business-34848. December 17th.

Authentic Leadership

It is interesting that once someone reaches the pinnacle of their company they are automatically referred to as a leader. Often this brings with it accolades for all success that follows. However, business success is complex and rarely can be ascribed to one person.

Margaret Heffernan, writing in the *Financial Times*, describes this as an 'attribution error' and challenges the notion of leaders as 'special people whose magical qualities generate brilliant decisions to produce enduring results'.[20]

It takes a great deal more than sitting on top of an organisational chart to be entitled to be called a leader. Leadership is not a title, it is a description of behaviour, and leadership qualities are exhibited by people at all levels of a company and at all levels of society.

Heffernan warns us against the risks of 'infantilising' or denying our own maturity and positive contribution as we engage in 'the cult of leadership adoration'. This reality carries with it the responsibility for all of us to lead, through our ability to be role models for others.

However, those in senior roles may influence the greatest number of people across the organisation, so to exhibit leadership qualities such as displaying the characteristics of kindness, compassion and empathy can be particularly impactful.

Expectations of companies and their leaders are changing and evolving – this concerns more access to the leader and creating a sense of connectedness rather than aloofness among them. The courage to state as the leader what you stand for is another important ingredient of success for today's leader. BlackRock's Larry Fink puts it this way:

---

20 Heffernan, M. (2023) Success is More Complicated than One Exceptional Individual. *Financial Times*, https://ft.com/content/c831fac2-3b75-4555-b9a3-5972a25d00c2. London, September 25th.

Your company's purpose is its north star in this tumultuous environment. The stakeholders your company relies upon to deliver profits for shareholders need to hear directly from you and to be engaged and inspired by you, they do need to know where you stand on the societal issues intrinsic to our companies' long-term success.[21]

One of the most admired corporate leaders in the area of responsible business is Paul Polman, former global CEO of Unilever. In 2021, he co-authored a book, *Net Positive: How Courageous Companies Thrive by Giving More Than They Take*, with Andrew Winston espousing his business philosophy.[22]

He tells of the significant changes he made very early in his tenure as CEO. They were designed to heighten sustainability initiatives across the company. In a bold move he cancelled quarterly financial market updates, used by fund managers as guidance for their investment decisions. He said he couldn't achieve the long-term transformation of the company if his horizon was the next quarterly briefing.

The investment community pushed back, creating concerns at board level. Polman told the story of how he made a judgement call that after a high-profile global search resulting in his appointment as CEO, it was unlikely the board would sack him this early in his tenure. He moved ahead with his way of doing business, which was to build sustainability into the very fabric of Unilever. He had the unwavering conviction that this would be the way to build a great global company. He states:

21 Fink, L. (2022) Blackrock. https://blackrock.com/corporate/investor-relations/larry-fink-ceo-letter

22 Polman, P. & Winston, A. (2021) *Net Positive: How Courageous Companies Thrive by Giving More Than They Take*. Harvard Business Review Press, Boston Massachusetts.

Solid data now shows that companies focussing on environmental, social and governance (ESG) performance, get equal or higher returns in the market.[23]

Unilever reaped the rewards of his visionary leadership. Its purpose-driven brands, the ones that connected to larger societal issues such as the provision of sanitation in developing regions and working to improve children's health, grew 69 per cent faster than the rest of the business and with higher margins underpinning the financial strength of the entire company.[24]

Journalist Peter Fisk, in writing about Polman's career, uses the Financial Times Securities Exchange Index as his benchmark and states that, 'During his time at Unilever CEO Paul Polman delivered financial returns more than double that of the FTSE index.'[25]

In support of this philosophy of caring for people, Polman noted that companies who put their people at the centre of their responses to challenging business conditions during the Covid crisis, emerged stronger than those who hadn't. He advocated for managers to truly get to know the people they worked with.

He was known for regularly holding calls with new starters to welcome them to the company. Quite different from the mechanistic approach where people were seen by some as units of labour.

He ensured that the culture of Unilever was to be ever watchful of the mental health of employees and to look for ways to support them in their lives as their personal circumstances changed. Initiatives included extended leave for new parents and caregivers.

Employee engagement surveys showed positive trends at Unilever. The measurement of employee happiness levels and intention to remain with the company grew each year and 90 per cent said they felt proud

---

23 Ibid.
24 Ibid.
25 Fisk, P. (2022) https://peterfisk.com/2022/08/net-positive-is-the-world-better-because-your-business-is-in-it-the-best-ideas-from-paul-polmans-book/

of the company they worked for. Three-quarters of new employees said that they applied for roles at Unilever because of the company's mission and values.

What distinguishes Polman from many other senior executives is his courage and his vision. Questions, as opposed to statements, can be immensely powerful in getting a concept across, and two of the most powerful from Polman are: 'What if companies operated in the service of their employees?' and 'Is the world better because your business is in it?'[26]

Authentic leadership also encompasses the principles espoused in Sisodia and Mackey's work *Conscious Capitalism* as regards understanding our impact on others:

> *It is about people who are aware of the impact their habits and actions have on their organisation and their environment … Conscious Businesses require authentic leaders that do not exercise dominance and control to reach a goal, but who are of service to the business, its people, its customers and the community.*[27]

Howard Shultz, founder of Starbucks, is another CEO often spoken about in discussions of aligning a values-based culture with strong commercial outcomes. He does, however, acknowledge the challenges, and in a 2014 interview for *Harvard Business Review* he stated that it 'has been difficult, and lonely.'[28]

26 Polman, P. & Winston, A. (2021) *Net Positive: How Courageous Companies Thrive by Giving More Than They Take*. Harvard Business Review Press, Boston Massachusetts.

27 Conscious Business Institute (2014) *Conscious Capitalism: how to make the most of the kindness in business*. Santa Barbara, CA, December 17th.

28 Ignatius, A. (2014) The Best Performing CEO's in the World. *Harvard Business Review*. November.

He was known as someone prepared to speak out on political and social issues yet simultaneously won Wall Street's respect. He did make the point however, that ultimately, 'The only ingredient that works in this environment is performance, so we have to perform'.[29]

Authentic leadership also requires the ability to manage disagreement which exists in one form or another daily in most workplaces, as work colleagues differ in their views on company strategy and its implementation. The leader must be open to alternative viewpoints, in fact seek them, and then respectfully moderate the ensuing discussion.

In meetings we are often confronted with a position that we disagree with, laying the grounds for conflict to result. Emotional responses and behaviours may ensue that cause the situation to escalate, with the consequences being unproductive, and at times damaging working relationships.

It is not uncommon to see the situation where one person makes a statement, another disagrees, perhaps vehemently with them; the first person then feels offended, even attacked, and becomes even more defensive and protective of their position. It's a downward spiral. To counter this cycle, we need to assume that the other party is actually 'coming from a good place' and 'speaking with good intent' and has a positive desire to improve the organisation.

Responses such as 'Could you elaborate on your idea?' or 'I'd like to better understand your thinking' show respect for the other person and a desire to understand. It will rarely result in immediate defensiveness, and you may also gain some additional information, or insights that may modify your own position.

Once you have listened, you have earnt the right to be listened to in return. This approach is particularly important when you are on a team, such as a senior executive team or a project team, and will be collaborating with the person on a continuing basis.

Importantly, Kirstin Ferguson reminds us that if you are the most senior person in a meeting, don't close off your session with 'does

---

29 Ibid.

anyone have something to add?' It's a conversation killer. It is far better to ask, 'what else do you think we need to consider?'

We should encourage a range of diverse views and one way to do this is to put people from different backgrounds with different expertise in the same room, around the same table – that way we'll hear different opinions. They are also likely to have different ways of expressing them.

The concept of 'assuming good intent' is not just applicable to one-on-one conversations or team meetings but when moving around the organisation on a day-to-day basis. Various leadership authors, including Richard Branson, have espoused the idea of, 'Rather than focussing on mistakes, a leader needs to catch someone doing something right every day.'[30]

Every company needs people who are focused on ensuring that rules are followed to ensure that good governance is maintained. However, this does not mean that people should spend all their time searching for infractions of the company's policies, and this should not be at the exclusion of providing praise and positive motivation for people doing the right thing.

Girish Mathrubootham, CEO and founder of Chennai-based software firm Freshworks, clearly enunciates the key to building an environment of trust:

> *The only thing that works in Freshworks, for a leader,*
> *is earning trust through a heart-led approach, which*
> *focuses on putting humans first, over business motives,*
> *and doing the right thing by them.*[31]

---

30 Branson, R. (2011) Richard Branson on the Power of Your People. https://www.entrepreneur.com/living/richard-bransons-8-keys-to-happiness-and-success/331932

31 Kumra, G. & Sengupta, G. (2023) https://mckinsey.com/featured-insights/asia-pacific/asias-top-ceos-embrace-change-with-boldness-and-resilience. January 13th.

Selfless Leadership

Civil society leaders are often among our most inspiring; those people who prioritise the wellbeing of others over their own personal gain. These are the unselfish people working for others, and a better society for all.

When asked to recall who they most admire (leaving aside family members), many people will bring up names such as Mother Teresa, Nelson Mandela, Martin Luther King and Gandhi (all of whom are quoted in this book). They share the traits of courage, determination, selflessness and kindness. They are the giants of advocacy and action for the vulnerable and the voiceless.

In Australia, we have our share of heroes, too. We are grateful to those who have taken a stand on behalf of those who are subjected to discrimination in society or who are particularly vulnerable.

Professor Tim Soutphommasane has challenged racism and championed diversity his whole life. During his time as Race Discrimination Commissioner at The Australian Human Rights Commission he launched the *Racism, It Stops with Me* campaign, and now continues his work as Chief Diversity Officer at Oxford University.

Former Socceroo captain, broadcaster and human rights activist Craig Foster is another powerful advocate for ending racism and for the rights of asylum seekers. He is the co-author of *Fighting for Hakeem* and spearheaded the grassroots community-led *Racism Not Welcome* campaign and is also a tireless advocate for Indigenous rights and recognition.[32] It was pleasing to see that Craig received recognition himself for this work when in April 2024 he was awarded an honorary Doctorate of Laws by the University of Wollongong.

Work in the fields of human rights and social justice is not easy, and those who stand up against discrimination are often victimised

---

32 Foster, C. & Engel-Mallon, A. (2019) *Fighting for Hakeem*, e-book, Hachette Australia.

themselves. Gillian Triggs, the former Australian Human Rights Commissioner, details in her book, *Speaking Up*, the challenges she faced and personal risks she took in undertaking her work, particularly at the time of publishing the commission's *Forgotten Children, a National Inquiry into Children in Immigration Detention* report in 2014.[33]

These children are of course powerless, voiceless and it is only through the actions of people like Gillian Triggs and the lawyers and others who work in this field that injustices can be highlighted and brought to the attention of the public.[34]

Indigenous leader Noel Pearson is another leader who has displayed great conviction and great courage for many years, never daunted by the criticism of so many who do not agree with his views. He was a tireless campaigner for The Voice to Parliament and is arguably the greatest orator that we have in this country today.

He speaks from the heart about respect for the rights of First Nations people and the importance of recognising them in our constitution. The Indigenous people of Australia through genomic testing have been shown to be the oldest known civilisation on earth, one with ancestries stretching back 65,000 years.

Elaine Pearson, Asia Director of Human Rights Watch, and author of *Chasing Wrongs and Rights*, is another person constantly speaking up for others.[35] She has worked tirelessly to end injustice such as human trafficking, and has also advocated for the humane treatment of refugees detained on Manus Island and Nauru and drawn the university sector's attention to the coercion of Chinese students in Australia.

Andrea Durbach is another powerful, courageous and committed advocate for human rights. She is a Professor of Law at UNSW and

---

33 Triggs, G. (2018) *Speaking Up*. Melbourne University Publishing, Melbourne.
34 https://humanrights.gov.au/our-work/childrens-rights/publications/forgotten-children-national-inquiry-children-immigration
35 Pearson, E. (2022) *Chasing Wrongs & Rights*. Simon & Schuster, Sydney.

founding director of the Australian Human Rights Centre (now Institute). She was born and educated in Cape Town South Africa where she practised as a political trial lawyer representing victims and opponents of the apartheid laws operating in that country. Her book *Upington* details her experiences as the defence lawyer for 25 Black people accused of murder.[36]

Julie Chai moved from a corporate career in human resources to champion the rights of a group she saw as facing discrimination in the workplace. She founded The Asian Leadership Project to provide a valuable forum that advocates for the elimination of discrimination against Asian staff within Australian companies. This career impediment is referred to as the 'bamboo ceiling'.

Audette Excel is someone who has integrated her profound desire to help others with her deep corporate knowledge. She has previously served as a non-executive director of Suncorp and is now on the board of Westpac. Her work is best characterised as 'bridging the world of business and the world of people living in extreme poverty'.[37] Her model is a fascinating one.

She founded Adara Partners and Adara Advisors, highly regarded corporate advisory firms which are comprised of some of the most experienced corporate advisors in the Australian financial and legal services sectors. These people work on a pro bono basis with fee income being channelled into Adara Group, which is an international development organisation working in Nepal and Uganda. They directly reach over 50,000 people in these regions annually and countless more through knowledge sharing.

Martin Luther King gives us hope that progress will be made when he says, 'the arc of the moral universe is long, but it bends towards justice.' However, it still requires brave people to stand up and it takes courage as one risks being ostracised, or viewed with suspicion,

---

36 Durbach, A. (1999) *Upington*. Allen & Unwin, Sydney.
37 www.adaragroup.org/about/

potentially making for an uncomfortable existence. The motivation to find courage and willingness to stand up for others in the face of potentially negative personal impact is indeed an act of selflessness and seems deeply rooted in kindness.

A wonderful sign seen on a church noticeboard exhorts us to find this courage – 'At the end of the day, I would rather be excluded for who I include, than be included for who I exclude.'

It is interesting to contemplate what the business world would be like if more corporate leaders displayed the same courage to transform their environments as the people previously mentioned are doing in society more broadly.

Although corporate leaders may not be the first to come to mind when we think of who we have most admired, if any leader chooses to align with their higher self, they will find opportunities abound in the workplace every day to display the qualities we all most admire. This will be a legacy worth leaving.

It is not easy navigating a corporate career, there are many mine-fields and many masters to serve. However, when the heads of our largest companies look back on their careers and look to single out their greatest achievement, will the answer be a movement in the com-pany's share price or will it relate to having hopefully made the lives of people, inside and outside the company, better?

Quiet Leadership

Leaders need to lead for everyone, and it is important to remember the different types of people within your care. One powerful approach to be mindful is to invite the quieter people into the conversation. In meetings they may well have been the ones who have listened the most intently and have reflected most deeply and who just may be able to offer the most wisdom.

It is good to remember that reluctance to speak up early in a meeting may simply be a preference, or it may sometimes be based on cultural norms. In some cultures, women are typically not encouraged to speak up. In some cultures, young people speaking up would be considered rude and in others to speak in a meeting with a more senior person in the room would be considered as challenging their ideas and thus unacceptable.

Two personality types that are well known, partly through the extensive usage of the Myer Briggs Type Indicator (MBTI) test in corporate settings, are extrovert and introvert. Both these personalities can bring benefits to any company, and both need to be honoured.

Susan Cain writes in such a moving way about the power of quietness, reflection and empathy in her seminal work *Quiet: The Power of Introverts in a World that Can't Stop Talking*.[38] The book is about the dichotomy between 'the man of action' and 'the man of contemplation' and how we need to honour both and find a balance between the two.

We should not fall into the trap of associating leadership with the loudest voice in the room. Quietness is not a weakness but a strength. Cain describes this beautifully as 'confidence is silent, insecurities are loud'.[39]

She issues us a challenge in her TED talk, which has now been viewed over 33 million times, dispelling the myth of linking talk with creativity – 'There is zero correlation between the person in a meeting doing the most talking and the person with the best ideas.'[40] Cain calls this out and says, 'The gregarious, larger-than-life leadership mould needs to be challenged.'[41]

The world has in many cases been shaped by extroverts, and the contribution that can be made by introverts has often been overlooked. Extroverts who have achieved leadership positions have achieved that

38 Cain, S. (2012) *Quiet, The Power of Introverts in a World that Can't Stop Talking*. Penguin Books, London.

39 Ibid.

40 Cain, S. (2011) The Power of Introverts. https://www.ted.com/talks/susan_cain_the_power_of_introverts

41 Ibid.

success through speaking, so it may not be easy to acknowledge the leadership potential of those with a quieter disposition. Nor to reverse this formula for success and learn how to listen and ask more questions.

If systems are designed by people with more outgoing personalities, it is likely that these qualities are what they will value most highly when recruiting others. The hotel chain Hilton Australia has recently instituted a policy of encouraging job applicants to post TikTok videos tagging Hilton when applying for jobs instead of submitting CVs. This could potentially disadvantage many people and indeed terrify a segment of the population.

Shade Zahrai, co-founder of leadership development and consulting firm Influenceo, believes, 'The corporate ladder isn't just for the loud; it's also for the thoughtful, the observant, and the introspective.' In her article 'Three Ways to Help Introverts Conquer the Corporate World' she offers the following advice:

1. Master the art of written communication.
2. Leverage your listening skills: the power of silent observation.
3. Seek one-on-one interactions: deep connections over surface networking.[42]

Senior managers have in many cases achieved their level of success by having knowledge that is valued within the company and be reticent to seek the views of others, for fear that this may in some way lessen their own credibility.

As new leadership paradigms replace the old, we will increasingly see the growth in appreciation for leaders who seek alternative views to their own, who listen and who acknowledge the contribution of others even if different from themselves.

Christine Holgate is one such business leader.[43] She embodies

---

42 Zahrai, S. (2024) Three Ways to Help Introverts Conquer the Corporate World. *Sydney Morning Herald*, January 28th.

43 Whittaker, M. (2023) She Who Delivers: the Fall & Rise Behind Christine Holgate. https://forbes.com.au/covers/leadership/christine-holgate-on-how-to-deliver-by-listening. April 19th.

the characteristics of courage and resilience while at the same time being renowned for her humility and lack of bravado, not necessarily traits that one might automatically associate with leadership. She is the CEO of logistics firm Toll Global Express where she grew the company's revenue by 17 per cent in 2023.

In 2024 Forbes Asia named her in their 50 over 50 Asian Women Leaders.[44] Characteristically she shifted the limelight from herself – 'Extremely humbled and proud that Forbes Asia have recognised our work at Team Global Express to grow a stronger, greener, logistics partner.'[45]

She is known for her willingness to listen to those working within the companies that she has led and has produced exceptional commercial results at natural health company Blackmores, Australia Post and now in her current role.

In following her career and observing her behaviour, one gets the sense that she is not managing according to a management playbook learnt in business school, rather this is simply who she is. This is how emotional intelligence plays out in a corporate setting.

Christine Holgate deeply cares about the people that she works with, and the hallmark of her management approach has been to show respect to people at every level of the organisations that she has led. Holgate commented:

> ... my learning is that whichever conversation you have, you treat people with respect. People can handle difficult conversations if they are respectful and you give evidence for why you're doing things, but if it's just bullying or disrespectful, expect people to object.[46]

44 https://forbes.com/sites/ranawehbe/2024/01/16/50-over-50-asia-2024
45 Ibid.
46 Christine Holgate (2024) LinkedIn post, January 18th. https://linkedin.com/feed/update/urn:li:activity:7153556273777524736/

It is likely that more will be learnt by asking questions and listening to the answers, than by talking. Questioning is one of the best tools to deepen understanding. Einstein famously said:

If I had an hour to solve a problem, and my life depended on the solution, I would spend the first 55 minutes determining the proper question to ask, for once I know the proper question, I could solve the problem in less than five minutes.[47]

Corrinne Armour has written *Leaders Who Ask. Building Fearless Cultures by Telling Less and Asking More*. Through her coaching and consulting work she is a tireless advocate for the power of listening as a means of leaders gaining a deeper understanding of their people. She sums up the power of listening beautifully when she states:

*When we **tell** people what to do, they may listen, but they are unlikely to commit to action and are even less likely to remember. When we **ask** great questions that lead to insight, there's an emotional component triggered in the brain that leads to commitment and accountability.*[48]

Somehow it seems that when a person is open to engaging in deep empathetic listening, they may be more inclined to then act with kindness, as they now have a better understanding of the other person and may feel more connection to them. In fact, in many cases, a precursor to kindness may be understanding, and through this connection acting in a manner that supports others.

---

47 Einstein, A. Einstein's 55 Minutes. https://ascd.org
48 Corrinne Armour https://corrinnearmour.com/author/

Humility is also linked to transparency, the willingness to admit that you don't have all the answers. Carolyn Dewar, co-author of *CEO Excellence: The Six Mindsets that Distinguish the Best Leaders from the Rest*, had this to say,

> *Resilience and humility go together. If you are grounded in your organisation's purpose, it gives you energy to navigate the storms. Humility also helps you to recognise that you don't know everything, so in moments of crisis you reach out for help, you learn.*[49]

While certain characteristics are likely to assist or impede a leader there is no right personality type that is superior to all others; different people will contribute in different ways. This applies both in leadership roles and throughout an organisation.

Introvert and extrovert are two personality types whose needs should be catered for when planning conferences, or large gatherings of staff. For instance, it is important to be aware that not everyone loves networking. It is not necessarily everyone's favourite time of the day, and in fact, in some cases people may find it exhausting or it may even fill some people with dread.

When organising a conference or large meeting it is worthwhile remembering that you are catering for a wide range of personality types. Build in time for breaks, and give people permission to be by themselves, which may take the form of giving people the time to go back to their room in the case of a residential conference, or of recharging by going for a walk or ensuring that there are places to sit quietly between sessions.

---

49 Dewar, C., Keller, S. & Malhotra, V. (2022) *CEO Excellence: The Six Mindsets that Distinguish the Best Leaders from the Rest.* Scribner Book Company, New York.

One characteristic of an empathetic leader is to be curious, and curiosity inevitably leads to questioning. When someone advances an idea, a true leader will not assert the seniority of their position at that moment, and even if they disagree, they will promote further discussion, unpacking the various layers of the proposition.

The importance of this is expressed by Kirstin Ferguson – 'The impact of any leader feeling they need to be the smartest person in the room can be devastating, especially for the most junior members of a team who revere the older, wiser leaders they work with.'[50]

Listening to and encouraging others to share their views earns you the right to then speak and guarantees you far greater attention from your audience, who are likely to emulate your empathetic listening style. It also shows respect and gives others confidence to contribute. There is nothing that kills creativity and lateral thinking more than a manager dismissing or shutting down a contribution from someone in a meeting. Hugh Mackay reminds us of one of life's truisms, 'Everyone's deepest need is to be heard'.[51]

The wisdom embodied in listening is not a new understanding. Over 2,000 years ago Epictetus reminded us that 'You have two ears and one mouth and it's best to use them in that proportion.'[52]

Brene Brown is considered a world expert on vulnerability and leadership. In her 2016 book *Daring Greatly* she describes vulnerability as 'uncertainty, risk and emotional exposure' far from the leadership archetypes that we are perhaps more use to seeing promoted.[53] She talks of stepping out of our comfort zone and into a world of uncertainty.

50 Ferguson, K. (2023) *Head & Heart, The Art of Modern Leadership.* Viking, Penguin Random House Australia.

51 Mackay, H. (2021) *The Kindness Revolution: how we can restore hope, rebuild trust and inspire optimism.* Allen & Unwin, Sydney.

52 Two ears one mouth. https://dailystoic.com/two-ears-one-mouth/

53 Brown, B. (2016) *Daring Greatly: How the Courage to be Vulnerable Transforms the Way We Live, Love, Parent and Lead.* Penguin.

This discomfort brings with it benefits, however, for any leader who wishes to create a sense of closeness with their people. Leadership coach and author of *Lead In*, Cathy Burke, says, 'Saying I don't know, makes leaders easier to know and be trusted.'[54]

Daniel Coyle in his book *The Culture Code* makes an important point, 'Vulnerability does not come after trust – it precedes that.'[55]

Courageous Leadership

It is good to be reminded that courage does not simply come in the form of the words spoken, but in the actions taken. A quiet person may speak less, yet their impact can be just as powerful and just as courageous.

In 1955 in Montgomery, Alabama, a diminutive African American woman named Rosa Parks was told to give up her seat on the bus for a white person. She simply said, 'No', which triggered a human rights protest that reverberated around a nation for years to come. It is amazing to see how often courage and quietness go hand in hand.

One famous example of actions over words was in the 1990s during the siege of Sarajevo, the capital of Bosnia Herzegovina. Vedran Smailovic, the lead cellist of the Sarajevo Opera, mounted his own form of protest amidst constant shelling and sniper attacks from the rooftops.

Over two years Smailovic braved the snipers and played in the streets and at funerals and in bomb shelters every day. He would walk out, set up his cello, and play Albinoni's 'Adagio in G Minor'. Inexplicably the snipers found themselves incapable of shooting at him while he played. He didn't speak one word; yet he embodied and displayed the highest form of courage, which is the willingness to lose

54 Burke, C. (2002) *Lead In*. Publisher Catherine Burke.

55 Coyle, D. (2019) *The Culture Code: The Secrets of Highly Successful Groups*. Random House Business, New York.

his own life to address injustice. If you are not familiar with 'Adagio in G Minor', please put those words into a search engine and listen quietly while contemplating the courage of this man. It is likely that you will be moved to tears.

Courage is a quality that we all need to find at various times in a range of situations. This generally manifests as the courage of one's conviction to do what we believe to be right. This applies whenever we see a situation that we are uncomfortable with. It is often people in less senior or less influential positions who will need to access the greatest courage in order to speak up.

Whistleblowers are a cohort who display great courage, and the price that is extracted on them is often extremely high. It is understandable why most people stay silent. It is the experience of many whistleblowers, across all sectors – government, corporate and civil society – that retribution often follows. As Bernard Keane writing in *The Mandarin* says, 'Retaliation is the reflexive response of systems of power to those who embarrass or threaten them.'[56]

Sam Salehpour, an engineer at Boeing, certainly experienced this when he raised safety concerns about the manufacturer's Boeing 737 Max 9 aircraft. He was threatened and harassed but continued to speak out.

Jeff Morris also knows this treatment only too well. His act of whistleblowing ultimately triggered the federal government's Royal Commission into Misconduct in the Banking, Superannuation and Financial Services Industry, which was established in December of 2017.

The naming of the commission did not denote an investigation to determine whether misconduct had occurred or not, often common in the terms of reference of a royal commission. There was already sufficient evidence of widespread misconduct, and the exploration of this was to be the focus of the commission.

---

56 Keane, B. (2023) https://themandarin.com.au/229061-whistleblowers-poorly-armed-in-fight-against-retaliation. August.

Morris uncovered corrupt practices within the wealth management division of Australia's largest bank, the Commonwealth Bank. It was an area of the bank that thrived on a culture of success fuelled by high commissions and big bonuses which likely encouraged advisors to steer clients from fixed deposits into riskier mortgage funds. Disturbingly it has been reported that no qualification was required by CBA other than completion of a one-week course, and their recommendations were later found to be compromised by self-interest.

One would assume that the actions of Morris showed him to be exactly the sort of courageous person one would want in any organisation. One prepared to speak up when governance was found to be lacking. Far from this being the case, Morris reportedly suffered constant surveillance and harassment, his reputation was slandered, he was sacked by the bank and later developed PTSD, quite likely from the trauma.[57]

While there is no suggestion that the chair at the time, Catherine Livingstone, or CEO Ian Narev, knew what was occurring, there is no denying that they were the stewards of an organisation whose culture seemingly permitted these practices, including this abhorrent treatment of an employee who had the courage to speak up. These revelations may well have been the catalyst for significant cultural change.

Whistleblowers have sought to highlight perceived wrong-doing in government as well. Among these are Bernard Collaery, a Canberra lawyer and former ACT attorney-general, who was subject to court action by the federal government for his alleged role in raising awareness about Australia's alleged bugging of the Timor-Leste cabinet in order to give Australia the upper hand in oil and gas negotiations in the 2000s.

57 Ferguson, A. & Christodoulou, M. (2023) The inside account of how Commonwealth Bank tried to bury the scandal that sparked a royal commission. ABC News, November 11th. https://abc.net.au/news/2023-11-11/the-dirty-tricks-the-cba-used-to-silence-whistleblowers/103086260

Another high-profile whistleblower case is that of Richard Boyle who worked for the Australian Taxation Office (ATO) and believed that the aggressive debt recovery practices launched against small business owners were unethical and heavy-handed.

Another concerned David McBride, a lawyer in the Australian army who grew increasingly concerned about what he believed was wrongdoing by some members of the Australian armed forces while he was serving in Afghanistan. In May of 2024 he was sentenced to nearly six years in gaol.

The Human Rights Law Centre (HRLC) is calling on the government to urgently reform whistleblower laws. The strengthening of legislation for the protection of whistleblowers is an area that requires urgent attention from government.

In a corporate setting companies need to view complaints raised by whistleblowers as opportunities to amend breaches of governance and strengthen their companies, rather than as a threat to be dealt with. Companies must seek to understand not only how breaches occur, but also why whistleblowers felt they had no other option.

As author Kirstin Ferguson says, 'If labels like being courageous were attached to people who spoke up, instead of labels like trouble-makers, the incentive for people speaking up would be very different.'[58]

Jim Detert, author of *Choosing Courage, The Everyday Guide to Being Brave at Work*, guides us as to what courageous leaders do differently:

- courageous leaders display openness and humility
- courageous leaders put principles first
- courageous leaders focus on making environments safer for others.[59]

58 Ferguson, K. (2023) *Head & Heart, The Art of Modern Leadership*. Viking, Penguin Random House Australia.
59 Detert, J. (2021) *Choosing Courage, The Everyday Guide to Being Brave at Work*. Harvard Business Review Press.

Every day in senior leadership roles, you are called upon to find some kind of wisdom inside yourself to make the best decisions. Leaders face many ethical conundrums, and this is one reason why leadership isn't necessarily easy; however, it does provide enormous opportunities for personal growth. In a fast-changing commercial environment a decision made one day may not be optimal the next. 'Set and forget' is not an option anymore.

One leadership characteristic that is not always acknowledged is having the ability to accept that you will not appeal to everyone. Leadership is not necessarily about popularity. Jim Detert in his HBR article 'What Courageous Leaders Do Differently' states that:

> *Good leadership is about being trusted and respected for the defensibility of the decisions you make. It's about courageous action to defend core principles, even when it costs something significant; potentially even one's own popularity or standing in the short run.*[60]

Courageous leaders are not afraid to do things differently. They are not afraid to swim against the tide and they are not afraid of criticism. They will hire people that others won't, they will use their position in society to advocate for human rights and they will not be afraid to explicitly state what their company's values are, and why their company is publicly standing with others in society as regards social justice issues.

Anais Nin beautifully enunciates the reward to be gained when we find the courage within us to act on our values – 'Life shrinks or expands in proportion to one's courage.'[61]

---

60 Detert, J. (2022) What Courageous Leaders Do Differently. *Harvard Business Review*, January 7th.

61 Nin, A. (1966) The Diary of Anais Nin. https://archive.org/details/diaryofanaisnin02nina

If you are a CEO and you publicly say that your company is supportive of marriage equality or of the recognition of Indigenous people in the Australian constitution you will be criticised in some quarters. Views are polarised with some ascribing self-serving, even sinister motives to CEOs who speak up. It seems unreasonable to label all leaders who speak out as having ulterior motives.

In fact, it can be argued that to stay silent diminishes who you are. Marc Benioff, Chair and CEO of Salesforce, is clear on his position:

> *What we are doing is advocating on behalf of our employees ... today CEOs need to stand up not just for their shareholders, but their employees, their customers, their partners, the community, the environment, school, everybody. Anything that is a key part of the ecosystem.*[62]

Self-awareness

Growing in self-awareness as individuals is fundamental to being a better human being, a better leader and a better contributor to society.

Philosophers down through the ages have grappled with the big questions in life. There is a wealth of wisdom to be gained from reading the writings of these ancient philosophers as the emphasis of their writings was often on self-knowledge. Plato is one who saw self-knowledge as fundamental to self-improvement and Aristotle said, 'Knowing yourself is the beginning of all wisdom'.[63]

Socrates's approach was not one of giving prescriptive formulas for how to live, but rather he urged us to ask ourselves questions to develop deeper self-knowledge. He exclaimed that 'the unexamined

---

62 Steinmetz, K. (2016) Salesforce CEO Marc Benioff: Anti LGBT bills are anti-business. https://time.com/4276603/marc-benioff-salesforce-lgbt-rfra. March 31st.

63 Aristotle. https://biography.com/scholars-educators/aristotle

life was not worth living' and said, 'I cannot teach anyone anything, I can only make them think.'

Socrates provides us with so much knowledge in this area. His approach was one of disciplined enquiry in which we didn't learn by simply accepting what others told us, but by questioning assumptions and thinking deeply as to our role in this life. An example of some of the types of questions that Socrates posed are:

- Who am I?
- What do I stand for?
- What are my values?
- What am I willing to fight for?
- What am I willing to share publicly?
- What is the one thing I would never compromise?[64]

Socrates's methodology extended to asking ourselves questions about how to behave in the world. He thought that understanding the perspectives of others would help him 'become a more excellent human being'. The most famous series of questions devised by Socrates were the six Socratic questions:

- What do you mean by that? (clarifying questions)
- What can we assume instead? (probing assumptions)
- What would an example be? (looking for evidence)
- What might an alternative be? (questions about perspectives and outcomes)
- What are the consequences of that? (questions that probe implications)
- What is the counterargument? (questioning the question).[65]

---

64 Socrates. https://www.cambridge.org/core/journals/think/article/abs/is-the-unexamined-life-worth-living-or-not/8D5EC7FCA494A8B9A5E5D02 BADAB6182

65 Socrates. https://biography.com/scholars-educators/socrates

The last question is an interesting one.

In a meeting this can be phrased as the question 'is it worthwhile exploring other approaches before we make a final decision?' or 'is it worthwhile taking a moment to see what the opposite to this might look like?' This contribution to the meeting, albeit short on words, may often be a timely intervention that prompts deeper thought on an issue. We should distrust 'group think' and always ensure that assumptions are challenged and the mechanics by which decisions are made are robust.

In building greater self-insight, it can be immensely valuable for executives to stretch their thinking by applying their centres of moral reasoning to life situations well outside their corporate environments. Harvard University Professor Michael Sandel's online courses, and book, *Justice: What's the Right Thing to Do?* are seminal works in ethical decision-making.[66]

To ponder ethical and moral considerations has long held a fascination for mankind. Some of life's deeper questions that we may choose to ask ourselves are:

- Is there such a thing as right and wrong?
- Is life, and decision-making, black and white?
- What do you do when you are unsure what the right thing to do is?
- Should our decisions always result in the greatest good, and if so, how do you decide what that is?
- Are we prepared to make a decision even if it will personally disadvantage us?

Business today finds itself in an interesting position with huge advancements taking place every day at speeds that could only have been imagined even decades ago. However, with these advancements comes challenges, and growth in self-awareness will assist enormously in tackling some of the ethical challenges that we are likely to face.

---

66 Sandel, M. (2010) *Justice: What's the Right Thing to Do?* Penguin, New York.

If we get these critical decisions right, we can create a prosperous world with enough for everyone. If we get them wrong, we will see further fracturing of the social fabric and at worst the irreversible degradation of the planet that we call home.

Corporate Awareness

The people at senior levels of organisations can have a significant influence on the culture of the organisation that they are responsible for. The culture that a CEO or board desires must be universally embedded at all levels, and they need to be able to verify that it is understood by everyone throughout the company and that day-to-day behaviour reflects this.

If they believe this has largely been achieved, then that belief needs to be tested. How do they know? How have they drawn that conclusion? How do busy executives focused on their own specific portfolio or company directors who may attend a board meeting once a month take the pulse of the organisation?

It is extremely difficult to ensure with great certainty that the company's values have truly been embedded. As the CEO of one large ASX listed company said to me, 'It's like being the mayor of an entire city.'

As a leader, when regrettable issues do occur it is important to seek to understand how these things occurred and ask oneself:

- What was I walking past?
- What might our managers have been condoning?
- What processes had proved to be inadequate in allowing unacceptable behaviours to exist?

Even if an organisation has a strong inclusive culture of respect which promotes the company's values, do all directors and senior executives embody these principles themselves in their behaviour inside and outside the organisation? How are they perceived by people across the company? What about at the management level of the organisation? Are these values understood throughout the organisation as being qualities that must be lived day to day?

The key is for directors and senior executives to get out of the boardroom and head office and talk to employees, suppliers and customers. Obviously, the board needs to respect that the day-to-day operation is the domain of the managerial team, however, visits to branches and various stakeholder groups by directors can be coordinated with the executive team and undertaken with their blessings. These need to move beyond the whole board undertaking a branch visit, which will inevitably produce a somewhat artificial experience.

Individual directors arriving early for a board meeting and having a coffee first in the company's internal café, or lunchroom, is often a good way to connect with those who work there. People contact is the best way to take the pulse of any organisation. The important point here is to get out and speak to people; after all what have you got to lose? As Professor Amy Edmondson, author of *The Fearless Organisation*, reminds us, 'you can't learn less!'[67]

Simply requiring staff to undertake annual online quizzes about the company's policies and values is no substitute for talking with people – the former does not embed cultural change.

When a positive culture is deeply embodied within an organisation there is far less risk of the company's values and standards of behaviour being transgressed, as opposed to situations where they have not been articulated well or when employees don't see the values being lived at all levels of the organisation. Role-modelling, constant messaging and staying in touch with everyone at every level are key for every leader.

One mindset shift which can assist in driving boards to take greater action on preventing issues such as workplace harassment is to view this as a workplace health and safety (WHS) issue, as well as

---

67   Professor Amy Edmondson (2023) Champions of Change online seminar, June 6th.

a human rights issue, as this is an area that most companies already understand and have taken a strong stance on, and where they have already adopted a preventative mindset.

Key Takeaways

- Kindness and empathy lead to an enrichment of corporate culture.
- The qualities of a leader are being redefined as heart-centred.
- Quietness can be a strength.
- Listening and asking questions are vital components of good decision-making.
- 'Everyone's deepest need is to be heard.' Hugh Mackay.
- Demonstrating curiosity is a safe method of speaking up.
- Self-awareness underpins moral and ethical decision-making.

Books Referenced

- Armour, Corinne, *Leaders Who Ask: Building Fearless Cultures* (2018)
- Aron, Elaine, *The Highly Sensitive Person* (2017)
- Brown, Brene, *Daring Greatly: How the Courage to be Vulnerable Transforms the Way We Live, Love, Parent and Lead* (2016)
- Burke, Cathy, *Lead In* (2002)
- Cain, Susan, *Quiet, The Power of Introverts in a World that Can't Stop Talking* (2012)
- Cameron, Alison, *Leadership for the New Millennium* (2020)
- Coyle, Daniel, *The Culture Code: The Secrets of Highly Successful Groups* (2019)
- Detert, J. *Choosing Courage: The Everyday Guide to Being Brave at Work* (2021)

- Dewar, Carolyn, Keller, Scott & Malhotra, Vikram, *CEO Excellence: The Six Mindsets that Distinguish the Best Leaders from the Rest* (2022)
- Durbach, Andrea, *Upington* (1999)
- Edmonson, Amy, *The Fearless Organisation* (2023)
- Ferguson, Kirstin, *Head & Heart, The Art of Modern Leadership* (2023)
- Foster, Craig & Engel-Mallon, Colleen, *Fighting for Hakeem*, e-book (2019)
- Janis, Irving, *Groupthink: Psychological Studies of Policy Decisions and Fiascos* (1982)
- Mackay, Hugh, *The Kindness Revolution: How We Can Restore Hope, Rebuild Trust, and Inspire Optimism* (2021)
- Pearson, Elaine, *Chasing Wrongs & Rights* (2022)
- Polman, Paul & Winston, Andrew, *Net Positive: How Courageous Companies Thrive by Giving More Than They Take* (2021)
- Sandel, Michael, *Justice: What's the Right Thing to Do?* (2010)
- Sisodia, Raj & Mackey, John, *Conscious Capitalism* (2013)
- Susman, Warren, *Culture as History* (2003)
- Triggs, Gillian, *Speaking Up* (2018)
- Twain, Mark, *Following the Equator* (1897)

CHAPTER 6

Creating a Kinder Future

Resources and Support

There is much work to be done in creating a fairer, more equitable world where kindness to people and planet is the norm, and no one person has all the answers. One of the true positives that can help us feel optimistic about the future is that we have a range of organisations working towards this very end.

These include those with a focus on the wellbeing of our people, equality and inclusion, sustainability, the health of the planet and human rights. These organisations include some of the finest people we have in our society, those who have devoted their lives to others. These people exist across all sectors – government, civil society, academic, consulting – and are also embedded in internal roles within corporations. They share their knowledge via courses, conferences, webinars and podcasts and disseminate it widely through their writing.

Creating a better world requires considered decision-making and two organisations that leaders can turn to for guidance on life's ethical questions are Sydney-based The Ethics Centre, founded by Dr Simon Longstaff, and Melbourne-based Cranlana Centre for Ethical Leadership, now situated at Monash University. People attend their programs from all states.

The Ethics Centre provides a consulting service to businesses to assist with upskilling their executives in decision-making and undertaking organisational reviews. It has also established Ethi-Call, a free advice line on ethical matters, and is the convener of Sydney's *Festival of Dangerous Ideas.* In 2024 it called on the federal government to provide funding for the establishment of the Australian Institute of Applied Ethics.

Cranlana holds regular two-day programs to assist leaders with the development of ethical frameworks, as well as its signature six-day Colloquium. Those who attend find the learning environment extremely stimulating and their participation extraordinarily beneficial and enriching.

The Vincent Fairfax Fellowship is another great resource. Cranlana is the current delivery partner, where Matt Beard is the Programme Director. The Fellowship was designed to equip Australian leaders with the conviction, skills and knowledge to make considered decisions, having regard to those affected and treating others as they would wish to be treated.

Anna Shepherd, founder of social enterprise Bambuddha Group, is a passionate leader who works in the field of promoting kindness in business. She has developed a Corporate Kindness Program to help leaders and businesses move the dial on kindness to people, customer, community and environment.

The United Nations can be a valuable resource to assist with this transformative work and much of the knowledge it has developed is accessible for business through membership in the UN Global Compact Network, the world's largest corporate sustainability network.

In Australia, this involves your company becoming a member of the UN Global Compact Network Australia (GCNA). Kate Dundas is the Executive Director and Fiona Reynolds is Chair. The local network provides access to a vast library of knowledge on sustainability and responsible business, and access to regular events.

There is also immense value for members in participating in Communities of Practice (COPs) where members from different companies share their expertise and learnings with each other to further the sustainability and human rights goals that they each have. This can occur even among competitors.

This division of the UN was founded by Kofi Annan in 2000 to bring business and government together with a charter to promote the take-up of the *UN Sustainable Development Goals (SDGs)* across 17 categories. They are:

1. No Poverty
2. Zero Hunger
3. Good Health and Wellbeing
4. Quality Education
5. Gender Equality
6. Clean Water and Sanitation
7. Affordable and Clean Energy
8. Decent Work and Economic Growth
9. Industry Innovation and Infrastructure
10. Reduced Inequalities
11. Sustainable Cities and Communities
12. Responsible Consumption and Production
13. Climate Action
14. Life Below Water
15. Life on Land
16. Peace, Justice and Strong Institutions
17. Partnerships for the Goals.

The UN Guiding Principles on Business & Human Rights is another resource that provides a valuable framework for business, which can often find discussions on their role in respecting human rights challenging.[1]

1　https://ohchr.org/sites/default/files/documents/publications/ guidingprinciplesbusinesshr_en

These principles were developed by a giant in the field of human rights, the late Professor John Ruggie from Harvard University, along with a team that included Australians Vanessa Zimmerman, founder of Australian-based human rights consultancy Pillar Two, and Rachel Davis, co-founder of New York–based Shift Project.

The framework is based on three pillars:

1. Protect – the state duty to respect human rights
2. Respect – the corporate responsibility to respect human rights
3. Remedy – access to remedy for victims of business-related abuse.

The Sustainable Supply Chain Ambition, produced jointly by the United Nations Global Compact Network Australia (UNGCNA) and Ernst & Young (EY) and authored by Farah Dirgantoro, is another valuable document.[2] The interdependencies of the different aspects of ESG are highlighted in this study. It specifically examines how businesses can have a positive impact on biodiversity, climate change and human rights through their supply chain processes. The five key recommendations were:

1. Moving from risk management to value creation
2. Creating visibility in supply chains using systems and data
3. Partnering with stakeholders
4. Demonstrating leadership and accountability
5. Developing proficiency at navigating the complex and changing reporting and regulatory environment.

One would like to think that the corporate sector views its domain as including its environmental footprint and at least some degree of social purpose. Even viewed through the lens of self-interest, business has a stake in a better world.

---

2   *The Sustainable Supply Chain Ambition*, (2023) United Nations Global Compact Network Australia/Ernst & Young, August.

Business likes predictability and continuity in order to plan and does not do well among chaos, and we have seen many instances of the corporate sector running to government to protect it, or bail it out, when these upheavals occur.

Regrettably, we still see a willingness to exploit the most vulnerable members of our society and sacrifice the environment in which we all have to live in order to create greater wealth. Quotes such as this one, attributed to the Cree tribe of Canada, are a stark reminder of the consequences of not taking action to arrest harm:

Only when the last tree has died, and the last river been poisoned, and the last fish been caught will we realize we cannot eat money.

Hopefully, we will find it within our hearts as a society to lift some of the most vulnerable people on our planet out of poverty even if only to avoid the prediction made by philosopher Jean-Jacques Rousseau in 1793 – 'When the people shall have nothing left to eat they will eat the rich.'[3]

One quote that has application in any discussion about a world that contains huge disparity of income and opportunity comes from the film *The Matrix*. These words were spoken by the character Morpheus in conversation with Neo:

What you know you can't explain, but you feel it. You felt it your entire life, that there's something wrong with the world. You don't know what it is, but it's there, like a splinter in your mind, driving you mad.

---

3   Rich, C. (2020) Eat the Rich: how an 18th century phrase has made a comeback. Vanderbuilthustler.com. September 14th.

It was highlighted by Matthew Sekol from ESG Advocate who is championing a greater corporate focus on ESG. Sekol states that, 'saving the company, the world and its people is undervalued.'[4]

He offers encouragement to those interested in building a profession in this field while at the same time offering a cautionary note that their passion for purpose may not always be matched by the company's focus on mere compliance and reporting.

Perth-based billionaire Dr Andrew Forrest is a person who could be known by any number of titles with entrepreneur, philanthropist, anti-slavery campaigner, environmental trailblazer and mining company chair among them.

In more recent times his focus has been on clean energy with the company he chairs, Fortescue Metals Group, developing strategies to move to green hydrogen, wind and solar and his initiative to create a new renewable energy company Squadron Energy. He takes a somewhat different approach to most in discussing the most impactful path forward in the quest to slow global warming.

He argues that despite the push for all of us to do our bit, there were about 1,000 people responsible for global warming, given their positions of power. As the Executive Chair of Fortescue Metals Group, one of Australia's largest iron ore producers, he does not leave himself off this list and has proclaimed that it is time to 'put heads on spikes, starting with mine, but please don't forget the other 999'.[5]

However, this responsibility, SDG 12, Responsible Consumption and Production, applies as much to us as individuals as it does to business. While we may well point the finger at high carbon emitting businesses, they only produce what they can sell, and it is up to us to consume responsibly. This challenges our notion of how much stuff we need to live a good life.

---

4   Sekol, M. (2024) The Plagues of an ESG Career, https://esgadvocate. substack.com

5   O'Malley, N. (2023) Inside Andrew 'Twiggy' Forrest's urgent global climate campaign. *Sydney Morning Herald*, October 28th.

In a first-of-its-kind study by researcher Erik Stokstad, published in the *Environmental Science and Technology Journal*, it was calculated that about six tonnes per year of food, fuel, clothing, and other supplies would keep each individual out of abject poverty.[6] A caring and compassionate society would not want to set consumption at a level that barely sustains life; however, at the other end of the scale the excesses are obvious.

Expressed as 'raw materials', the study showed that to have just and sustainable living standards would mean each person would consume between eight and 14 tonnes of raw material per annum. In developed countries, using data from Germany and the US, current consumption is more than 70 tonnes per person.

The issue is that although the earth can provide enough for everyone while not being degraded to unsustainable levels in the process, the total population consumes too much, and consumption is in no way equitable. We are prepared to consume far more than we need, while leaving millions in poverty and despite our consumption levels being unsustainable by the planet. An equitable world would be a worthy goal but at the very least it is our responsibility to reduce the gap.

One initiative that is focused on reducing the negative environmental impacts of the fashion and textile industry is The Fashion Pact. It was launched by French President Emmanuel Macron in 2019 and is industry CEO led. Today more than 60 CEOs representing over 160 brands, approximately one third of the global fashion industry, have joined.

The industry draws many of its resources from nature, not only in materials but also water, with a high potential to damage the environment upon which it relies through wastewater, chemical leaching and plastic pollution, much of which ends up in the world's oceans. We can

---

6   Stokstad, E. (2023) How much stuff does it take to not be poor, about 6 tons per year. https://science.org/content/article/how-much-stuff-does-it-take-not-be-poor-about-6-tons-year. September 20th.

all play our part by not participating in the fast fashion phenomena that inevitably results in the improper disposal of millions of tonnes of clothing.

Women who wish to make a significant personal contribution to mitigating the effects of climate change are encouraged to join 1 Million Women. They are a community of members who to date have pledged to reduce their consumption resulting in a reduction of 703,316,318,354 tonnes of carbon pollution.

There are a number of organisations that can be drawn on for support in addressing specific areas of inequality. They can help with facilitating a greater take-up within your company of gender equality initiatives as they have developed significant expertise that can be used by organisations to develop their own internal programs. This is through providing knowledge, membership and certification which highlights publicly a company's commitment.

In an Australian context, these include the Workplace Gender Equality Agency (WGEA), Family Friendly Workplaces (FFW) founded by Emma Walsh, the Champions of Change Coalition led by CEO Annika Freyer, Perth-based CEOs for Gender Equity, initially spearheaded by Tania Cecconi, and now led by CEO Ashley McGrath, and online media site Women's Agenda, co-founded by Angela Priestley and Tala Lambert-Patel. UN Women works globally to address the inequality faced by women.

The responsibility of a company is not restricted to establishing an environment of equality within its own four walls and extends into its supply chain, which will invariably be populated by vulnerable people subjected to exploitation and forced labour.

Again, there are organisations that can assist such as The Responsible Business Alliance (RBA), which is a membership-based organisation, and Electronics Watch, headed by Bjorn Claessen, which works with companies engaged in public procurement. In 2021 it signed an agreement to work in close cooperation to assist members with their supply chain challenges.

Rapid technological advancements present us with opportunities to increase our positive social impact, particularly in areas such as analysing complex supply chains. This is another example of 'tech for good'.

Newer modern slavery legislation will see companies face stricter requirements for performing due diligence on suppliers; as opposed to simply listing intended actions, in modern slavery statements.

In March of 2024 we saw the adoption of the Corporate Sustainability Due Diligence Directive (CSDDD) by the European Union. This should have a positive and broad-reaching impact on not only European companies but those non-European companies doing business in Europe.

This directive will regulate how large companies will regulate supply chain sustainability due diligence and make those companies liable for impacts they cause, thereby driving commitment to raising the bar among their suppliers.

Platforms to interrogate complex supply chains to deeper levels are giving organisations greater visibility than ever before and are available for any company wanting to genuinely tackle this issue.

In 2024 Grace Forrest, co-founder of Walk Free, was honoured with the Roosevelt Freedom from Fear Award for her work in eradicating slavery. She is the first Australian woman to receive this award.

She draws a clear distinction between transparency and due diligence laws. She makes the point that transparency law makes a business look at their supply chain with a view to uncovering areas of concern. Due diligence law requires an organisation to prove what they are doing to mitigate the harm to workers in the supply chain. Proactivity versus reactivity – 'It shows a proactive will to protect, with a legal framework around it.'[7]

Some organisations that have developed tech platforms to fight modern slavery are Informed 365, Fair Supply, Freedom Seal Global,

---

7   Forrest, G. (2024) Instagram talk, posted February 20th.

FRDM, EcoVardis, SlaveCheck, TraceSCI, with ongoing research and development being undertaken by Sydney University through the OAASIS Project (Open Analysis to Address Slavery in Supply Chains).

Most of the big consulting firms have human rights or modern slavery practices as well as some law firms. Organisations with deep specialised expertise who can assist with consulting and staff training are Anti-slavery Australia, founded by Jen Burn, and Be Slave Free, founded by Fuzz and Carolyn Kitto.

One organisation with specific expertise in the safeguarding of workers in the commercial cleaning industry is the Cleaning Accountability Framework (CAF). It works to achieve fairness for workers in the commercial cleaning sector, an issue disproportionately affecting women. Most cleaning in today's corporate offices is outsourced, and therefore exploitation, harassment and wage theft are regrettably all too common in the sector, often from unscrupulous operators preying on recent arrivals to Australia who are either unaware of their rights or are too afraid to speak up.

As individuals we also need to take personal responsibility for our purchases, and one simple way is for everyone to install the Good On You app on their phone. This app, developed by an Australian not-for-profit, is free to download, and rates garment manufacturers in three categories – Labour, Environment and Animal. Good On You also posts content on social media sites to help consumers decide how ethical and sustainable manufacturers are, and to flag areas of high risk.

Finding Our North Star

Making the decisions necessary to implement more responsible business practices are nuanced, often complex, and often require wisdom to be brought to bear. This is all made ever so much easier when you have already decided who you are, and what you stand for, both as an individual and as a company. To quote social activist Mechai Viravaidya, 'Business people need ISR (individual social responsibility), as well as CSR (corporate social responsibility).'[8]

The creation of organisations which operate in a manner that honours higher values will be achieved when the leader sets this as an unambiguous vision, does not waver and everyone within the organisation plays a role in contributing to the attainment of this goal.

The analogy for leaders here is the way that sailors previously navigated using a sexton to plot their course against the North Star. If you deviated by even a few degrees, you didn't arrive at your destination. Leaders today need to find their North Star and never deviate. This is also known as using your 'moral compass'. Aligning decisions to your moral compass will make decision-making a great deal easier.

Moral courage is the presence of the strength to make the right and moral decision, even if it might be to our personal detriment. Moral courage explains some of the world's greatest successes, and the absence of it some of our greatest failures.

Moral failure is when we overlook poor behaviour. As David Morrison, Chief of the Australian Army, said, 'the standard you walk past is the standard you accept.'[9] The powerful line was written by his speech writer, Cate McGregor, however, it was Morrison who delivered it publicly, drawing a line in the sand as regards sexism in the armed forces.

Companies need to know where their moral compass is pointing, and stay true to that, and not succumb to situational morality in tough times. This occurs when the right decision is made, but circumstances change, and we convince ourselves that it is no longer the standard to apply.

---

8   Viravaidya, M. (2023) EFMD Global Asia Annual Conference, Bangkok, Thailand, November 7th.

9   Harte, M. Australian of the Year David Morrison on Gender Equality in Australia. https://engagingwomen.com.au

These moments are when our character is being tested. When a leader deserts their principles, the opposite of 'staying the course', and convinces themselves that it's fine to do so, this is known as *ethical fading*. We are now on a slippery slope, and if we can justify one less transparent decision, what might come next?

A parable about choices, which embodies indigenous wisdom, is one often quoted by legendary rugby league football coach Wayne Bennett when speaking to his players. It concerns an old Cherokee man who is teaching his grandson about life.

> *'A fight is going on inside me,' he said to the boy. 'It's a terrible fight, and it's between two wolves. One is evil: he is anger, envy, sorrow, regret, greed, arrogance, self-pity, guilt, resentment, inferiority, lies, false pride, superiority and ego. The other is good: he is joy, peace, love, hope, serenity, humility, kindness, benevolence, empathy, generosity, truth, compassion and faith. The same fight is going on inside you – and inside every other person, too.'*
>
> *The grandson thought about it for a minute and then asked his grandfather, 'Which wolf will win?' The old Cherokee replied: 'The one you feed.'*[10]

There is no doubt that whether we choose to feed our higher, more benevolent self or choose the alternative, that choice will determine which part of our nature will begin to dominate our thinking and our actions.

A wise leader will still consult others, listen to a range of opinions and stress test their assumptions. Yet at the end of the day leadership

---

10   Webster, A. (2023) *The Wolf We Feed*. Pan MacMillan, Australia, Sydney.

is about leading, and if you are the CEO the final decision will rest with you.

Sometimes people will challenge the leader around where a company should set the bar on issues of honesty, openness and transparency. The argument is that surely regulators have already done this for us, and all a company now needs to do is operate within the law that has been handed down. This is not leadership, this is the mindset of a follower, slavishly pursuing a doctrine of compliance.

Society's views are changing. Society is starting to judge companies much more around their ESG credentials, their environmental, social and governance position on a range of issues. Not just consumers making purchasing decisions but when people are making decisions around who they want to work for or whether they remain with an organisation.

In many cases the corporate world has operated based on rewarding poor behaviour and propagated the philosophy that kind people don't have what it takes to be successful.[11] This flawed doctrine has no place in a kinder, more sensitive world and as we see a greater number of leaders with higher levels of emotional intelligence running our companies, we will appreciate that kindness in business is not a weakness but a strength, one that has the power to transform company performance and to create a better world.

When you have found your own personal North Star and sought to advance ideas that will make the world a better place, you may have discovered that it isn't always easy to get traction with others in order to see that change materialise. If it were easy, the world would have changed a long time ago.

This can be especially true if you are not in a senior leadership position and seek to influence those with the power and resources to create real change. In some cases, as an agent of change, you will be met with apathy or resistance, and at times encounter decision-makers

---

11 Tharoor, S. & Zacharias, J. (2023) *The Less You Preach the More You Learn.* Aleph Book Company, Delhi.

who lack the courage to use their influence to make significant change, and yet the world needs you to continue your work.

Commercial selling skills can be valuable in framing discussions in which you are seeking to influence more senior decision-makers. One of my favourite expressions regarding commercial sales is 'selling is not telling'.

The principles of professional selling dictate that before you can expect the other person to appreciate what is important to you, you first need to understand what is important to them. It may then be possible to tailor the discussion of your product or service as being a solution to their challenge.

This applies equally to 'selling' an agenda of change, hence in any discussion with a senior decision-maker you need to suspend your desire to tell them all about your vision and show genuine interest in them and their role, and hence any discussion should commence with questions.

These questions could be around their highest priorities for the company, their current challenges, what's keeping them awake at night and perhaps even what legacy they'd like to leave. As you listen, you will probably be surprised how often their vision for the company aligns with yours.

You have shown respect by listening and have now earnt the right to put forward your ideas. There is also now relevant context for your discussion that will help you frame your points around their aspirations. You are likely to find that there will be greater receptivity by doing this.

Final Thoughts

There is much work to be done to transform the corporate sector, yet there is reason for real optimism. Globally we are increasingly seeing big shifts in company strategy that consider the wellbeing of people and planet. In many cases these were unimaginable even some years ago.

One example of this is that we are also seeing more women on boards and in senior management positions. Narelle Hooper and Rodin Genoff in their book *New Women, New Men, New Economy* have said:

> *The marketplace is choosing for us. Across the world we see organisations with more women in leadership roles delivering superior financial returns, increasing productivity and tapping the ingenuity of their people to tackle wicked problems.*[12]

Yes, progress in this area in Australia has been slow, despite the efforts of highly respected and courageous leaders such as Liz Broderick, Founder of the Champions of Change Coalition, Governor-General Sam Mostyn, Ming Long and Sunita Gloster, past and current Chairs of the Diversity Council of Australia, Georgie Dent, CEO of The Parenthood, and many others.

As evidence of some progress we now have six of the top 20 Australian companies headed by women. The Australian Institute of Company Directors (AICD) *Gender Diversity Report* published in October 2023 showed that within these 20 companies 40 per cent of board seats are now filled by women.[13]

Elizabeth Knight, writing in the *Sydney Morning Herald*, points out, 'What passes for success, or progress, is still a low bar.'[14] However, Michelle Jablko, CEO of Transurban, states:

---

12 Hooper, N. & Rodin, T. (2015) *New Women, New Men, New Economy*. Federation Press, Sydney.

13 AICD (2023) Top 20 ASX boards reach 40 per cent women. https://aicd.com.au/board-of-directors/diversity/women/top-20-asx-boards-reach-40-per-cent-women. August 7th.

14 Elizabeth Knight, (2023) Why appointing a female CEO to run a big company doesn't feel like progress. *Sydney Morning Herald*, August 16th.

Let's at least acknowledge that progress is being made, however, I find it interesting that the company boards who appoint these female board members and CEOs themselves remain stubbornly male dominated with only about 11 per cent of the top 200 companies being governed by female directors.[15]

Not all boards are progressive in their thinking concerning important policies that have a direct effect on the wellbeing of employees and many fail to act, preferring to wait for legislation that forces them to reform.

We see positive moves in Australian government legislation that will apply from July 1st 2025 to pay superannuation on government-funded paid parental leave. We are also seeing increased workplace protections for workers which companies are now obliged to adopt. And some companies are taking leadership positions such as Medibank, which led the charge on many of the initiatives to support families years ago, well before being required to do so by law.

Global research undertaken in 2023 by communications firm Edelman across 27 countries gives us insight as to where the corporate sector sits in the eyes of the public.[16] They measured the public's trust in four sectors in society – government, business, media and civil society. Business came out on top, measured at 62 per cent on the *Edelman Trust Barometer*, with government the lowest at 51 per cent.

The corporate sector, much maligned for decades, is emerging as one on which the public are prepared to pin their hopes. This is likely to be due to a two-fold shift. Business is becoming a better contributor to society, while at the same time faith in other sectors may regrettably be in decline. Hopefully in future surveys we will see John F. Kennedy's aphorism of 'a rising tide lifts all boats' manifest.

---

15   Elizabeth Knight, (2023) Why appointing a female CEO to run a big
     company doesn't feel like progress. *Sydney Morning Herald*, August 16th.
16   Trust Barometer (2023). https://edelman.com

There may also be a simple irony – at least with business you know what their primary motivation is, and people do like certainty. As former Australian Prime Minister Paul Keating said, 'In any two-horse race always back self-interest, at least you know they're trying.'[17]

In encouraging signs, we see concern for planet manifesting in the financial services sector. Bank Australia operates with 100 per cent renewable energy and was awarded Green Bank of the Year in 2023. The Commonwealth Bank announced in July 2023 its plan to transition out of financing oil and gas projects. Westpac has already announced its move away from financing coal projects, with the National Australia Bank setting interim targets.

At this point in time ANZ bank remains Australia's biggest funder of fossil fuels, with $18.6 billion to the coal, oil and gas industries in the seven years since the Paris Agreement, which came into force in 2016. Unlike its competitors, ANZ appears content to provide funding with $2.6 billion for fossil fuel projects in 2022.[18]

The positive funding decisions of some banks may admittedly be pragmatic ones, based on risk profiles of certain sectors. In this case, that the assets of fossil fuel companies backing the loans may indeed end up as 'stranded assets' worth a fraction of the loan itself. Self-interest can at times produce positive outcomes.

New Zealand is also showing very positive trends. ESG Enterprise states:

... between January and September 2020, $9.7 billion was added to responsible investment funds. The figures establish that ESG is becoming a critical part of portfolios for many ESG investors.[19]

17   Dobell, G. (2014) Australian Strategic Policy Institute. https://aspistrategist. org.au/canberras-unholy-trinity/. October 20th

18   Market Forces (2023) https://marketforces.org.au/campaigns/banks/anz/

19   ESG Enterprise. https://esgenterprise.com/esg-news/esg-top-rated-new-zealand-company/

In encouraging signs, the government's rollout of wind and solar to achieve their 2030 clean energy target is backed by business including the country's three biggest energy companies, AGL, Energy Australia and Origin. Fatih Birol, the executive director of the International Energy Agency (IEA), sees reason for optimism:

> *Despite the scale of the challenges, I feel more optimistic than I felt two years ago. Solar photovoltaic installations and electric vehicle sales are perfectly in line with what we said they should be, to be on track to reach net zero by 2050, and thus stay within 1.5C. Clean energy investments in the last two years have seen a staggering 40 per cent increase.*[20]

This does not mean that there is room for complacency. Fatih Birol also noted that greenhouse gas emissions from the energy sector were 'still stubbornly high', and that the extreme weather seen around the world this year had shown the climate was already changing at frightening speed.

The IEA, which called solar 'the cheapest source of electricity in history', has called on developed countries with 2050 net zero targets to bring them forward by several years, in a report entitled *Net Zero Roadmap*, published in September 2023.[21]

Former Chief Scientist Alan Finkel shares similar concerns about greenhouse gas emissions from the energy sector and has stated that the percentage of fossil fuels in the energy mix has only moved from 87 per cent to 84 per cent in the last three years.

Leading independent research company Rhodium Group has stated that on current projections we are a long way from reaching

---

20 Harvey, F. (2023) Staggering green growth gives hope for 1.5 degrees, says global energy chief. *The Guardian*, September 26th.

21 https://iea.org/analysis?type=report

carbon neutral by 2050. The key area lagging behind is air travel, predicted to rise by 77 per cent.

However, there are positive initiatives being undertaken such as the European Green Deal which aims to make Europe 'climate neutral' by 2050 through the greater adoption of green technologies. The corporate world should be supportive of this as it likes certainty to facilitate planning and is aware that global warming will not emerge in a linear, predictable fashion.

Ensuring a 'just transition' should be an important focus for governments and business leaders as we grapple with the urgency of acting on climate change. The London-based Institute for Human Rights and Business, led by John Morrison, defines this as the consideration that needs to be given to those individuals and communities who may personally suffer negative consequences of transitioning out of high carbon activities and into the green economy. We need to ensure harm to workers, communities, countries and regions is avoided while maximising the benefits of climate action.

Business leaders must also grapple with the dilemma that the E and the S of ESG are inextricably linked and at times seem to be in competition. An example of where they overlap is in the mining of cobalt for lithium-ion rechargeable batteries used to power electric vehicles and in many forms of technology.

Activist and researcher Siddharth Kara forces us to confront the moral implications of our move to a cleaner environment in his book *Cobalt Red: How the Blood of the Congo Powers our Lives*.[22] He details the human rights abuses of Congolese people, often children, working in appalling conditions in militia-controlled cobalt mines, including the use of child labour in these toxic pits. Given that 75 per cent of the world's cobalt is mined in the Congo, the world's large technology companies and manufacturers cannot look away and ignore these abuses.

---

22 Kara, S. (2023) *Cobalt Red: How the Blood of the Congo Powers Our Lives.* MacMillan, New York.

The conundrum presented by conflicts between the 'E' and the 'S' exists in the manufacturing of solar panels also. More than 80 per cent of the solar panels manufactured today are done so in China, with most coming from Xinjiang Province, allegedly using Uyghur forced labour.

A good example of a company confronting this moral dilemma is First Solar, a leading US solar panel manufacturer, which conducted an audit that found that migrant workers in its operations in Malaysia were victims of forced labour, after a recruitment company had used unethical practices. CEO Mark Widmar didn't bury the report – instead, he chose to share it in plain sight along with his plans to remedy the situation and put in safeguards to ensure there was no reoccurrence.[23]

We need to see more of this openness, honesty and courage from our business leaders. In the case of Uyghur forced labour, we need to develop alternative sources of supply which may hopefully force higher standards by current producers. German firm BASF announced its withdrawal from the region in early 2024.

The unwillingness of business more broadly to act in a similar manner to Widmar has been a failure on an epic scale and must be addressed urgently. The US Customs and Border Protection *Uyghur Forced Labor Prevention Act* is designed to support enforcement of the prohibition on the importation of goods into the United States manufactured wholly or in part with forced labour in the People's Republic of China, especially from the Xinjiang Uyghur Autonomous Region, or Xinjiang.[24]

---

23 Penn, I. & Swanson, A. (2023) Solar company says audit finds forced labour in Malaysian factory. https://www.nytimes.com/2023/08/15/business/energy-environment/first-solar-forced-labor-malaysia.html. August 15th.

24 Uyghur Forced Labor Prevention Act. https://cbp.gov/trade/forced-labor/ UFLPA

One of the world's largest rubber glove manufacturers, Top Glove, in Malaysia, was accused of using forced labour to lower manufacturing costs. The world needed large quantities of PPE (personal protection equipment) during the global Covid pandemic.

The National Health Service of the UK government continued to place orders with Top Glove, finding alternatives more costly and choosing to place the wellbeing of UK citizens ahead of the wellbeing of exploited migrant workers in Malaysia. The US government banned the same imports to drive change. We need more decisions based on ethical principles and less on commercial expediency.

To further drive home the point that we must take action on the major challenges facing the world today, Australian philosopher Toby Orb published *The Precipice, Existential Risk and the Future of Humanity*, in which he put the chances of human extinction occurring in the next hundred years at one in six.[25]

While there have been numerous doomsday predictions, there is no denying that we have created a world in which we are currently pushing the boundaries. We are experiencing a dangerous level of geo-political conflict, we live with the ever-present threat of nuclear weapons and climate change is undeniably occurring. Scientific and technological advances such as genetically engineered pathogens and artificial intelligence, while heralded as advances, carry with them the potential for unintended consequences.

Apathy is the enemy of progress. It is vital that our leaders have the courage to take action and do what is right for the wellbeing of all people, the protection of biodiversity and long-term health of the planet. These are the moral and ethical demands of our time, yet the rewards of doing so await every company. As Alison Taylor writes in the article 'Ethics Pays':

---

25   Orb, T. (2020) *The Precipice, Existential Risk and the Future of Humanity.*
Bloomsbury Publishing, London.

Building an ethical culture is a challenging task that offers enormous long-term rewards. Companies with ethical cultures will have more sustainable growth, retain and attract the best employees, earn public trust and consumer loyalty, and be far better placed to survive disruptive political, social, and environmental forces.[26]

The redefining of business success is just one part of a deeper societal transformation that is required. We must see an honouring of kindness and other values such as thoughtfulness, empathy, compassion, fairness and respect increase in society more broadly. One day, possessing kindness may be seen as the ultimate measure of success in our society.

Governments, too, need to reassess. As with corporations they are equally caught up in worshiping at the altar of growth, in their case growth of the economy, which society at large has accepted. Yet some are starting to question the wisdom of this, including economist Ross Gittins – '... despite all the handwringing over our lack of productivity improvement, would it be so terrible if the economy stopped growing?'[27]

Kyle Westerway writing in *Forbes* provides this insight:

... it's going to be a generational project to rebalance things. We're seeing the start of that as stakeholder capitalism and ESG [environmental, social and governance] are becoming a part of the mainstream conversation. Maybe we're at that moment in a pendulum's arc where it pauses and starts to begin its trajectory back in the other direction. I hope we're there because we need to reset.[28]

26   Taylor, A. https://ethicalsystems.org/ethics-pays/
27   Gittins, R. (2023) Big business should serve us not enslave us. *Sydney Morning Herald*, September 13th.
28   Westerway, K. (2022) Jack Welch: The Man Who Broke Capitalism. https://forbes.com/sites/kylewestaway/2022/05/31/jack-welch-the-man-who-broke-capitalism/May 31st.

This transition towards organisations honouring higher values and treating all stakeholders with grace and dignity may not be smooth or without upheavals, and will certainly have its critics; however, it has started, and as with all evolutionary processes is taking us on to a better world.

As for where the power to change the world lies, people often believe that governments lead the country. Governments don't lead, people do. Government policy is predicated on polling advising them what voters want.[29] The same is true of the corporate sector as regards consumer intentions.

Some people are critical of companies as being blockers of social progress; however, companies too do their research to ascertain what consumers, potential business clients and investors want. So, at worst they can be accused of being laggards rather than leaders. The message here is that we all have the power to play a role as change agents, by sending a message as to what kind of world we want to live in.

If we want companies to change, we as individuals need to change: change what we buy, who we buy from, what companies we invest in and who we are prepared to work for. We as individuals, united in an underlying common desire for a better world, are the leaders. We will drive 'the kindness revolution' that Hugh Mackay speaks of by setting higher standards for ourselves, and it will be based on each of us asking ourselves, 'how can I be kinder?'[30]

Steve Farber, author of *Love is Just Damn Good Business*, incites us to go beyond kindness – 'When love is part of an organization's framework and operationalized in its culture, employees and customers feel genuinely valued.'[31]

One day all businesses will focus on creating environments that foster a sense of belonging and connectedness and embracing kindness

---

29 McKenzie-McHarg, V. (2023) Power Plays panel, Byron Writers Festival, Byron Bay, August 12th.

30 Mackay, H. (2021) *The Kindness Revolution: how we can restore hope, rebuild trust and inspire optimism*. Allen & Unwin, Sydney.

31 Farber, S. (2020) *Love Is Just Damn Good Business*. McGraw-Hill, New York.

as a core value. Success will be redefined and kindness in business will never be seen as a weakness, only as a strength. The days of putting the toughest CEOs up on pedestals will be over, and in their place will be the kindest; those who contribute to the stock of social good.

Toxic workplaces will be replaced with cultures of trust where concern for each other will be the norm, an ethos extended to suppliers, customers and communities. This will require that we all find within ourselves a generosity of spirit, so that we can lift everyone up, with no exceptions.

In this world it is likely that listening will be as valued as talking. Empathetic listening, a skill used by those seeking to understand others, will be valued. Coopetition, the act of cooperation between competing companies where their combined resources can create social good, will be widespread. Greed and shortsightedness will give way to moral and ethical decision-making – this will become the norm. What is required is an authentic and long-term commitment, from all of us, to living differently and to doing business differently.

If you are in a position of power and influence and are still unconvinced by the contribution that kindness can make to your business success, just ask your people – your suppliers, your clients and customers, and regulators – what characteristics they would like to see embodied in the organisation that you lead.

Although you don't have to be the CEO or chair of the board; we can all contribute to our work environments in a positive way, and through them our communities. Influence wherever you can. A kind word for someone who would appreciate your encouragement, being empathetic towards someone who has just started in the company and doesn't know anyone yet, or finding the courage to speak up for someone who you feel needs your support. Small actions of kindness can have monumental effects in the lives of others.

To change the world, hope on its own is not enough. We need to engage with issues using 'active hope' to respond in the most effective manner to the aspects of society that we seek to change.

Joanna Macy, who is described as an eco-philosopher, and scholar of Buddhism and resilience expert Dr Chris Johnstone, enunciate this principle in their book *Active Hope: How to Face the Mess We're in Without Going Crazy*. They state, 'Active Hope is waking up to the beauty of life on whose behalf we can act. We belong to this world, and we are here to play our part.'[32]

Whether you are a visionary corporate leader, an employee with a good heart or someone outside the corporate domain altogether who simply wants to live in a fairer more equitable world, the bottom line is that it all starts with us. We are all powerful, well beyond the limits of our own belief systems, and every one of us can contribute to building a better world.

One of the greatest contributions that we can make, in the great drama that is life, is simply to be a kind human being. A smile, an uplifting comment, a helping hand for someone, demonstrating acceptance and respect for all people no matter how different they may be to ourselves.

The great power of kindness is that the ways to be kind are limitless and the beautiful thing about kindness is that every act of kindness has a multiplier effect well beyond the initial action. Some of the most admired people in history have provided us with wisdom, inspiration and encouragement to be kind:

Mother Teresa – 'We ourselves feel that what we are doing is just a drop in the ocean, but the ocean would be less because of that missing drop.'

Mahatma Gandhi – 'Be the change you want to see.'

Nelson Mandela – 'It's in your hands now.'

Thank you for the contribution that you are already making to a kinder world.

---

32 Macy, J. & Johnstone, C. (2012) *Active Hope: How to Face the Mess We're in Without Going Crazy*. New World Library, Novato, CA.

Key Takeaways

- We must rise to the moral and ethical challenges presented by artificial intelligence.
- Seek out the guidance and support that is available to build responsible businesses.
- We can all contribute to our work environments in a positive way.
- The ways to be kind are limitless.
- We are living in a world of positive change.

Books Referenced

- Farber, Steve, *Love Is Just Damn Good Business* (2020)
- Fox, Catherine, *Stop Fixing Women* (2017)
- Kara, Siddharth, *Cobalt Red: How the Blood of the Congo Powers Our Lives* (2023)
- Macy, Joanna & Johnstone, Chris, *Active Hope: How to Face the Mess We're in Without Going Crazy* (2012)
- Orb, Toby, *The Precipice, Existential Risk and the Future of Humanity* (2020)
- Tharoor, Shashi & Zacharias, Joseph, *The Less You Preach the More You Learn* (2024)
- Webster, Andrew, *The Wolf We Feed* (2023)

PART 3

A Case Study

I have been impressed time and again by the schizophrenic character of many businessmen. They are capable of being extremely far-sighted and clear-headed in matters that are internal to their businesses. They are incredibly short sighted and muddle-headed in matters that are outside their businesses but affect the possible survival of business in general.

Milton Friedman
A Friedman doctrine: The Social Responsibility of Business Is to Increase Its Profits

CHAPTER 7

A Company that Cares

Communication

The company that I am most qualified to talk about is Konica Minolta Australia, where I spent the last 15 years of my 35 years in the corporate sector, the last eight as Chair and Managing Director. It is a wholly owned subsidiary of Konica Minolta Inc in Japan, a global technology company.

The primary product offering is in the field of printing and scanning devices, and document management software which overlaps with those of some of the better-known global technology brands such as Xerox, HP and Canon, all of whom are much larger. During the company's first 40 years in Australia, it had been run by Japanese executives sent from Tokyo on a four-year assignment.

In 2013 the company held its annual conference to kick off the new Japanese fiscal year, and as the current managing director was due to be replaced, it was assumed that one of the five people attending the conference from the Tokyo head office would be announced as his replacement.

The most senior person in attendance surprised everyone when he announced that I was to be the new managing director. At the time I held a national role as the General Manager of Sales. I walked up on stage, turned to the audience of some 300 employees and channel partners, and said, 'I want us all to work together to build a company that cares. That cares for the people who work here, that cares for our customers and that cares for our community.'

The next day when the conference was over, I walked into the office for the first time as managing director, and the real work began. The first thing I did was to write to everyone in the company to share this vision, as many were not present at the conference.

I had never been a managing director before, and I imagine that conventional wisdom on leadership at the time may have emphasised instilling the troops with confidence that the right person had been appointed to be in charge and that I knew exactly what I was doing.

I took a different approach. In my email I said, 'There is only one problem with my vision statement, and that is that I don't know how to achieve it, and I need your help. I need you to share your ideas with me and I want to hear your opinions on what needs to change.'

As our understanding of leadership archetypes has grown, it could now be considered that I did, in fact, show the qualities of a leader by acknowledging my inadequacies and demonstrating vulnerability and even humility. This one short address at the conference, and the subsequent email the following day, lit a fire of change within our organisation that lasted for years.

We followed up with a voluntary survey using a tool known as the Market Responsiveness Index (MRI) from boutique consulting firm Market Culture. This firm, founded by Linden and Chris Brown, authors of a *Customer Culture Imperative*, had spent years helping companies in Australia and the US build cultures that connect the people within those businesses with their customers.[1]

We were a mid-sized company of about 400 people at the time and over 90 per cent of people responded to our survey. There were survey questions asking people to rate the company against certain criteria,

---

1   Brown, L. & Brown, C. (2014) *The Customer Imperative*. McGraw-Hill, New York.

but also free-text fields where they could enter suggestions and reflections of their own, and we received 800 comments from the people who responded.

I sent a note to everyone thanking them and letting them know what the response rate had been and the main themes that had emerged. I advised them that rather than asking someone else to prepare a report with the best ideas in it, I had read every one of the 800. I felt that if they had taken the time to share their thoughts, I should take the time to read them. The message was a respectful one and that we were all in this together.

This may hardly seem like ground-breaking management strategy; however, it was the first time that the people, who were at the heart of our organisation, had been asked for their ideas on how to build a better company.

Overwhelmingly, the feedback fell into two categories. The thing people wanted the most was better communication, from top down and between departments. They felt the company was too siloed.

We took some very visible actions to respond to these requests. This included structural changes within our buildings and far greater communication on an ongoing basis such as the sharing of monthly financial results with all team members and regular communication from myself and other senior executives.

I had always felt uncomfortable that although we were open plan, except for offices for managers, our Human Resources and Legal Departments were walled off with several offices inside. I'm not saying that no department in any organisation should ever be partitioned off, but it just wasn't working for us. This area was referred to as 'the compound' and the physical separation served to create a barrier between our people and the very department responsible for them. One of the first actions I took was to have the walls removed.

The offices that housed the managers within the company had been created with grey film on the glass-fronted walls that restricted visual contact between those in the department and the manager. Most managers liked their privacy; however, I had the film on the glass removed.

Changes were needed at my level within the company as well. Rather than moving into the previous managing director's office, which was very isolated, I turned that into 'the quiet room', an area with soft furnishings where anyone could take a break.

I moved into a glass-fronted office in a high traffic area near the internal café and practised some good old management principles from the '80s such an 'open door policy' and 'management by walking about'. People now had far greater accessibility than ever before to the person responsible for the company.

Not everyone was onboard with the changes. It is only natural that when you have people who have been in an organisation for a very long while, that change can be disruptive.

One day the manager of a department came to see me and said that she didn't like what I was doing. She wanted everything to stay as it had been. She also said that her two supervisors felt the same way. I listened to her concerns, asked her to elaborate and then talked about why change was necessary and the fact that I was being guided by the responses that I had received from the survey.

She had created a niche for herself that was working well for her and her key staff, and I was not able to convince her to try an alternative way of operating. Regrettably, I lost three experienced women who all resigned on the one day. I still reflect on whether I could have managed this situation better.

Purpose

The second most common theme that came out of the survey was that people said they wanted more purpose. They had heard about companies, much larger than us, that had well-developed community engagement programs that allowed staff to volunteer with charity partners, salary matched giving programs, things of that nature, and in 2013 we didn't have any of those initiatives inside the company.

There had been some reticence among some members of our senior management ranks when I originally made the decision to send the survey that asked people what they wanted. The assumption was that we would be swamped with unreasonable requests around pay increases and conditions. I found the societal focus from our people enormously encouraging.

Behavioural economist Dan Ariely outlines in his book *Predictably Irrational* that money is not the sole or even the most important motivator for people.[2] I sensed that higher wages are not what people would ask for. Instead, our people asked us to implement ways for them to give to the community.

As purpose was number two for our staff I wrote to everyone again and asked them what that looked like and how they wanted that to manifest. One recurring theme was to start working with charity partners. We asked them to vote in three categories – Social, Environmental and Health. They chose The Smith Family, which works with underprivileged children to support their ongoing education, Landcare, an environmental organisation restoring native bushland, and the Breast Cancer Network of Australia (BCNA), which provides vital support for those diagnosed with breast cancer.

This wasn't just an exercise in donating once a year; we worked very closely with these organisations. Our people volunteered in their offices when requested, we used Landcare's bush regeneration days as team building events for various departments, individuals took part in fundraising for our partners, and some staff undertook roles as mentors for young people through the Smith Family.

One of our partner events was the Field of Dreams held each year by BCNA. It would invite supporters to turn up at the Melbourne Cricket Ground (MCG), don a pink poncho, and assemble in the

---

2   Ariely, D. (2008) *Predictably Irrational.* Harper Collins, New York.

centre of the ground within the outline of a pink woman which was the logo of the organisation.

It took 15,000 people to fill the outline and they invariably achieved this despite asking these people to brave the cold of a Melbourne winter's night. A photo, illuminated by the floodlights of the MCG, was then taken from above and used throughout the year for promotional purposes. This is the power of the not-for-profit sector to garner support when the organisation is perceived as authentic and genuine and performing a valuable service for others.

Can you imagine a for-profit corporation achieving this with unpaid volunteers? If you received an invitation from Telstra, our largest telco, inviting you to come out at night and be photographed forming a giant orange T to help it promote its business, how do you think you would react?

Cambodia

Shortly after establishing these partnerships, we held our annual incentive trip for our highest performing salespeople and dealers in Cambodia. Our keynote speaker for the awards dinner was Somaly Mam. She had spent some 20 years of her life rescuing children and teenage girls who had been trafficked into the brothels of the main cities of Cambodia. She had been trafficked herself as a teenager. Her story had been published as *The Road of Lost Innocence*.[3] Her organisation was called AFESIP, an acronym for the French Agir Pour Les Femmes en Situation Precaire or 'Acting for Women in Distressing Situations'.

On the night, she brought five young women with her who themselves had experienced sexual violence and had gone through the process of rehabilitation and reintegration and were now in their first year of university, thanks to funding from overseas. We could see that

---

3   Mam, S. (2011) *The Road of Lost Innocence*. Virago Press, London.

with positive intervention young lives could be changed. The wonderful actress and human rights advocate Susan Sarandon has been a long-time supporter of AFESIP's work.

There is an expression in the human rights world, 'once you know you can't unknow, and once you've seen you can't unsee.' So, upon returning to Australia, we added a fourth category to our not-for-profit program in order to support this work.

I explained that the cause was helping young women who had been trafficked and others who had been subjected to sexual violence in various ways, and we would now be supporting the work of AFESIP. This was done through an Australian-based fundraising charity called Project Futures that had been established by Stephanie Lorenzo some years earlier. Our people were delighted.

We then commenced annual funding that would permit those young women, and others who followed, to complete university and be provided with laptops and other support. On a return visit to Phnom Penh in April of 2024 I had the privilege of spending time with these young women who now work at the AFESIP centre helping others.

This program has grown considerably now and I also had the privilege of meeting with the nearly 20 young women who are currently in university. They are studying to be lawyers, psychologists, nurses, business managers and accountants.

Our simple act of kindness changed lives and at the same time gave our own people the greater sense of purpose that they had requested. Everyone benefitted.

After some time, we asked our team members if anyone was interested in seeing firsthand the difference that their donations, matched by the company, were making and established annual trips. We provided all staff with two days per year of volunteering leave and provided an additional week for those who attended these trips to Cambodia.

About 10 people would attend each trip and we even had one of our suppliers, AirRoad Express, send people along. They became very generous donors to support the work being carried out in Cambodia by AFESIP. Even following his retirement the founder of AirRoad, Tim Payne, has personally continued his very generous personal support for the work of AFESIP.

There are bogus orphanages in Cambodia and other poor countries, where children are deliberately kept in poor conditions with busloads of tourists pulling up and donating, thinking they are helping improve the lives of the children. This has given rise to the term 'orphanage tourism' in a similar manner to 'voluntourism', the practice of volunteering in poor countries, which can at times take the jobs of locals.

AFESIP is not an orphanage. There is no government agency that assists victims of trafficking or rape victims and while the Cambodian police will pursue perpetrators and legal authorities will prosecute, they rely on AFESIP and others to care for victims. Before we offered our support, I did a great deal of due diligence on Somaly's personal story and the organisation, and over 10 years later continue to be an advocate for its vitally important work.

I often took a week of my annual leave to visit outside of these company trips. On several occasions, I accompanied Somaly during her outreach work into the slums. She would take food, soap and condoms to groups of women who worked as prostitutes. They had not been trafficked and were not in forced labour, but economic circumstances forced them into this work. Their clients were local men paying one or two dollars per visit to the homes of these women. This was the only way the women could feed their children and pay the rent on the hovel they lived in.

One day we pulled up in Somaly's car, and the women all recognised her and called out excitedly. They were as grateful for the fact that someone cared enough to visit them, as they were for the items she brought with her.

When I stepped out of the car, Somaly called out to the group of 20 or so women, 'Who remembers David?' (from my previous visits). Lots of hands shot up. Somaly turned to me and said, 'Oh David, all the prostitutes in Phnom Penh love you!' I quickly jumped in with,

'Somaly, on my next visit, my daughters Beth and Nina are coming with me, so you can't say that, as they might get the wrong idea!'

I later discussed with Somaly my level of discomfort around my participation in these visits. My concern was based on the whole idea of the 'white saviour' coming to help the vulnerable and oppressed. I really had difficulty reconciling this in my mind, and suggested that we should just transfer funds and not visit.

Somaly then recounted several stories about how these women felt about my visits. One had said, 'We smell so badly we don't even like to sit next to each other yet he always comes and sits and has lunch with us whenever he visits Cambodia.' There was no running water or sanitation in the slums. She said it meant so much to them. Another said, 'He's the only man I have ever met in my whole life who didn't bash me.' I found my visits humbling and life-changing.

Modern Slavery

When we came back from that first Cambodian trip where Somaly Mam spoke to our group, we began studying the widespread issue of women being trafficked.

This led us to Walk Free, part of the Minderoo Foundation, founded by the Forrest family. It had funded research by the Gallup organisation, a political polling company, which also does social research.

It had produced the *Global Modern Slavery Index*, research that attempted to quantify the number of men, women and children in the world today trapped in modern-day slavery.[4] The research indicated that there were over 40 million people in the world in some form of forced labour.

Global Estimates of Modern Slavery published by the International Labour Organisation (ILO) and Minderoo in 2023 now has that

---

4   Global Slavery Index (2016) | Walk Free Foundation, https://walkfree.org/global-slavery-index

figure at closer to 50 million.[5] The research showed 41,000 people in Australia were trapped in forced labour in businesses, in domestic servitude and in forced marriage.

It is worth remembering that behind every product that is manufactured with slave labour is an individual person with their own story, usually one of just wanting to provide for their family. Millions of people are forced to work in dangerous sub-standard conditions with little regard for their wellbeing or their lives shown by their employer. Exploitation does sit on the same continuum as slavery. It's all a matter of degrees of abuse and whether the individual has any agency or choice.

In our case at Konica Minolta, we initially started off supporting an organisation fighting against the sexual slavery of young women in Cambodia but had now learnt that many of the slaves in the world today were, in fact, in corporate supply chains. Ending slavery in corporate supply chains will be a hard nut to crack; however, there are resolute people working in this field with considerable knowledge that can be drawn on.

In our case that included Vanessa Zimmerman, Founder and CEO at Pillar Two, Carolyn and Fuzz Kitto, founders of Be Slavery Free, John McCarthy, Jenny Stanger, Alison Rahill and Carsten Primdal at the Catholic Archdiocese of Sydney Anti-slavery Taskforce, Sonja Duncan at SD Solutions, and Justin Dillon at FRDM, whose supply chain monitoring system we implemented.

While we gravitated towards smaller firms for advice, there were others working in the field of human rights embedded in much larger institutions and organisations whose assistance in helping to grow our understanding of a new and complex field was greatly valued.

These included Jen Burn, founder of Anti-slavery Australia, an organisation working within the University of Technology Sydney

---

5   Global Estimates of Modern Slavery: Forced Labour & Forced Marriage, https://www.ilo.org/publications/major-publications/global-estimates-modern-slavery-forced-labour-and-forced-marriage

(UTS), Justine Nolan, Executive Director at the Australian Human Rights Institute (UNSW) and the Chief Purpose Officer at KPMG Richard Boele, and Victoria Whitaker, Head of Climate & Sustainability at Deloitte.

The free self-paced online training provided via the Anti-slavery Australia website is a great place for any individual or organisation to start increasing their knowledge in this area.

Thai Fishing Story

Slavery crossed our path again on another of the annual incentive trips, this time in Thailand. One evening we were on a clipper ship, an old four-masted sailing ship, and following dinner, there was a talk about Thai culture in the ship's library.

There was an opportunity to ask questions of the cruise director, and my daughter Nina, who was accompanying me, captured the following discussion.

Somebody commented that it was pitch black outside except for all the lights that were dotted around on the ocean and asked what the lights were. The cruise director said that every light represented a Thai fishing vessel, and the lights were used to attract the fish at night.

She said that recently, they had jumped in a little dinghy during the day and went over to one of the ships. They asked if they could come on board and talk to them about the sort of seafood they were catching.

The captain of the fishing boat must have felt obliged to say yes and the cruise director stepped on board. The first thing she saw was an emaciated person sitting on the deck with a collar around their neck which was chained to the deck of the boat.

With considerable alarm, she asked who he was and why he was chained up. The captain simply stated that he was a slave, and with a sweep of his arm to indicate all the other boats on the ocean, explained that most of them had slaves. He added that this one was shackled to the boat as he was a troublemaker, but not for much longer as they were planning on throwing him overboard.

He then offered to sell her the slave, and they negotiated the price, $US500. She went back to the ship, returned with the money, and bought this human being to set them free.

She didn't realise it at the time, but she had paid a lot more than what it costs to buy a person to work for you for the rest of their life. The captain would have paid a slave trader at the docks no more than $US100. The cruise ship then deviated from its normal course and took the man they had rescued to a police station.

It turned out he was from Myanmar. He'd signed a contract with a recruiter who'd gone through the villages there, offering good jobs in Thailand. He was told that he could go there for two years and earn enough money to completely change his family's life, but he had been tricked and ended up as a slave on this vessel.

Regrettably, it is a quite common story and in 2019 slavery in the Thai fishing industry became the subject of an Australian-made film, *Buoyancy*, produced by Causeway Films. It was an honour to be invited to speak at an event as part of the launch of the film at the Melbourne Film Festival.

In this case the slavery concerns seafood that ends up in the products of global food producers for human consumption and as pet food, and finds its way into our supermarkets and restaurants. However, our 'Road to Damascus' moment was realising that if slavery could happen in the supply chains of this sector it was surely happening in the tech sector, with most manufacturing now based in lower labour cost jurisdictions.

These incidences of slavery that we'd encountered ourselves fuelled our desire to try and do something to ensure that there was no form of slavery in our own operation, regarding any of the goods or services that we procured for use in our business.

I knew we didn't have forced labour in our offices, or even our direct domestic suppliers. Identifying and addressing slavery is more complex than looking at your direct operations. Each business has a long, and often opaque, supply chain. They in turn all have their own suppliers that they buy raw materials and components from, used in the manufacturing of their products. In some cases, these can extend for 10 tiers deep or more.

Imagine how many different companies have made small components that ended up going into a smart phone or laptop or any other piece of complex technology. Many different suppliers across multiple countries, which is where the problem comes in. Smaller companies, local companies that we've never heard of, often using third-party labour hire firms for their labour force. These predators trawl though impoverished villages selling dreams that turn into nightmares.

Our Supply Chain

We were determined not to look away and continue as normal, and although our level of knowledge was low, we were committed to doing something. Although we were not a manufacturer, as is the case with most companies we purchased finished goods from other suppliers.

Starting to open up discussions with them about their supply chains introduced complexity into what was otherwise a relatively simple, often transactional relationship. However, we decided that the degree of difficulty should not be the determining factor as to whether we started this journey or not, certainly not when human lives were at stake.

We were growing, but still only a 500-person company. Yet we created the dedicated role of Ethical Sourcing Manager and in 2015 appointed Laura McManus into that position. She came from Walk Free, and her knowledge of human rights and modern slavery was invaluable for us in starting our program. She is now working on a far bigger stage as Human Rights Manager for Woolworths, the largest supermarket retailer in Australia.

She developed a suite of documents and policies such as a company Human Rights Statement, which we held ourselves to account against, a Supplier Code of Conduct, that we measured our suppliers' conduct against, and an Ethical Sourcing Roadmap to set out the timelines of actions and achievements that we had set ourselves over the next 18 months. These milestones proved to be somewhat unrealistic, but again we were new at this, and it simply meant revising our expectations.

We started initially by gathering our largest suppliers together. We freely admitted that we were at the early stages of building our knowledge but asked suppliers to join us. We also built relationships with external experts to help inform our work. We were supported by a number of NGO organisations and people from different sectors who were dedicated to ending modern slavery, and for that I am extremely thankful.

Now, we didn't manufacture anything in Australia ourselves, but we bought a lot of manufactured goods. Uniforms for our service personnel and T-shirts with the Konica Minolta logo on them for staff, also office furniture, office supplies, technology and marketing merchandise.

We had never really thought about where these things came from. Who grew the cotton, who made the T-shirts? How were the people treated? Were they paid a living wage? How many different companies participated in the manufacture of all the other things we bought? Raw materials, components and finished goods all had to be transported. How were these people treated? So, we started to ask these questions. There was no law compelling us to do so, this was not about compliance, it was just the right thing to do.

We had our first challenge when our marketing department wanted to purchase 300 T-shirts for a forthcoming conference. They were going to be branded with Konica Minolta and the theme of the conference, and the marketing department wanted to investigate how the things that we were buying were made.

A person from our marketing department came to me and said that they had investigated the situation – there was good news and bad news. They had talked with the company that we usually bought the T-shirts from, and in turn they had gone to their supplier and asked questions about where and how the products were made. They had got a lukewarm response, as the order wasn't big enough to warrant that importer doing any research into the manufacture of the product.

Nevertheless, the company we dealt with had gone on and found another supplier who was able to verify that their goods were ethically produced going right back to where the cotton was grown. But the bad news was that it would cost more for those products.

I asked the marketing person, 'Just so I fully understand – your question is, should we continue to buy the cheap product that may be made by people in some form of slavery or should we buy the more expensive product that has not involved the exploitation of workers involved in its production? Is that the question?'

The person simply smiled, turned and walked away, and of course, bought the ethically sourced product. Things were starting to change in the way that we'd previously done business. It felt good to be trying to do the right thing; to walk the talk.

It is estimated that one third of all workers are not paid enough for their labour in order to afford a decent standard of living. Kindness to others can manifest in many ways and ensuring that those people, who make the things we use in our businesses, are paid a living wage is surely one of them.

We of course make clothing purchases as individuals as well and I have since made contact with several Australian companies that provide ethically sourced clothing. One is Melbourne-based Etiko (meaning ethical in Latin) founded by Nick Savaidis, and another is Queensland-based Outland Denim, founded by James and Erica Bartle.

My daughters Beth Brady and Nina Cooke and I have visited the Outland manufacturing facility in Kampong Cham in Cambodia.

It is a model of how to run a caring business. Many of the women who work there have previously been trafficked and following their rescue been offered jobs by Outland and a chance for a new life. The story of each woman is stitched in to the lining of the garment.

In 2018, I was invited to go to the United Nations in Geneva and speak at the Business and Human Rights Forum about the work of Konica Minolta in Australia. While I was there, I was privileged to hear a talk by Indonesia's Fisheries Minister, Susi Pudjiastuti. She spoke of Indonesian government vessels intercepting fishing boats and finding slaves who in some cases had been held captive for over 20 years. They had worked for up to 20 hours a day, paid nothing and never been permitted to step off onto land.

A government decree had now been issued requiring all fisheries companies to submit a detailed human rights audit that included all vessels. However, there were still 250,000 Indonesian crew on ships with foreign flags working all over the world who had no protection under Indonesian law.

The Thai government also made moves towards greater scrutiny of fishing vessels following international condemnation. Public activism can have a positive effect for those being exploited. Thai Union, a global seafood company with plants in multiple countries, and which counts John West Foods among its brands, is one company looking to raise standards. The European Commission has subsequently removed Thailand from its list of 'warned countries' due to efforts made to improve human rights among seafarers.

Recognition

We thought we were playing catch-up with our ethical sourcing program, but it may have been more a case that our attempts to eliminate slavery were more the exception rather than the rule in corporate Australia, and our actions started to catch the attention of people outside the company.

In 2017 we were awarded The Freedom Award by Anti-slavery Australia. We were the first company to receive this award which had previously been bestowed on NGOs, government departments and individuals working in this field.

The organisation was founded by Professor Jennifer Burn and resides within the Faculty of Law at the University of Technology Sydney, doing work to support people in Australia who have been subjected to slavery.

It is doing exceptional work with those who have been forced into marriage against their will and who need to turn to someone who can discuss options with them and assist with legal matters where required.

In 2018 we were awarded the top Business Award for that year by Ros Croucher, the President of the Australian Human Rights Commission at their end-of-year awards luncheon. Some of the largest companies on the ASX had been shortlisted, along with a major national law firm. The work that was being acknowledged was across a broad field, however, it was our work in ethical sourcing that set us apart.

When I was leaving the awards ceremony, I was asked by someone who had attended, 'What has been the main achievement in the area of modern slavery that you received the award for?' I said, 'Well we've actually achieved very little so far, but I believe the award is an acknowledgement that we've started.'

In 2019 it was my great privilege to receive an invitation to join 300 sustainability leaders at the United Nations in New York, where we were addressed by Al Gore, Jacinda Ardern and others. I had also been invited to speak that week on the importance of gender equality at the UN Trailblazing Women Conference. It was General Assembly Week when the world's leaders were in the main chamber next to where our meeting was held.

Greta Thunberg and Donald Trump found themselves uncomfortably in the same room at the same time. You may remember her powerful speech that included her chastisement of the whole chamber,

'How dare you continue to look away and come here saying that you're doing enough?'[6]

It is vitally important that all companies make a commitment to eliminate slavery from any aspect of their business. The 50 million people in forced labour today are voiceless. We who have power need to be their voice. This is not an issue of discretionary kindness; it is morally unacceptable to turn away.

Culture

Demonstrating concern for others in society and concern for those within your organisation are not the same. Doing good, and being good, are two entirely different things. Therefore, it was important that we also had a focus on the wellbeing of our own people, especially after stating that we wished to become 'a company that cares'.

There are many factors that underpin a company's culture. We were never perfect, and I certainly made mistakes along the way, and there are many things that upon reflection I would have done differently. We didn't always live up to the high standards we espoused, and there would have undoubtedly been people who felt let down at times. However, the intention was always to positively impact the internal culture of the organisation through actions that aligned with the company's values.

One example was when we gathered everyone together for a kind of opening ceremony after we had refurbished our head office in Sydney. This included a traditional Indigenous smoking ceremony, which has been practised by First Nations people for centuries and is one of the oldest ceremonies still practised in the world today. This cleanses the area and promotes the protection and wellbeing of visitors.

There was a new showroom, meeting rooms and alcoves where people could meet informally. We named each area after one of our

---

6   https://un.org/development/desa/youth/news/2019/09/greta-thunberg/

team members, either still working with the company or someone who had made a significant contribution during their time with the company. Very few people knew who the rooms had been named after as we had taped over the titles of the rooms and unveiled them one by one.

I believe people really appreciated our gesture of acknowledging those who had made a particularly important contribution to our culture. Our Perth office had come up with this idea for their office opening, and we had now adopted it for the Sydney head office.

We should never forget the power of small gestures that acknowledge people. On one man's last day with the company, he referenced his first. He said he would never forget that on his very first day I had taken the trouble to stop by his workstation, say hello and introduce myself. That simple act, perceived as one of kindness, stayed with him during his entire time with the company.

We had two intakes per year of about a dozen undergraduate students from Macquarie University. This was known as the Pace (Professional And Community Engagement) program and was an assessable part of their degree.

The concept was that they could learn from us, however, I saw an opportunity for us to learn from them. I would welcome the group on their first day and tell them that I wanted them to speak up in meetings and share their perceptions of the company and question the decisions that they were observing us making. (Of course, this would not be easy at first.) I told them, 'I would rather have one student with fresh ideas in our business than 10 consultants from McKinsey.' Young people, not yet encumbered by traditional business thinking and models, can bring invaluable fresh perspectives.

Konica Minolta was greatly assisted by Paul and Rosanna Hawkins, co-founders of innovation agency Crazy Might Work. As a part of implementing their design thinking programs, we selected 20 people from across the business representing all states and a diversity of ages, genders and roles to help us design a better company. Through the excellent facilitation of Crazy Might Work we were encouraged to think far more broadly, and at times completely outside the square. It was a transformative process.

In any company it is important to establish an environment of 'psychological safety' and Professor Amy Edmondson elaborates on this in her important work *The Fearless Organization*.[7] She is an acknowledged world expert in this field and describes such an environment as one in which it is 'safe for interpersonal risk-taking and that speaking up with ideas, questions, concerns, or mistakes will be welcomed and valued.'

It is an environment where people know that it is safe to express their views even if counter to those of the most senior people, or those adopted by the broader company. Psychological safety is permission for candour. Positive signs that this type of environment exists include people feeling comfortable in asking questions and contributing to discussions. There needs to be strong intent at senior levels to create psychological, physical and emotional safety at work.

However, some cultures are not supportive, and negative characteristics that impede psychological safety are things such as domineering management behaviour and the tolerance of everyday sexism, bullying and harassment. Other signs are cultures where the norms are to routinely work long hours, often unpaid, in order to advance one's career.

Wage Parity

One of the first things I did as managing director was to ask for analysis to be undertaken to ensure that there had not been a history of discrimination around salaries. When completed it was determined that there were a small number of cases of women being paid less than men for performing the same role, with no explanation other than gender.

---

7   Edmonson, A. (2023) *The Fearless Organization*. Wiley, Hoboken, NJ.

I was advised that if we had used a professional services firm to conduct this work, their recommendation would be to correct this over the next three pay increase cycles; that is, over the next three years.

This approach seemed to me to be a bit like discovering that someone was being bullied and saying to them that we were going to ensure that they were bullied a little bit less over the next year, a little less again over the following and at the end of three years we'd make sure that they were not bullied at all.

I had appointed a new People & Culture Officer whose vision for the company aligned with mine and I knew that this senior executive change would be an important factor in the company's transformation. Following the salary audit, she ensured that those people who had been underpaid received a salary increase commensurate with their male peers, as of the next pay run.

One of my great regrets looking back is that I didn't have the thought to pay these people what they were due retrospectively, to the day they joined the company.

Parental Leave

One area of policy-making which was not driven by any legal requirement in 2018, and which was not common at this time among most companies, was parental leave above the levels mandated by government. This seemed like a good way to support our staff at such an important time in their lives.

Leave provisions at the time were 12 weeks for maternal leave for the person giving birth, and two weeks paternal leave for their partner. Like most companies we were simply complying with the law at that time.

We felt that the legislative bar had not been set at the right level, so we decided to remove the terms 'maternal leave' and 'paternal leave' and just call everybody 'parents' and treat them the same and we extended 12 weeks' leave to both. It was also extended to people who were adopting and included provisions for still birth.

Legislation has caught up with this thinking and these types of changes are commonplace now, however we implemented these things early on, following on from other trailblazers such as Medibank.

Our view was that we should not wait for some external body to tell us what was right, but we should think these matters through ourselves and act according to what we determined was the right thing to do.

We also made the leave quite flexible. We felt that we weren't in the best position to tell our people how best to use that leave; to do so would have seemed counter-intuitive. The only requirement we had was that they had to use the 12 weeks up within three years of the birth or the adoption, but we were flexible with how they took that leave, such as in one block or one day a week or saving it up for a future date.

When the team that put the policy recommendation together said we could announce it and put it on the intranet tomorrow, I asked, 'What happens if one of our people gave birth to a child today?' The answer was that they would miss out because the policy would only apply from tomorrow.

I said that it just didn't really feel like a kind approach. Somebody said we could bring it back to the first of the month. I said, 'Yes, that seems better, but what happens if your child was born on the last day of last month?' In the end we decided that in the same way that the leave could be taken at any time in the next three years, the leave would actually apply to any birth or adoption that had taken place in the last three years.

It was retrospective on a pro rata basis, diminishing in length the further away the birth had taken place. This new policy didn't apply to many people but those people that it did apply to were extremely appreciative. And for many people that it would never apply to, it confirmed in their minds that they really were working for a company that cared about its people.

Another regret is that we didn't introduce superannuation payments on parental leave, which if implemented would contribute at least in some small way to the disadvantage experienced by women in the workforce following the birth of a child.

Domestic Violence Leave

We also implemented a policy to support people experiencing domestic violence. We had a woman who was a survivor of domestic violence come to our office and talk to our staff to reinforce why we were creating a new policy and she certainly helped to inform our work.

When she talked, I was struck by the inter-relatedness of what she had been going through at home and her workplace. She would sometimes flee the house to get away from her attacker and would head straight to her car, and lock the doors, so that at least momentarily she was safe inside the vehicle.

Her abuser would be so outraged that he would do things like smash the side mirrors or kick a side panel of the car. But it was a company vehicle so she would have to report the damage at work.

Often while attacking her, he would grab her mobile phone to make sure she couldn't call anybody for help, and would also smash that. Again, it was company property, and she would have to report that she had damaged the phone.

She would make up excuses and say, 'I'm so sorry I've damaged the car again in the car park at the supermarket,' or 'I've dropped my mobile phone again.' She developed a reputation for being careless with company property, but she was just too embarrassed to tell people the truth.

It made me realise there needed to be greater awareness inside our own organisation of when certain occurrences might be linked to traumatic events going on in the lives of our people. Statistics suggest that one in four women will experience some form of family or domestic violence, be it physical, mental, emotional or financial in their lives.

We knew that we must have women working with us who were going through these experiences, and we must also surely have people who are perpetrators of domestic violence. Sometimes the perpetrator will be a woman, however, this is far less common than male perpetrators.

We decided that we would have several of our staff trained at the University of NSW, not as counsellors but to gain skills in offering a greater degree of empathy and understanding for the people going through this experience. This ensured that there was at least one person in each branch around Australia that somebody needing support could go to, outside of their direct manager, or even outside of the People & Culture department. People really appreciated that initiative.

We were also one of the first companies to create a domestic violence leave policy, which provided two weeks of extra leave on top of sick leave and annual leave. We also did something which was, and perhaps still is, controversial.

We extended that leave to not only the victims but also to perpetrators. People who were perpetrating domestic violence and wanted to stop and wanted to go to counselling during work time. That was criticised in some quarters.

I was told that I had provided an incentive for perpetrators, in the sense that if you are an abuser, you get extra holidays if you work at Konica Minolta. I thought about this very deeply and I came to the conclusion that a person would not commit these acts or come forward with a bogus claim of being a perpetrator of domestic violence just to get some time off work. That didn't really make sense to me.

Respect at Work

A natural extension of this was to make sure that people working at Konica Minolta felt safe on all levels in our offices. This was so basic and fundamental to our efforts to create an environment of physical, emotional and psychological safety.

The Australian Human Rights Commission report by Commissioner Kate Jenkins, *Respect@Work*, dealt with the high incidence of harassment in the workplace.[8] I didn't see evidence of those things taking place, but we still didn't think we were a perfect workplace where these things weren't happening.

We started to talk to all our people about ensuring that we respected each other, and that we wouldn't tolerate any form of bullying, sexual harassment or discrimination against people based on ethnicity, gender, sexuality or any other reason.

I visited every branch and as well as addressing everyone in a town hall style meeting, I also met on a separate occasion during the visit with all women in every branch.

I still had much to learn. I had originally suggested that we go out for breakfast. It was pointed out to me that this timing would exclude women in every branch as the morning was often their busiest time at home, getting kids organised for the day or doing school or childcare drop-off. I still don't know why I had this blind spot and didn't think of this myself.

So, we either went out to a café during the day or met in an internal meeting room. I started each meeting by simply asking them to tell me what it was like to be a woman working at Konica Minolta.

It became clear that one issue was that some men often didn't realise that their actions were causing others concern. Much of this fitted into 'everyday sexism', such as men walking out of a meeting, leaving their coffee cups behind, with the assumption that the women in the meeting would tidy things up.

One other example was the telling of a joke that may have seemed very funny to most of the group listening but caused distress to others. We had just started a marketing campaign called 'Rethink', as in rethink the way you use technology in your office, so we used this same campaign internally to combat harassment.

---

8   *Respect@Work: Sexual Harassment National Inquiry Report* (2020) Australian Human Rights Commission.

The idea was for people to become aware of the impact that they had been having on others, and rethink. Also for those who saw poor behaviour to speak up by only needing to use this catch phrase.

Commercial Success

Business is not about winning awards – it is about producing commercial results, so I was particularly pleased when we also saw a steady increase in our revenue and market share. I intuitively felt that there was a link to our attempts to try and be a better company in the holistic sense.

In the ensuing years we won many large contracts and naturally I wanted to know why these new clients had chosen us. Invariably they would say they had undertaken an exhaustive study, the evaluation team had determined that the products from various suppliers, the service levels and the pricing was about the same. Therefore, there was no reason to go through the disruption of changing from their current supplier to us.

However, these days their internal governance policies required them to look more deeply into who each prospective supplier was as a company. They no longer just looked at what it was that suppliers wanted to sell them, but now looked at who the companies were. One new client put it nicely; he said, 'We don't just look at the nice new shiny car anymore, we now also look under the hood.'

They would say that when they evaluated Konica Minolta, they saw that our values and their values were closely aligned, and they felt that we were a good fit for them, and that's why they were awarding us this contract.

On one occasion for an exceptionally large national contract, we were notified that we had been selected as the preferred bidder and time had been allocated for the negotiating of the contract terms and conditions before signing could take place. We met for one day a week for six weeks. It was a drawn-out process – at various stages we were requested to do something we were not sure we could deliver on, and we were not prepared simply to agree to get the contract signed.

Eventually the contract was signed, and in the following week I received a letter from the lead solicitor representing the client to say that in all his time undertaking this type of work he had not seen a negotiation conducted so respectfully and transparently.

He singled out our attitude of ensuring both parties' needs were met, rather than just pushing for the best outcome for ourselves. He predicted that if we adopted the same attitude in the ongoing management of the contract with his client that the contract would be renewed, and we would be the supplier for many years to come. It has proven to be the case.

The business didn't just grow due to large corporate contracts. We also had many smaller companies, state and federal government departments print shops who used digital presses awarding Konica Minolta contracts. Our business grew every year for 10 years, which was inexplicable in a declining sector, where businesses were significantly reducing their purchases of printing and copying equipment to produce hard copy documents as they moved to the digital storage of information.

Moving the Dial

I find one of the best ways to illustrate the positive impact of displaying kindness to people is to tell the following story.

One year I invited everyone who had worked in the company for 25 years or more to come to Sydney, and I took them out for dinner. A simple act to say thank you for your loyalty. I chose a suburban restaurant for our cheap and cheerful night out and we had a very enjoyable evening. All those attending were field service engineers, the people who come to your office in order to ensure your equipment is functioning properly.

At the end of the meal, one man asked, 'Could I please say

something?' He was a quiet man who had not spoken all night. He stood up, in the middle of the public restaurant, and other diners looked around to see what was happening. I imagine this was the first speech that he had ever made in his life.

He said, 'For over 25 years, I have worked in this company, however I have never told anybody where I worked. I just didn't see the point. I came to work, and I did a fair day's work for a fair day's pay, and that's how I've fed my family. But now, I tell every single person I meet that I work for Konica Minolta, and why would I do that? It's because I feel so proud to work for a company that would care about young women on the other side of the world who have been trafficked into a life of sexual slavery.'

He had worked in the company for over 25 years, but on the engagement scale, he was disengaged. However, the engagement dial had now gone from disengaged to engaged, and it kept going, resulting in him becoming a loyal public advocate and champion for Konica Minolta.

We had treated him well enough for those 25 years that he had stayed, however, it was not enough for him to feel any real sense of belonging and purpose beyond his day-to-day job. The change which he felt was the positive, unintended consequence of showing kindness to a vulnerable group of young women in another country. Many other people came up to me over my time as Managing Director, expressing similar sentiments of pride in our company.

In all my time in the corporate world I never saw any initiative that was as powerful in providing motivation and a sense of purpose and belonging for people, than when a company decides to make kindness a priority and focuses on the wellbeing of people, both inside and outside the organisation. This is where we see the virtuous circle of profit and purpose at work.

Business has enormous capacity to contribute positively to all aspects of our lives, while simultaneously fulfilling its commercial objectives. I would encourage every organisation to take up the challenge to bring profit and purpose into alignment where you will find that values really do create value.

This will result in kinder more nourishing workplaces; a fairer more equitable society; and a more positive and sustainable future for our planet. It will also elevate our own lives as we start to expand our positive impact in the world. Alison Cameron describes this as leading with grace which facilitates 'the movement of authenticity, truth and love through the world'.[9]

Most poignantly, Paul Polman invites all business leaders to ask themselves the following question: 'Is the world a better place because my company is in it?'[10]

Key Takeaways

- Share a vision to build a company that cares.
- Create an environment where ideas percolate up, as opposed to being top down.
- Create an environment of psychological safety.
- Confront human rights issues in the business.
- Being good (internally) and doing good (externally) are two different things.
- Embracing diversity and gaining exposure to other cultures broadens our awareness and provides valuable learnings.
- Business has the power to help create a better world.

---

9   Cameron, A. (2020) *Leadership for the New Millennium*. Living Essence Publications, Currumbin QLD.

10   Polman, P. & Winston, A. (2021) *Net Positive: How Courageous Companies Thrive by Giving More Than They Take*. Harvard Business Review Press, Boston Massachusetts.

Books Referenced

- Ariely, Dan, *Predictably Irrational* (2008)
- Brown, Linden & Brown, Chris, *The Customer Imperative* (2014)
- Burke, Cathy, *Leadership Insights: Practical Wisdom* (2023)
- Edmonson, Amy, *The Fearless Organization* (2023)
- Mam, Somaly, *The Road of Lost Innocence* (2011)
- Cameron, Alison, *Leadership for the New Millennium* (2020)
- Polman, Paul & Winston, Andrew, *Net Positive: How Courageous Companies Thrive by Giving More Than They Take* (2021)

About the Author

David Cooke is an Australian business leader noted for his public advocacy of responsible and sustainable business. *Kind Business* is his first book.

He is a sought-after conference speaker, and his work includes addressing boards and senior executive teams as well as conducting in-house management workshops on ethical decision-making. David was named in the Top 50 ESG Influencers globally by Onalytica. He consults through his firm ESG Advisory https://esgadvisory.com.au.

In 2013 David was appointed as the first non-Japanese Managing Director of Konica Minolta Australia, and prior to that held management positions with Canon and Rank Xerox during his 35 years in the corporate world.

This led to the awarding of the Australian Government's Workplace Gender Equality Agency's citation as an employer of choice. He is a Member of the Champions of Change Coalition.

While leading Konica Minolta, he created the roles of Chief Sustainability Officer, Corporate Social Responsibility Manager and Ethical Sourcing Manager; positions that were all taken up by female leaders.

In 2017 the company was the first in Australia to be awarded the Anti-slavery Australia Freedom Award and in 2018 received the Australian Human Rights Commission's top Business Award.

In 2018 he was invited to speak on Business and Human Rights at the United Nations in Geneva, Switzerland. In 2019 he was invited to speak at the UN in New York on Gender Equality at the UN's Trailblazing Women conference.

He is the former Chair of UN Global Compact Network Australia, the world's largest corporate sustainability network, and former Chair of the Australian Human Rights Institute Advisory Committee (UNSW), and was formerly a non-executive director of Sustainalytics Australia, prior to its acquisition by Morningstar.

He has served on several NGO boards, and the Federal Government Advisory Group on Business and Human Rights and is an Adjunct Professor at UTS Business School. He is also currently an ambassador for Family Friendly Workplaces and the Byron Community Centre, which provides support services for the homeless in Byron Bay through the Fletcher Street Cottage.

David completed his doctorate in 2008. David's dissertation was titled *The philanthropic contract: building social capital through corporate social investment*, which dealt with the business case for profit–making corporations contributing to society through partnerships with civil society or NGO organisations.[1]

Emerald Publishing awarded David its Global Responsible Leadership Award for Social Impact in 2011. David's academic writing can be accessed via https://works.bepress.com/david_cooke/.

In 2014 he was awarded the Top Alumnus of the last 20 years by the Southern Cross University Business School. He was named one of the Top Changemakers to Watch in 2022 by CEO Magazine Global – 'Not content to take the world as it is these innovators have stood up and pushed for change, from environmental action to social justice.'

In 2022 he was awarded an honorary doctorate (*honoris causa*) for

---

1   Cooke, D. (2008) The philanthropic contract: building social capital through corporate social investment, https://works.bepress.com/david_cooke/

his work by Edith Cowan University (ECU) in Western Australia. In granting the honorary doctorate the Chancellor of Edith Cowan University, the Hon Kerry Sanderson AC CVO, stated:

> *ECU values your significant and exceptional achievements, and the mark you've made, in developing innovative and socially responsible initiatives in business. Your efforts to address human trafficking and sexual slavery are applauded by this university.*

Acknowledgements

I would like to start by thanking my wonderful daughters, Beth Brady and Nina Cooke, for all their emotional support and encouragement, not to mention their multiple readings and valuable suggestions. Next, experienced journalist Alison Paterson, who at the request of friends, read my first draft and emboldened me to keep going. Also, Claire Summerer, who contributed her great insights throughout the writing process.

No book can ever reach its final stages without expert editing, and for performing this invaluable role with such professionalism, sensitivity and warmth I would like to thank Karen Comer. The multiple tasks involved in self-publishing from project management to printing were expertly undertaken by Michael Hanrahan and Anna Clemann at Publish Central. Thank you.

I would also like to acknowledge all the people who I write about in the book and whose work I have quoted. In many ways this book is a guide to your own writings and insights and I hope many readers of *Kind Business* will avail themselves of your wisdom. Finally, thank you to everyone who through their acts of kindness leaves the world a slightly kinder place at the end of each day.

ESG Advisory (https://esgadvisory.com.au) is the consulting and speaking vehicle through which Dr David Cooke shares the themes presented in *Kind Business*. This includes in-house consulting, conference keynotes, workshops and board and management presentations.

- Kind Business: values create value.
- Business as a force for good – profit and purpose.
- Business and human rights, modern slavery and ethical sourcing.
- Ethical decision making.
- Building strong corporate cultures.
- Building successful corporate / not-for-profit partnerships.

ESG advisory assists clients to embed these principles to become truly responsible to their broader ecosystems and become agents of positive transformation.

This knowledge is applicable to any board, senior executive team or individual willing to engage in a fearless and courageous way to transform their corporate culture, achieve true sustainability and advocate for the values that the world today is so greatly in need of.

The goal of this work is to invite everyone to be a voice for the voiceless, for the marginalised and for the vulnerable in the world, to those corporate leaders with the resources and power to uplift them and in so doing create a fairer, more equitable world.